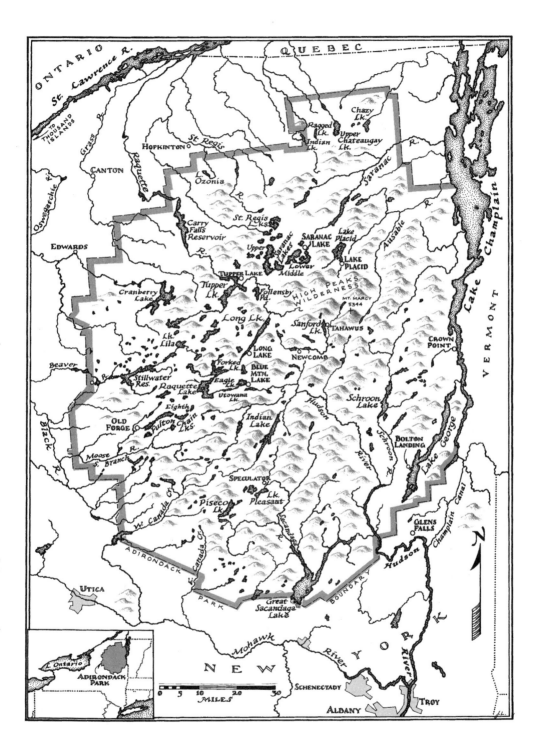

THE ADIRONDACKS

A History of America's First Wilderness

PAUL SCHNEIDER

A John Macrae Book ◆ Henry Holt and Company ◆ New York

Henry Holt and Company, Inc.
Publishers since 1866
115 West 18th Street
New York, New York 10011

Henry Holt® is a registered trademark of Henry Holt and Company, Inc.

Published in Canada by Fitzhenry & Whiteside Ltd.,
195 Allstate Parkway, Markham, Ontario L3R 4T8.

Library of Congress Cataloging-in-Publication Data
Schneider, Paul
    The Adirondacks: a history of America's first wilderness / Paul
Schneider.—1st ed.
        p.   cm.
    "A John Macrae book."
    Includes index.
    1. Adirondack Park (N.Y.)—History.   2. Adirondack Mountains
(N.Y.)—History.   I. Title.
F127.A2S35   1997   96-39844
974.7'5—dc21   CIP

ISBN 0-8050-3490-0

Henry Holt books are available for special
promotions and premiums. For details contact:
Director, Special Markets.

First Edition—1997

Designed by Paula R. Szafranski

Printed in the United States of America
All first editions are printed on acid-free paper. ∞

10   9   8   7   6   5   4   3   2   1

For Nina

CONTENTS

INTRODUCTION

In a sense this book is a romance, a story of first love between Americans and a thing they call wilderness. For it was in the Adirondacks that masses of (non-Native) Americans first learned to cherish the wilds as a place of solace and recreation. It was by no means love at first sight. For centuries, beginning with the almost simultaneous 1609 arrival of Henry Hudson on the river that bears his name and of Samuel de Champlain on the lake that bears his, explorers and colonizers approached these woods and waters as a residence of evil, or they eyed them lasciviously as a place of opportunity. Trappers trapped them nearly dry of furs. Soldiers hacked their way across them in pursuit of personal and national glory. Farmers eked a living out of rocky fields, miners prospected mightily, and loggers logged. In short, the Adirondacks were little different from the rest of the New World.

But at some point during the nineteenth century, we began to see this northeast corner of New York in a new light. Recreational hunters and anglers were in the vanguard, but they were not alone. Something about these particular woods and waters drew the leading painters, scientists, writers, and philosophers. They were followed by masses of the newly middle-class. The sick came to be cured, and the weary to be rested. The newly super-wealthy came and built sprawling fantasy camps deep in the forest. An industry of guides and rustic lodges appeared to service the visitors—the birth of what is now called ecotourism. A woodsy new language, literature, and design aesthetic bloomed and prospered. With each generation, a new idea of the meaning of "wilderness" was imported to the area, refined, developed, and to some degree implemented.

Between 1885 and 1894 a series of laws and constitutional amendments laid the groundwork for what is now the Adirondack Park. At six million acres, it is bigger than Yellowstone, Grand Canyon, and Yosemite combined. It's as big as the entire state of New Hampshire. There are thousands of lakes, tens of thousands of miles of rivers and streams, hundreds of mountains, and countless trees here. It's an unusual park, though, roughly split between private land that is to varying degrees vulnerable to future development and public "Forest Preserve" that is enshrined in the constitution of the state as "forever wild."

The story of this century has been the struggle to transform that initial romantic infatuation with the wilds of the Adirondacks into a sustainable marriage—to find an acceptable definition of wilderness that can survive our culture's seemingly insatiable desires. Depending on whom you ask, the park today is either an important, albeit still seriously flawed, model of peaceful coexistence between civilization and the wild, or a dysfunctional pipe dream. The proper meanings and uses of "wilderness" are not yet settled.

Nor have old conceptions and habits regarding wilderness fully given way. There are still trappers seeking furs in the Adirondacks; guides guiding initiates; loggers, farmers, and owners of fabulous great camps. There are philosophers and righteous prophets in the Adirondacks. Part of this book is about a few of the above who allowed me to accompany them into their own particular Adirondack wildernesses.

It is always a temptation to indulge a metaphor to its limit, to say that America's early fear and loathing of the wilderness in the Adirondacks and elsewhere was simply that of a child who views the other sex with alarm. And that the speculating, cutting, and clearing that followed was the hungry desire of adolescence, which gave way in time to a romantic infatuation driven by an image of the beloved at least as much imagined as real. The fabulous sprawling camps built around the turn of the century were showers of gifts intended as devotional tokens, but they were really subconscious attempts to remake the real woods into our fantasy "wilderness." And finally now, at last we are mature in our relationship to the Adirondacks, complete in our understanding of the wilderness. It's chafing at times, yes, and there's renegotiating to be done, but we're solidly wedded.

But the temptation to make finite proclamations is better resisted. If there's one thing the history of the Adirondacks teaches, it's that the meaning of wilderness, like love, changes as soon as it's defined.

PAUL SCHNEIDER
New York City
September 1996

A Few Words about Boundaries

For the purposes of readability, I use the term "the park" rather freely to describe the area currently within the boundaries of the Adirondack Park, or "Blue Line." I do this even though much of this book describes events that took place before the creation of the political entity called the New York Forest Preserve in 1885, of the Adirondack Park in 1892, or, most important, of article 7, section 7 of the 1894 New York State Constitution, which deemed that the lands of the Forest Preserve "shall be forever kept as wild forest lands." Some of the material in the book, for that matter, predates the entity called New York State.

1   *The Trapline*

It was very odd. There were no signs of a struggle. There were no plants torn up, no disturbed mud. All four of the long, sharpened wooden stakes with forked tops that Bob Inslerman had pushed firmly into the lake bottom were still in place, exactly as he left them the day before. But the trap was nowhere to be found. In twenty-odd years of taking beaver, muskrat, mink, and otter on the Saint Regis Lakes, nothing quite like this had ever happened before.

Inslerman stood up and adjusted his yellow rain pants. He shrugged. He shook his head. He leaned back over the bow of his sixteen-foot Starcraft aluminum boat and poked around in the mud with a short gaff, and then reached around some more with his hands. The trap was of a type called a Conibear, with two sets of jaws that form a sort of tunnel when open, and close over the body of an animal that passes through them. It is typically set along a beaver path, or, as in this case, in the water at a break in the reeds used by the animals as a passageway. It is considered to be more humane than the foothold trap, as its prey inevitably dies quite quickly. There is no way for a beaver caught in a Conibear to drag the trap off without disturbing the stakes that hold it in place.

"It's just gone," Inslerman said finally. His gray-and-black beard was about ten inches above the tea brown water. "Gone," he said again. Twenty feet away the beaver lodge, a medium-sized pile of mud and chewed sticks, sat stoically in the November shower.

Perhaps a duck hunter was out earlier that morning and took the trap, Inslerman thought out loud as he stood again and moved back toward the stern of the boat. Or maybe someone opposed to trapping—a friend of the beaver, so to speak—removed it. But why would a trap thief take the time to replace the stakes so carefully? He gazed absently across the lake to the campus of Paul Smiths College, where he knew some of the students and faculty opposed killing wild animals for any purpose.

It seemed unlikely, though, that a college student would come out this far on such a drizzly morning. And he knew for a fact that the people who own the summer place nearest to the lodge would not disturb the set, even if they were still around this late in the season, which they were not.

As a member of the lake property owners' association, Inslerman has a fairly good idea of the trapping views of most of his neighbors. "They're from Manhattan," he said pointing to the camp, "and they're very active in Audubon, and they like to go out birding a lot. So even though this is state land, I never used to trap for beaver here out of respect for them. I figured they would be opposed to it." Though over the years he occasionally met the camp's owners during the summer social season at the lake, for a long time Inslerman never even told them that he was a trapper. There are plenty of places to trap without being right in front of somebody's summer home.

Then the beavers ate the telephone line to the camp. Not just once, either. The third time it happened the woman of the house called the Department of Environmental Conservation and asked to be connected with her neighbor Bob Inslerman. When he is not on vacation trapping, Inslerman is a regional wildlife manager for the state of New York. His professional territory includes roughly half of the Adirondack Park, and an increasing part of his job over the past five years has been responding to complaints about overzealous beaver. It's more often birch trees that need rescuing than telecommunications equipment, he said.

An adult beaver can weigh sixty pounds, which is about the size of a full-grown Labrador retriever. Inslerman categorizes the animal as a "large mammal," along with the deer and bear rather than with the muskrat and otter. At four feet long, it's a good deal bigger than the cuddly children's image of the busy little animal merrily singing as it works.

It does, however, work. In the 1950s Inslerman's predecessor at the DEC, a man named Greenleaf Chase, counted the beavers in a remote valley in the northern part of the park. On one river he found that a colony of several hundred had stepped a feeder stream all the way up the side of a mountain to its headwaters. On the other side of the ridge was a large stand of poplar and birch, which beaver like more than almost anything besides the smell of each other. But there was no stream there. So the busy rodents raised the water level of the top pond so high that the stream crested the ridge and flowed down the other side—into a different watershed altogether. There they constructed a whole new series of dams and feasted on the grove.

One-quarter of a beaver is tail. Six inches wide and one inch thick, the most remarkable thing about it from a biological viewpoint is that it is covered with scales like those belonging to a fish. Meat from the back end of the beaver is said to even taste and smell like fish, at least when compared to the front, which is decidedly more mammalian.

Mammalian, that is, with a full line of accessories for water life. Valves close off a beaver's nose and ears when underwater, and thin goggle membranes come down over its eyes. Skin flaps behind the front teeth allow it to haul logs around the pond without swallowing water. Two oil glands between the back legs supply a daily dose of preening oil, which the animal combs into its fur with a special toenail.

Next to the oil glands lie the castor glands. They are about the size of tangerines and the few ounces of castor that comes out of them is umber in color and, as one writer put it, "thicker than Grand Marnier." A few daubs of the stuff are the best way to lure a beaver into the jaws of a trap, because a male beaver, especially, is likely to investigate the scent of a stranger. Trappers used to call castor "barkstone," and fine perfumeries still occasionally use it to add an element of wildness to their concoctions.

"When she called about the telephone wires I said to her, 'Well, we could issue a nuisance trapping permit and you could hire someone to come and reduce the size of the colony,' " Inslerman continued, " 'but I know you're uncomfortable with trapping. So let's think about other ways to control them.' And she said, 'No, I don't care. I want them out. Who do I call?' " Inslerman chuckled.

"And I said to her, 'Well, I happen to be a trapper.' "

In the distance, the base of Saint Regis Mountain appeared out of the mist for the first time of the morning. Inslerman started his ancient Evinrude WinSpeed outboard and guided the boat very slowly up a winding swampy slough not far from the beaver lodge. There was a line of muskrat traps up at the end that he wanted to check. As plentiful as beavers are these days in the park, there are even more muskrats. Muskrats, Inslerman explained, breed two or three times a season, with litters of four or five at a time.

Most of the Adirondack Park, he added, is prime muskrat habitat. There are more than four thousand lakes, ponds, swamps, and bogs tucked away in the park. There are thirty thousand miles of rivers, streams, and brooks. The headwaters of the Hudson are within the park, as are major tributaries to the Mohawk and Saint Lawrence Rivers, and Lake Champlain as well. Once a traveler is west of the High Peaks, which rise quite steeply from the eastern boundary of the park, the Adirondacks seem more a place of water than of mountains.

There are, however, plenty of peaks. Stretching from Lake Champlain in the east to Utica in the west, and from eleven miles south of the Canadian border in the north to just north of Schenectady

"Mountain View on the Saranac," 1868, by Homer Dodge Martin. COURTESY OF THE ADIRONDACK MUSEUM, BLUE MOUNTAIN LAKE.

in the south, the Adirondack Park is larger than Yellowstone, Grand Canyon, and Yosemite national parks combined. A fifth of New York State is inside the "Blue Line," which makes the park larger than New Jersey or Massachusetts. At six million acres, it's about the size of New Hampshire. There are within its borders roughly two thousand peaks that by regional standards qualify as mountains. Of those, more than a hundred rise above three thousand feet, and more than forty are higher than four thousand feet. Two in the northeast quarter of the park, Marcy and Algonquin, have summits greater than five thousand feet.

These are not towering giants by western standards, or even by comparison to the White Mountains of nearby New Hampshire. The five overlapping ranges of the Adirondacks are compressed and confused to a degree that can make for some fairly formidable hiking nonetheless. In thirteen and a half miles, the trail over the Great Range from the village of Keene Valley to the summit of Mount Marcy entails a vertical ascent of some nine thousand feet.

In addition to beaver and muskrat, there are black bear, white-tailed deer, red fox, gray fox, coyote, bobcat, otter, fisher, mink, raccoons, weasels, and some forty other species of mammals in the park. Three hundred different kinds of birds spend all or part of the year in the park. There are brook trout, lake trout, brown trout, rainbow trout, landlocked Atlantic salmon, and at least seventy other fishes. There are turtles, salamanders, snakes, frogs, toads, skinks, and newts. Ninety percent of the animal species that inhabit the eastern half of the United States can be found living somewhere, at some season, in the Adirondacks.

More than wildlife, and more even than mountains and water, this Adirondack wilderness is one of trees. There are sugar maples in the park, and black maples, striped maples, red maples, silver maples, mountain maples, swamp maples, and box elders. There are black oaks, northern red oaks, chestnut oaks, bur oaks, swamp white oaks, white oaks, American beeches, and here and there some surviving American chestnuts. There are fourteen species of willow, as well as various sumacs, ashes, buckthorns, lindens, tupelos, cherries, elms, and hickories. The deciduous trees dominate, but there are also eastern hemlocks, Scotch pines, white pines, pitch pines, red pines, and jack pines in the park. There are red, black, white, and Norway spruces. There are tamaracks, the conifers that shed their needles every fall like leaves, and there are balsam firs.

A conservative estimate of the number of trees in the Adirondacks—well, a true conservative wouldn't venture to guess how many trees there are—but there are probably in the neighborhood of a billion. A single freak storm during the summer of 1995 knocked down an estimated ten million trees across an area the size of the state of Rhode Island. Damage was quite severe, especially in pockets of the Five Ponds Wilderness Area in the northwest sector of the park. Massive logs were piled twenty feet high in places there. Yet the impact of the loss of even those millions of trees was more political than biological. Commercial interests immediately agitated in Albany for permission to undertake "salvage" logging operations, while ecologists insisted that the long-term effects of the storm on the forest were likely to be negligible.

In most places the forest is relatively young; second or third growth after successive waves of farmers, loggers, charcoal makers had taken what they wanted. But not everywhere. There are groves of hardwoods in the Pigeon Lake Wilderness Area, west of Raquette Lake, that were probably never cut. Some of the birches there belie the reputation of that family of trees for slender delicacy; mature yellow birches, for instance, with trunks that two adults standing with arms outstretched cannot reach around. Along the Powley Road, south of Piseco Lake, there are spruces six feet around at the base that are probably close to three hundred years old.

And at a place called the Pine Orchard, a few miles east of the Sacandaga River in the section of the park called the Wilcox Lake Wild Forest, are three-hundred-year-old giants that centuries ago would have warranted protection by the English Crown for the sole use of the mast makers of the Royal Navy; straight-grained white pines six feet in *diameter* and perhaps two hundred feet tall.

There are many such patches of original forest sprinkled around the park, places that by virtue of remoteness or lack of the species sought by loggers at a given time managed to escape the depredations of earlier generations. North of the Stillwater Reservoir in the northwest sector of the park is the 93,000-acre Five Ponds Wilderness Area, more than half of which constitutes the largest remnant of virgin forest in the eastern United States.

The most optimistic recent estimate, by the writer and mathematician Barbara McMartin in her fascinating and exhaustive analysis of the changes in the forest, is that there are half a million acres of true old-growth forest in the park. Of these, some 200,000 acres have probably never been logged. The rest, though technically not "virgin," were cut so long ago—125 years or more—and so selectively that biologically speaking they have recovered completely. There are perhaps a million additional acres where only a well-trained forest ecologist can recognize the mark of past human intervention, not so much by the age of the existing trees but by the relative absence of the logger's favorite species, spruce.

The mark of humanity past and present is by no means absent from the Adirondacks, however. One of the most unusual aspects of the Adirondack Park, as parks go, is that people can actually own property and live within its borders. In fact, the state of New York owns only 43 percent of the land inside the Blue Line. These 2.6 million acres, the Adirondack Forest Preserve, are probably the best-protected wild lands in the country.[1] Any change in their "forever wild" status requires that an amendment to the Constitution of the State of New York be approved by two consecutive sessions of the Legislature and then ratified by a referendum of the voting public.

The rest of the park, 3.4 million acres of it, is private property of one sort or another. There are rules and regulations regarding its use, but it is all to some degree either developed or vulnerable to development. According to the most recent census, 130,000 people live on private land within the park year-round, mostly in the many villages and hamlets, but occasionally in remote roadless areas. Another hundred thousand or so move there seasonally from more crowded sections of the Northeast. In all, ten million people are thought to visit or at least make a scenic drive through the park each year.

There are traffic jams on the Fulton Chain Lakes among the boats on their way down to Old Forge to see the Fourth of July fireworks. There can be a hundred hikers on the top of Mount Marcy on the right day in August, though this is largely due to the near universal desire to climb the highest peak in the state rather than the loneliest one.

---

[1] There are equally well protected Forest Preserve lands south of the Adirondack Park in the Catskills.

And around the shores of the Saint Regis Lakes, where Inslerman traps, are the "camps" of summer people, including the more than sixty buildings that make up Topridge, once the summer residence of Marjorie Merriweather Post.

Here and there, throughout the park, are the former and current woodland palaces of the superrich families that also built the great mansions of Newport, Rhode Island, Fifth Avenue, and elsewhere. Here, too, are the summer retreats of thousands of families of more modest tastes and means. Here are summer camps for children, and members-only clubs and rustic hotels for their parents. Here are sub-divisions, condos, motels, theme parks, water slides, golf courses, tennis courts. Here are (and were) factories, hospitals, mines, logging operations, paper mills. Wal-Mart hopes to build a superstore inside the park.

More people arrive every year. According to the Adirondack Park Agency a thousand new houses are built inside the Blue Line every year; ten thousand every decade. Some who love wilderness say the implications for the future of the park are obvious and ominous. They agitate for stronger controls on development. The gloomiest among them moan that the place is already ruined, or fast getting there. But the visionaries see the Adirondack Park's mix of private and public lands as a model, however flawed, for other places where people and wilderness hope to coexist. To them the park could be a rough proto-type for the sustainable development of the world.

On the other side are those who complain that all attempts to fur-ther limit the fragmentation of the park's open spaces are, at worst, the work of "ecofascists who want to take man out of the equation." They see a selfish greed of wealthy hikers, fishermen, rock climbers, and bird-watchers from downstate. The most bitter among them look at the preponderance of low-wage service jobs in the Adirondacks and blame the locked-up resources of the Forest Preserve, or the regula-tory overburden of the state government. They look at the park and see not a model for anywhere else to emulate, but a magnification of everything that they feel is wrong with America.

It's a debate that in recent years has not always been carried out in a civilized tone. Eggs have sailed. Barns have burned. Lives have been anonymously threatened. There are humans in the Adirondacks, to be sure, often of the highly politicized sort.

This process of redefinition is nothing new. One of the few things that can be said with apolitical certainty about the lands of the Adirondack Park is that ever since the arrival of Europeans in the vicinity almost four hundred years ago, the meaning and value of "wilderness" has been in flux. Generations came to these hills and lakes to try out their ideas of material and spiritual progress. Occasionally these concepts grew out of an attempt to listen to the land. But most often, then as now, people arrived from elsewhere with their notions of what that wilderness should be, and what it meant, already in place.

In this respect, the history of the Adirondacks is not so different from that of the rest of the country. Somehow here, though, unlike so many other places in America, the wildness survived and even recovered lost ground. It persists.

This could be a result of the fact that it was in the Adirondacks, as much as anywhere, that Americans first learned to love wild places. Virtually every formulation of the wilderness idea in popular American culture has produced its Adirondack variety. The tradition of ecotourism here goes back at least as far as Ralph Waldo Emerson's 1858 camping trip to Follensby Pond—the famous "Philosophers' Camp." Adirondack history is the story of Americans out of doors.

Or it could be merely by historical accident that the Adirondacks largely escaped the filling-in that took place in the rest of the eastern United States; more fertile grounds for development lay elsewhere.

But whether by political design or economic serendipity, the essential truth remains that there is today in northern New York State a larger and healthier helping of wild open land than anywhere else east of the Mississippi River. "New York," as Thoreau observed in 1848, "has her wilderness within her own borders."

Located in the crowded northeast corner of the country—a mere half day's drive from New York City, Boston, or Montreal—the vast wild spaces of the Adirondacks are something more than an anomaly begging an explanation, though they are certainly that. To the unsuspecting inmate of this age of global warming and ozone depletion, the discovery of such riches here at the busy end of the twentieth century comes almost as a shock. It's like hearing for the first time that peregrine falcons are nesting on the stone pinnacles of the Brooklyn Bridge.

"Eagle Lake," 1881, by John Lee Fitch. COURTESY OF THE ADIRONDACK MUSEUM, BLUE MOUNTAIN LAKE.

Add the knowledge that only a century ago most contemporary popular reports said the park was largely hunted out, trapped out, fished out, and logged-over, and the shock of finding such a large and relatively healthy serving of wild land in the Adirondacks transmutes almost to wonderment. This is not the direction we are used to hearing the environment take. It's as unexpected at the end of the twentieth century as finding a contented man in his middle age tending a trapline way up some deserted and wild creek as the last leaves of autumn lap along the shore. Trappers, one might have thought, belong to some other era's idea of wilderness.

"Look at that," Bob Inslerman said, pointing to a small pile of reeds floating under the overhang of low bushes and sphagnum moss at the water's edge. "A muskrat pulled those there to eat."

A foot or two down the bank a tiny trail headed up onto the boggy land. It was no more than a few inches wide, recognizable only to someone who is familiar with the morning habits of muskrat and mink. The eyes of most people who travel on Adirondack lakes are drawn inevitably to the profiles of the surrounding mountains, or to the spiky silhouettes of white pines and hemlocks against the skyline. The eyes of a trapper, on the other hand, constantly survey the exact line where the water meets the land. Inslerman can spot a freshly gnawed cattail root from forty or fifty feet away. "That trail looks good, doesn't it?

"Like most of us people," he said, "animals are often lazy. Instead of going around this little point of land here, they will cut over it, making that little trail."

The "little point" jutted into the water all of about three feet, meaning a muskrat shortened the morning commute by six feet every time he walked over it. Inslerman took up his position on a board resting on the gunnels at the front of the boat. His boots dangled in the water on either side of the bow as he paddled around to the other side of the little tongue of land. Where the trail came back to the water, sure enough, a good-sized muskrat had stepped on the pan of one of Inslerman's leghold traps. When it felt the jaws close on its hind leg, instinct told the animal to head for deep water. There it quickly drowned.

Once in the boat, it didn't look much like a thing a person would want to wear. It looked like a drowned rat, albeit one with webbed feet and a thick soft brown pelt. Inslerman pressed as much water out of the fur as he could and put the animal in a wooden crate before leaning back over the bow to reset the trap.

He squeezed the long spring flat with one hand and pried open the trap's jaws with the other. Then he flipped a short lever called "the dog" over one of the jaws and set it lightly into a slot on the pan, setting the trap. It's worth being careful at this point, but an accident is only likely to result in a handful of bruised fingers. At five inches long, the foothold traps Inslerman uses for muskrat and mink seem much smaller than those in the imagined bygone days of Jim Bridger and the other mythic trappers of the Far West. They look almost like toys. Nevertheless, the technology and strategy of trapping are essentially unchanged after almost two hundred years. And the object of the game, the collection of furs for sale on the international market, is several hundred years older still.

A few minor adjustments to make sure the jaws lay flat, and that the pan didn't rest too high, and the trap was ready to place back at the outlet to the little trail. A trap should sit about an inch below the surface of the water; if set too shallow it is more likely to catch an animal by the front leg. A muskrat's front leg is quite thin, making it more likely to "ring off" if the chain somehow gets fouled and the animal remains in shallow enough water to thrash around.

A ring-off leaves a trapper with one foot and the muskrat with three. That this is neither uncommon nor deadly became apparent later in the afternoon, when two traps produced three-legged muskrats. One of them was quite large and fat and had lost its leg in a trap so long ago that the fur had completely grown back over the wound. The other was somewhat more recent, with a bit of rotting bone still visible.

Inslerman can remember the locations of seventy-five or a hundred different sets without the aid of markers, though an early snow makes his job much more difficult and occasionally he'll tie a little bit of surveyor's ribbon near a new set so he doesn't forget it as he paddles by. Often he can spot the cutout "V" on the pan of an undisturbed trap from his seat at the bow of the boat, and he just paddles on to the next spot. Other times there is clearly a dead animal in the trap. Usually, though, the best sign that a set has been successful is that the trap is not visible and there is no sign of a struggle. Then he rests his belly on the bow of the boat and leans over to find the trap.

At one such set he stopped prodding around the lake bottom with his gaff long enough to exclaim, "Whew, I just got a strong whiff of mink," and then he pulled up a foot-long specimen. The smell was sharp and musky and particularly strong near the mink's hind end.

"Trapping in the Adirondacks," 1870. Engraving by J. P. Davis after a painting by Winslow Homer. COURTESY OF THE ADDISON GALLERY OF AMERICAN ART, PHILLIPS ANDOVER ACADEMY.

Unlike the nine pudgy muskrats taken that day, the feel of a mink's body in the hand is that of a carnivore, sleek and bony. It was the first of two minks taken that day.

There would be no beaver, though. Late in the afternoon, in a particularly deserted stretch of his trapline, out of sight of any of the camps along the shore, Inslerman checked two more Conibears he'd set not far from an active lodge. All along the banks nearby were trails where beaver had scuffled up into the forest in search of their preferred foods.

Both of the traps were mysteriously sprung. Not gone this time, just sprung. Usually if a beaver springs a Conibear, say with a stick he's carrying, he is obliged to leave the stick in the trap. There were no sticks in either trap. And no beaver either. It was odd.

The water was glass flat. Inslerman stood in the bow for a moment, thinking. It began to rain for the thirtieth time that day. There was no one in all this wild land, it seemed, other than a pair of lonely trappers in an old tin boat.

"I love it right here," he said at last, "you would think you were somewhere in the middle of Canada, or Alaska."

After resetting the traps, with a twig he took a dollop of thick orange jelly from a plastic vial and marked a few of the Conibear stakes with it. The odor of barkstone was distinctly sweeter than that of the mink. Sweeter, and wilder.

2 *Mohawks and Missionaries*

On September 19, 1609, a member of the crew of the *Half Moon* wrote in his journal that "the people of the country came flocking aboard and brought us grapes and Pompions [pumpkins], which we bought for trifles. And many brought us beaver skins, and otter skins, which we bought for beads, knives, and hatchets." The little Dutch ship was anchored as far up the Hudson River as was possible on the incoming tide, near present-day Albany. Its captain was Henry Hudson, and it was the first European ship on the river. The international fur trade had arrived in New York.

The "people of the country" who carried the pelts through the woods to the riverbank, or paddled them down the river to sell to men on the *Half Moon,* were almost certainly members of the powerful and well-organized Haudenosaunee, more commonly known as the Iroquois Confederacy. At that time, the ancient confederacy consisted of the Seneca, Cayuga, Onondaga, Oneida, and Mohawk peoples. Virtually all of what is now upstate New York was under their control, and early European maps sometimes called the region Irocoisen.[1]

---

[1] The first known European map of the region, made in 1570 by Abraham Ortelius, calls all of northern New York "Avacal." Governor Pownall's map of the colonies of 1776 says of the park area: "This vast tract of land which is the Ancient Couchsachrage, one of the Four Beaver Hunting Countries of the Six Nations."

More specifically, the majority of those earliest fur traders were probably from the easternmost Haudenosaunee nation, the Mohawk. The name "Mohawk" derived from the Massachuset nation's word for "maneaters"; the Mohawk's own word for themselves sounded something like "kaynekero-nu," and meant "People of the Place of the Flint."

Individual Iroquois could hunt and travel anywhere within the confederacy, and intermarriage was a significant part of the glue that held the Haudenosaunee together, but there were specific boundaries between member nations. The line between the Mohawk and their western neighbors, the Oneida, ran north to south from somewhere around the present town of Waddington on the Saint Lawrence River to Utica on the Mohawk River. To the east, Mohawk influence stretched to both sides of Lake Champlain. There were conflicting claims by various non-Iroquois peoples to various corners of what would become the Adirondack Park, but the bulk of it was Mohawk territory.

This doesn't mean these original proprietors ever lived in the Adirondacks on a year-round basis. Iroquois hunted in the lower regions of the park fairly regularly, but their relationship to the more mountainous areas was squarely based on the very different realities of preconquest America. As big and wild as they seem today, the Adirondacks then were a mere fragment of a game-filled forest that stretched virtually unbroken for more than a thousand miles in every direction except east.

The Adirondacks stayed largely empty of people in those days for the same reason they were later bypassed by white settlers; it was much more practical for humans and other large mammals to make their homes in the surrounding lowlands. In the fertile Mohawk River valley to the south of the park, the Mohawk raised crops of corn, beans, and squash. There they had three great palisaded river towns named Ossernenon, Canajoharie, and Teantontalogo.

"Haudenosaunee" means "People Who Live in the Longhouse," and like the other nations of the confederacy, the Mohawk built multifamily homes that were rarely more than 15 feet wide but were regularly more than 150 feet in length. Individual families came and went through their own entrances to the longhouse, and tended their own cooking fires.

Like most Native Americans, they did not have livestock, though they did have well-trained hunting dogs. Some medical historians have postulated that this is one reason they were ultimately so tragically susceptible to the various poxes of the Europeans, most of which were originally diseases that affected livestock. Nor, apparently, were the Mohawk particularly impressed with the idea of animal husbandry.

"Leave these filthy swine that run about among your houses, feeding on garbage, and come and eat good food with us," a Mohawk diplomat named Kiotsaeton who traveled up through the park to Montreal lectured the French in 1645. "Our country is full of fish, venison, moose, beaver, and game of every kind."

Rather, the Haudenosaunee used their vast forest holdings as a range from which to draw protein to supplement their crops, the way a fishing village might make use of the sea. But their relationship with the wilderness was neither as passive nor as simplistic as the term "hunter-gatherer" typically implies. There is ample evidence that they consciously managed their game resources. Some early European witnesses of hunts noted that the Haudenosaunee avoided killing does. And though it ultimately broke down under the pressure of the international fur market, there was a prohibition on the destruction of entire beaver colonies.

"The Indians have a yearly custom (which some of our Christians have also adopted) of burning the woods, plains, and meadows in the fall of the year," Adriaen Van der Donck wrote in *A Description of New Netherlands* in 1655. Burning produces prime browse areas for deer, a notion that Van der Donck said was not lost on the Iroquois. In the park, says Philip Terrie in *Wildlife and Wilderness,* the grasslands along both the Moose and the Oswegatchie Rivers may originally have been created as hunting grounds by this method.

The cliché "impenetrable" forests in which the Iroquois and other Native Americans lived did not possess the quality of "otherness" that most modern European and American notions of wilderness usually imply. This was not only because they possessed the mythic "Indian" ability to survive in a general way, which they certainly did, but also because they very specifically knew their own turf. The principal routes through the forest, like the canoe carry from the Hudson River to Lake Champlain, or the route up the Fulton Chain Lakes to the

Raquette River and then over the Indian Carry to the Saranac Lakes, were worn a foot or more deep by centuries of foot traffic. When the Iroquois formed into teams of a hundred or more for lacrosse, a game they invented, their "field of play" wasn't a field at all but a vast, vaguely defined area that ranged over miles of woodland.

In their view of things, the confederacy—and indeed the world— was one Great Longhouse. Physically, metaphorically, and spiritually the forest was the bulk of that longhouse. It was the greater part of home. The Seneca kept watch over the western door. The Onondaga tended the central council fire, where important confederacy matters were decided by consensus. The Mohawk were the keepers of the eastern door.

But in the seventeenth century the Dutch, followed by the English, were knocking on the eastern door and offering all manner of blandishments. The pelts traded to Hudson's crew in 1609 were probably not from what is now the park, as a whole continent of good hunting began at the shore of the river, but the desire for beads, knives, hatchets, and especially cloth, guns, and eventually rum proved to be great. Furs rapidly began flowing out of even the most secluded corners of the Great Longhouse, including, ultimately, the Adirondacks. Though it wasn't immediately apparent, the arrival of Europeans in America made it a "New World" for the native peoples as well. The Haudenosaunee, who had always hunted and trapped for their food and clothing, and to some degree always carried on trade with other Native nations, became market hunters.

In 1610, only a year after Hudson's "discovery" of the river, the merchants who had funded his voyage commenced sending regular trading ships to Albany in search of pelts. They were not disappointed. More ships crossed; more furs were brought down the rivers and sold. In 1624 the first colonists arrived, most of whom set up not, as might be assumed today, at the mouth of the river on Manhattan, but in Albany. They built a fort there, which they named Orange. But lest there be any confusion about their true intentions they called the town that grew around it Beverwyck. As the name suggests, they were not there to tame the lands to the north, or even conquer them. They were there to do business with the residents of the wilderness. In good years during the next few decades, sixty thousand beaver pelts purchased from the Iroquois sailed from Beverwyck to Europe.

Also just outside the eastern door of the Great Longhouse, only this time to the north in Canada, the missionaries and traders of New France had constructed an altogether separate empire based on trading for furs with the traditional rivals of the Iroquois, the Wyandot (Hurons) and various peoples of the Algonquian language group. The first fur taken from the park and sold to a white man almost certainly didn't go down the Hudson to Albany and Amsterdam, but down the Saint Lawrence and thence to France. The people who met Hudson's ship probably knew to bring furs because French ships had been trading for furs with the Algonquins at the confluence of the Saguenay and Saint Lawrence Rivers almost every spring since the 1540s.

The Iroquois Confederacy was completely surrounded by people of the Algonquin lineage, and relations between the two groups were always somewhat strained. In the park, this took the form of regular skirmishes with Algonquins from across the Saint Lawrence River, including a group called the Montagnais who lived entirely by the fruits of the forest and who maintained a conflicting claim to hunt in Mohawk territory. The French called the Montagnais the "paupers of the wilderness" because they had no territory of their own and would occasionally show up starving at the gates of Quebec. And tradition has it that the Mohawk scornfully called them Adirondacks, or "Bark Eaters," because they were supposedly reduced by hunger to peeling trees in the winter in order to eat the soft inner layer of bark.

The fur trade with Europe significantly upped the stakes, turning a relatively stable if occasionally violent Iroquois-Algonquin balance into a highly volatile and deadly flux. Nor could the French and English be described as particularly peace-loving during the period. Directly between the two competing fur capitals lay the Adirondack Mountains, which meant that long after the major sources of fur moved west, the region would remain extremely important to soldiers and smugglers, Native or otherwise.

The principal highway between Canada and British North America throughout the colonial period was along the eastern edge of the park. Canoes were portaged from the Hudson and Mohawk Rivers to the southern tip of Lake George, from where it is a relatively short, thirty-five-mile paddle to Ticonderoga and Lake Champlain. Or they were carried directly to the southern tip of Champlain, via "the Drowned Lands," to somewhere near the present-day town of Whitehall. Once on Champlain, it was possible to paddle all the way down the lake into the Richelieu River and on to Montreal.

It was along this route that the French earned for themselves and their Algonquin allies what has often been described as the implacable and history-changing enmity of the Iroquois Confederacy. A few months before the *Half Moon* dropped anchor at what would become Albany, the French explorer Samuel de Champlain became the first European to walk on land that is now part of the Adirondack Park. His predecessor, Jacques Cartier, may have seen the High Peaks in the distance when he and his crew carried a thirty-foot cross to the top of Mont Réal in Canada on a crisp fall day in 1535. But Champlain actually came up the lake from Canada and shot a few Iroquois with his harquebus.

Almost as soon as Champlain arrived in Quebec on his third voyage to America in 1608, the Hurons told him of a great body of fresh water to the south. He wanted to see it, and with two other French soldiers and sixty Huron and Montagnais warriors he set off in early July of the following year. Once the twenty-two canoes made their way past the rapids on the Richelieu River and put in on the lake, the party switched to paddling only at night so as not to alarm the Mohawk owners of the place. While the sun was up, the explorer and his companions peered out from behind logs and branches at the water and the Green Mountains rising on the other side. From his hiding place, Champlain thought the lake beautiful enough to name after himself.

On one such day on the Adirondack side of the lake, while sleeping off a night's paddling, Champlain dreamed that he saw some Iroquois warriors drowning in the lake. He wrote later that in this dream he wanted to rescue the floundering men, but his Algonquin friends stopped him. Let the Iroquois dogs drown, he was told. When he awoke and described his dream to his real-life Algonquin companions they interpreted it as a good omen. And back in their canoes that night they did, in fact, encounter a band of Haudenosaunee. This was around ten o'clock on July 29, most likely on the Ticonderoga promontory.

Both parties agreed that the required battle should not take place in the dark, and it was scheduled for the following day. The Iroquois made camp on shore. The Algonquins with Champlain, meanwhile, lashed their canoes together and commenced the required war ceremonies in their boats. According to Champlain this lasted nearly all night, punctuated occasionally with epithets shouted across the water at the enemy. The next day's fighting, however, was brief.

The Algonquins landed at dawn and the three Frenchmen hid in the woods. Two hundred Iroquois warriors in full battle dress, which included paint, feathers, and armor that Champlain described as "woven from cotton thread and with wood," marched out to meet the enemy. Champlain now came forward clad in his metal breastplates. These are traditionally described as shining brightly in the morning sun. But even if his armor was slightly tarnished from a winter's service in the New World, the Iroquois had never seen such regalia before. Far more important than the metal on his chest, though, was the lead in his gun.

"When I saw them making a move to fire at us," Champlain later wrote in his journal, "I rested my musket against my cheek, and aimed directly at one of the three chiefs. With the same shot, two fell to the ground; and one of their men was so wounded that he died some time after. I had loaded my musket with four balls. When our side saw this shot so favorable for them, they began to raise such loud cries that one could not have heard it thunder."

Arrows briefly flew in both directions, but before Champlain even had a chance to reload, one of his European companions fired from his hiding place in the woods. This apparently was too much. The Iroquois fled into the forest, Champlain reports, "whither I pursued them, killing still more of them, and took ten or twelve prisoners."

The standard wisdom is that the Iroquois, being Indians, never forgot. "It was an evil hour for Canada," wrote Francis Parkman, the greatest chronicler of the forest wars that burned off and on between the French and English and their Native allies for the next 150 years. "My pen has no ink black enough to describe the fury of the Iroquois," wrote the Jesuit missionary Father Ragenau to his superiors in France in 1650.

No doubt in hindsight Champlain's hasty intervention in an ancient rivalry was ill advised, and certainly the Iroquois were incensed by it. But the Mohawk and their allies had many more compelling reasons than the loss of a few warriors to side with the Dutch and the English in the fur trade, and to harass the French. Since they undoubtedly understood the geography of the eastern half of North America better than the Europeans, they recognized as fast as anyone else the new order that was being established. Furs that went down the Saint Lawrence River in Huron canoes did not translate into trade goods for the Haudenosaunee. And like the Europeans, they wanted as big a piece of the fur trade as they could get. Iroquois diplomacy and warfare for the next hundred years or more was based largely on that goal.

It is the warfare that is typically remembered. In 1642 the Iroquois attacked and virtually eliminated the remnant Huron nation.[2] The Huron had once been the most numerous and wealthy people of the Great Lakes region, but the combination of European disease and Iroquois aggression—made much more potent by the addition of Dutch firearms—was too great to withstand. After the particularly bloody year of 1649 the Huron were gone as a power. Most were either dead, Christianized, or assimilated as prisoners into the Haudenosaunee.

In short order the same fate befell several other French-influenced nations. The Petun, the Neutral, the Tobacco, and the Erie all disappeared. Any canoe moving up and down the Saint Lawrence was a target. For a decade virtually all communication between Montreal and the interior of New France, as Canada was called, was cut off by Iroquois raids.

One such raiding party brought the first European to Lake George. Father Isaac Jogues was thirty-five years old in 1642 when his Jesuit superiors ordered him to journey up the Saint Lawrence with supplies for the mission among the Hurons on the lake of the same name. The previous year he had traveled almost all the way to Lake Superior and back. He was a veteran "Black Robe," as the Algonquin called the missionaries. He knew the dangers involved in travel to the west.

But for the Jesuits the wilderness was neither the Great Longhouse it was for the Iroquois, nor simply the foreign trading opportunity it was for the Dutch in Albany. The New World was a cosmic battleground. There were only three hundred Europeans in all of New France at the time, an empire that included not only Canada but most of the Mississippi Valley. They lived on the edge of a continent of evil, a place of the devil where the mettle of true Christians could be tested.

It was a testing, of course, that reaped a healthy profit in the fur trade for both the Society of Jesus and the King of France. But Father

---

[2] The Huron were actually of the Iroquoian, not the Algonquian, language group, but they were not a part of the Haudenosaunee.

Jogues did not endure what was to come for the love of money. Furs could be traded quite well from the safety of a fort, as in Albany. Or from a ship, for that matter, as the French did for decades before the founding of Quebec. Jogues and other individual Jesuits like him went into the wilderness for the purpose of winning souls.

In this, the strategy of the Black Robes was quite different from that of the third group of Europeans in the same corner of the New World. Jogues might have sympathized with his contemporary William Bradford's description of the unbroken forests and pristine waters of New England as "hideous and desolate." But unlike Jogues, the Separatists of the Massachusetts Bay Colony came to the wilderness to remove themselves from a corrupt and corrupting Old World. They came to create a perfect society on what they considered to be open real estate. The wilderness of forest surrounded them, but it was not the focus of their effort as it was for the Jesuits. The Pilgrims' project was themselves. Just as the ancient Hebrews had gone into the desert for forty years for purification, Cotton Mather, already a third-generation American, thought of the wilderness as a way station "thro' which we are passing to the Promised Land."

This English proclivity to build new societies *outside* of the wilderness would, in a less religious form, ultimately rise to overpower both the Dutch attempt to simply tap the riches of the wilds, and the Jesuit effort to create a Roman Catholic society *within* the wilderness through conversion. However at the time of Jogues's capture in 1642, the fields of the Lord in the Adirondacks and elsewhere were available for redemption.

In Jogues's descriptions the unredeemed Iroquois were "demons," to be sure, but there was no intrinsic reason they could not, like their more pliable neighbors the Hurons, become "pillars of that rising Church." And to suffer while transforming such devils into pillars, that was a blessing.

Thus, when Jogues later catalogued for his superiors in Rome the myriad tortures he endured during his trip through the park, he prefaced it by saying, "Our Lord favored us with his Cross." Throughout the report, sprinkled between horrific indignities, are statements like "God alone knows for how long a time and how many blows that were dealt on my body, but the sufferings undertaken for his love and glory are filled with joy and honor."

The 1642 raid that captured Isaac Jogues took place on the second of August on the Saint Lawrence River. There were about forty in the French party, most of whom were Hurons in various stages of conversion to Catholicism. When the Mohawks attacked, about half of these —primarily those who were unconverted—wisely disappeared into the forest. Jogues, too, managed to find a relatively secure hiding place in the rushes at the edge of the river. But when he heard the cries of René Goupil, one of the two French civilian volunteers traveling with him and his little flock of church pillars, he turned himself in.

According to reports in *The Jesuit Relations,* the remaining Frenchman, Guillaume Couture, also surrendered voluntarily, but somehow as he entered camp a scuffle broke out and a Mohawk warrior was shot. "The remaining four sprang upon [Couture], stripped off all his clothing, tore away his finger-nails with their teeth . . . and thrust a sword through one of his hands," Jogues wrote.

At this point Father Jogues managed to get loose from the men holding him and ran to his companion and threw his arms around his neck, but he was promptly dragged back off and beaten until senseless. When he came to, he received the same fingernail treatment that Couture had endured.

Fingernail removal was apparently a regional practice; thirty years before, Champlain had reported that the Hurons were biting the nails off of one of their captive Iroquois until he ended the man's misery with a bullet. René Goupil's manicure followed Jogues's, but for some reason the captured Hurons were left unharmed for the time being.

Ultimately about seventy Mohawk warriors, well armed with guns purchased or received as gifts from the Dutch at Albany, captured twenty-two prisoners and set off up the Richelieu River for Lake Champlain. After eight days that Jogues remembered as a haze of fever and mosquitoes, they camped at one of the islands at the southern end of Champlain and were joined by another, larger war party of around 130 Iroquois heading north.

That afternoon Jogues and his fellow prisoners were made to run the famous gauntlet, and this time the Hurons were not spared. All of the Iroquois warriors, now numbering around two hundred, armed themselves with clubs or switches of thorns cut from the forest and formed two lines facing each other up a hill. The prisoners were stripped and made to run naked up the incline between the lines while there was "a rivalry among [the Iroquois] to discharge upon us the most and the heaviest blows."

Jogues collapsed halfway up the hill. Partly, he said, it was out of weakness. And partly it was because he accepted "that place for my sepulcher." But he was not killed, and later that night Iroquois youths amused themselves by plucking out his beard.

The next day they reached Ticonderoga and portaged their canoes over the same land where many battles would be fought in the next century. Jogues and the other two Frenchmen became the first, if most unfortunate, white men to see Lake George. Jogues said the Iroquois called the lake "Andiatarocté," or "Place Where the Lake Closes." Early European maps called it "Lake of the Iroquois," or "Heiro-coyes," from which James Fenimore Cooper got "Horicon" for *The Last of the Mohicans*.

The party landed at the head of the lake and then marched over-land to the Mohawk River, perhaps turning south when they reached the Sacandaga River. It took thirteen days to reach the first of the Mohawk towns, Ossernenon, which like other Iroquois towns was usu-ally referred to by Europeans as a "castle" because of the wooden pal-isade that surrounded the longhouses. By then, Jogues reports, his wounds were "putrid to the extent of breeding worms."

Again they were made to run the gauntlet, which was made some-what worse this time by the iron rods that many of their new tormen-tors had purchased from the Dutch and used in place of the traditional sticks. Jogues called it the "narrow road of Paradise." Again, he says, he fell, but this time he got up and staggered through to the town. This newfound endurance may have raised the Black Robe somewhat in the estimation of his captors; it was considered a matter of honor among both Iroquois and Algonquin warriors to endure the tortures of their enemies without showing pain or fear.

After the gauntlet, Jogues and his companions were allowed a moment of rest before an Algonquin prisoner, one of Jogues's converts, was ordered to cut off the priest's thumb with a clamshell. She com-plied. And that night the youths dropped hot embers on the staked-down men.

They were displayed for two days on a wooden platform con-structed for the purpose and then taken on a victory tour of sorts to the other two main Mohawk towns. In Teantontalogo, Jogues reports,

he somehow managed to baptize some new Huron prisoners that were
brought in from another raid.

Ultimately Guillaume Couture was adopted by a family, as most
Iroquois prisoners were, and his suffering abated. René Goupil, however, was killed with a hatchet and his body dragged through the village and left in a ravine. Jogues found the corpse and buried it under
some rocks in a stream, but the next day when he went to the river to
give it a proper Christian burial he was unable to find it. So he
chanted a service of the dead over the water. It was the first of October. The foliage would have just been coming into its full glory.

Late in the season Jogues was taken along as a firewood boy of sorts
on the fall hunt. It was probably a grand affair, as Iroquois hunting
methods required large parties of hunters and were attended with
much ceremony. Before the arrival of metal traps at the end of the
1700s, beaver were usually taken by breaking down their dams and
then spearing the animals as they tried to escape the pond. Or, in winter, the Iroquois chopped a few holes in the ice, to which the beaver
would go for air shortly after the lodge was destroyed. Teams of hundreds of hunters sometimes drove deer into lakes, or down long fences
that took days to construct and funneled the herd to where other
hunters were waiting with clubs and hatchets. Smaller furbearers
were caught in snares, nets, cage traps, or with dogs. Guns were
reserved for moose and the occasional bear.

The hunt most likely was to the north, perhaps to the Moose River
plains. If so, Jogues probably added the interior of the park to his list
of "first European to see" achievements. But he didn't stay the whole
time. For some reason the women on the hunt particularly despised
the priest, perhaps because he refused to eat any game that he
believed had been offered to pagan gods. He was sent back to the village early.

After a while his suffering abated, and he began to believe that
God must have intended him to minister to the Mohawks and their
prisoners. The captors, for their part, came to believe that their Black
Robe prisoner was unwilling or unlikely to escape. He was permitted
to wander unmolested from town to town as a sort of national mascot
or curiosity. Occasionally, more French and Huron prisoners were
brought in and Jogues converted some of them. He baptized one
woman while she was being burned at the stake. He later reported

that he converted seventy Mohawks and other Haudenosaunee by the following August.

Around this time he escaped; he might pass out of the purview of this book except that he returned to the Adirondacks a few years later. The Mohawks had taken him along on a fur-trading trip to Albany, which at that time consisted of a log fort and about thirty houses belonging to Dutch traders and farmers. When the Dutch saw him they encouraged him to sneak onto a vessel leaving for Europe, and after a night spent agonizing over whether his true mission was to convert the Mohawks, he agreed. A rumor that his captors were outraged over a message he had sent from Albany to the French in Canada, and that they planned to kill him as soon as they got back to the Mohawk River, may have helped clarify God's plans for him.

Jogues's luck, however, was not yet improved. He and his captors were staying in a hundred-foot-long barn that was home to a Dutch farmer, his Mohawk wife, and a small herd of cattle. The plan was for Jogues to slip out in the evening and make his way down to the shore of the river, where a boat would be left for him to row out to the waiting ship. On his first attempt to leave the barn, however, he ran into the farmer's dog, which bit him in the leg, and he was forced to return to the barn to get a bandage. His captors decided to sleep on either side of him to prevent another attempt.

At dawn, though, he sneaked out again, managed to elude the cur, and limped down to the river. But by then the falling tide had left his boat high and dry on a large mudflat. He shouted to the ship, which he could plainly see anchored in the river, but no one heard him. Finally, by rocking the boat backward and forward, he was able to wiggle it across to the water and row to the safety of the ship. It was almost a year since he had set off on the Saint Lawrence in his canoe.

Two days later the anger of the Mohawks at Jogues's disappearance caused the officers of the Dutch vessel to lose their courage, and they put the ragged priest back ashore and left town on the outgoing tide. His next hiding place was beneath the business office of a Dutch trader. Through cracks in the ceiling he could see and hear his former captors come in above him to sell furs. Six weeks later, if only to get him out of the basement, the Dutch took up a collection and paid the Iroquois a modest ransom of three hundred livres.

Jogues was on the next boat to Manhattan, already a cosmopolitan place where eighteen languages were spoken. One of the city's five hundred residents gave him a new set of clothes for his trip back to Europe. This made the crossing more comfortable than it might have been, as he was forced to sleep on deck because there was no room for him below. But at Falmouth, England, Jogues stayed alone on board while the entire crew went ashore to celebrate the crossing in the sailor's manner. As soon as darkness fell, a band of harbor thieves came aboard, beat the priest up, and stole his new hat and coat.

Finally, Jogues arrived in France on Christmas night in 1643. He became a minor celebrity and the dinner guest of choice in the royal courts of Roman Catholic Europe. He had, after all, been to hell and back. In still, quiet moments however, his God continued to tell him that the Mohawks needed him. That spring he procured a special dispensation from the pope allowing him to say the mass despite the otherwise disqualifying fact that he was now physically handicapped, and he returned to Montreal. There, a truce between the French and the Mohawk was being negotiated based on an exchange of prisoners.

It was at this conference that the Mohawk chief Kiotsaeton commented on the good fishing back home. Then, as now, the Iroquois were renowned for their eloquence and political sophistication and Kiotsaeton's long and beautiful speech was duly recorded in the *Jesuit Relations* of 1645. The translator was Jogues's old companion Guillaume Couture, who had risen to a position of some influence in Ossernenon. With the thumbless Father Jogues listening in the audience, Kiotsaeton calmly explained to the French that the Mohawk always intended to return the hapless priest, if only he hadn't been prematurely stolen by the Dutch.

Though the French believed that they had just concluded a general truce with all five nations of the Haudenosaunee, they soon found out that they had made a separate peace only with the Mohawk. Still, they hoped to make it succeed, as the Mohawk considered Montreal, Three Rivers, Lake Champlain, Lake George, and the Adirondacks to belong to themselves. The governor of New France felt that a person of relative importance should go down to the Mohawk River to seal the deal. Father Jogues was selected.

He delivered a few canoeloads of gifts in mid-May of 1646, and might have stayed on indefinitely except, according to some sources, his new Mohawk friends warned him that he would be killed if members of other Iroquois nations found him around. So he returned to Canada. But God's work was still unfinished, and the proselytizer set off up the Richelieu and Lake Champlain for the third time in September of that year. It would be his last trip.

On the lake, Jogues and his companions learned that the general mood of the Mohawk toward the French had soured. According to both the Jesuits and the Dutch in Albany the primary reason was that some of the assimilated Hurons in the Mohawk villages had told their captors, not incorrectly, that ever since their people had begun associating with the French they had been plagued with strange and incurable diseases. A strange plague had, in fact, broken out among the Mohawks after Jogues's last visit.

Jogues's Algonquin escort immediately turned back, but the stalwart missionary and one French volunteer continued on up the lake. Though there were some among the Mohawks who hoped to preserve the peace, the majority apparently did not agree with Jogues that his holy mission was among them. The priest was soon apprehended on Lake Champlain and taken up Lake George as a prisoner for the second time. This time he took it upon himself to name it Lac Saint Sacrement, a name it kept among Europeans for a hundred years.

Again Jogues was marched overland to the villages, where this time he was unceremoniously killed with a hatchet. The "peace" had lasted less than a year.

Father Isaac Jogues was only the most famous of hundreds of prisoners taken by both sides during the "beaver wars" of the seventeenth century. The majority of the captives were not Europeans, though more is known about white prisoners because the primary sources for the period are the Jesuits and various New Englanders. Most who were captured by the Iroquois were, like Couture, eventually completely and willingly assimilated into Haudenosaunee culture or, like Jogues, killed. But not all.

Occasionally prisoners taken by one side or the other escaped and made their way back home. Depending on the circumstances of their escape, some no doubt crossed land in the park. One such woman came floating down the Saint Lawrence River to Montreal in the spring of 1647. She was a converted Huron whose Christian name was Marie; her story was included in the *Jesuit Relations*.

She escaped at night from her Onondaga captors outside the main village of the Oneidas, about thirty miles west of the park. To avoid making footprints in the snow, and presumably to confuse her captors, she didn't go immediately northeast toward home, but headed instead even farther west along the well-traveled path between the various nations of the Iroquois. Only when she reached Onondaga, the capital of the confederacy, did she cut back east, toward the Adirondacks, but more importantly, toward home.

Hungry and dressed in only a light tunic against freezing Adirondack nights, Marie lived out a legendary survival story. She fed herself on roots and the inner bark of trees, and a few turtles that she collected while traveling. She twice tried to end it all by hanging herself from a tree, but later told the nuns in Montreal that the Catholic God persuaded her to want to live.

Life was somewhat better after she found a hatchet in an abandoned camp, with which she was able to fashion the bow-and-arrow-like friction device with which the Iroquois (and many other Native Americans) traditionally ignited fires. The tiny fires provided warmth, but were quickly stamped out before the smoke could give her location away.

Her lot improved even more when she overheard a party of Iroquois hunters approaching and hid beside the path until they had passed. She then followed their trail back to their canoe (most likely constructed of red elm bark rather than canoe birch, which was rare in Iroquois country) and solved the problem of its being too large for solo paddling by chopping it in half and patching it back together in a more manageable size. By the time the Haudenosaunee hunters returned to find half their boat missing she was gone.

Depending on how far west she was, she may have been on a tributary to the Grass River or the Saint Regis River. If not, it may have been the Oswegatchie. At any rate, she ultimately paddled into the Saint Lawrence. After a two-month journey, she arrived back at Montreal to resume her Christian education with a canoe full of duck and goose eggs she had collected, freshly speared and smoked fish, and a generous quantity of dried venison from deer that she had driven into the water and then chased down and slaughtered with her hatchet.

The fighting and the prisoner taking continued off and on for most of the century. But each time that Iroquois expansion and European dis-

ease eliminated another Algonquin nation, the French simply reestablished their trading relationship with the next tribe west. Worse, as the
century progressed, the demand for furs proved too great for Haudenosaunee game management techniques. By 1670, according to
some sources, most of the important furbearers were gone from the
Adirondacks and the other New York hunting grounds.

Iroquois political expansion then took on an added urgency. Their
effective dominion ultimately extended from the Carolinas to the
Mississippi Valley to Hudson Bay. By the turn of the century Iroquois
hunters were routinely traveling a thousand miles on the fall fur hunt
in order to have sufficient furs to sell to the Albany traders in the
spring.

From early April to the end of June, Native trappers from the north
and west traveled by canoe to Albany with the previous season's haul.
The town had a government-sanctioned monopoly on the fur trade in
New York, which the English preserved when they took over the colony
in 1664. This policy suited the Iroquois, as the Albany cartel remained
steadfastly opposed to any promotion of white settlement above them
on the river. For more than a century, until their monopoly was broken
in 1725 by the founding of a trading post at Oswego on Lake Ontario,
the clique of fur traders in Albany and exporters in Manhattan who
together ran the New York colony didn't particularly care what happened in the wilderness to the north. The Dutch believed, among
other things, that the northern woods were populated by unicorns,
which in their minds was reason enough not to go there. As long as the
furs flowed out, the burghers were happy.

Everything was ultimately sold to somebody in Albany, but the
principal goods the Indians wanted in exchange for their furs were
wampum, rum, gunpowder, and most importantly wool cloth. Actual
guns were less important than might be imagined, since most got
their armaments as gifts from either French or English authorities.
For a long time Jew's harps were hot sellers.

There were definite fashions among the Native buyers, though,
and the smart trader had to keep up with them. A cloth called duffels,
from the town of Duffels near Antwerp, was in demand for a while
because it made nice blankets. But a wool fabric called Strouds, after
the town where it was made in England, was in the long run the most
popular trade item. The Iroquois were choosy shoppers, and wouldn't

accept fabric that was inadequately dyed. The favored colors were blue and red, the darker the better. Nor were Native buyers inclined to want cloth if it wasn't sufficiently luxurious.

"Those Savages who come to trade here will have good, choice goods, and do understand them to perfection," a trader named Livingston wrote to his supplier in London in 1734.

The trade was highly regulated. In order to prevent inflation, there were limits to the presents a merchant could give a Native trapper. Incoming trappers were not allowed to be swarmed by merchants haranguing them and promising them deals just to get them into their establishments. Nor were Natives allowed to enter private homes; they were required to sleep in special dormitories outside of town. This segregation only applied during the trading season, however, supposedly to prevent the use of rum behind closed doors as an inducement to lower prices. Natives could, and often did, stay with their white associates in the off-season.

There was also a prohibition against extending credit to a Native, though many traders did. In the early 1700s a man named Evert Wendell Jr. kept an account book of such deals. He drew pictures of the number of furs he was owed by Native trappers—twenty-five beaver here, fifteen marten there, a bearskin, and so on. The trapper was then obligated to do all his trading with Wendell until enough skins were delivered to retire the debt. If payments were tardy, Wendell simply added more skins to the account as interest. Sometimes he kept a man's gun as security.

Wendell also offered Native trappers goods on consignment for sale back in the interior, though this too was technically against the law. He traded with both men and women, noting in his logbook that the women were less likely than men to allow themselves to be cheated.

Not surprisingly, perhaps, prices paid to Indians were low relative to the trader's profits even when the prohibition on rum was observed, which was not always the case. The markup between the price paid to a Native trapper and the price received for a fur in Europe was almost a thousand percent. Furthermore, demand was stable; in 1638, King Charles I of England decreed that "nothing but beaver stuff or beaver wool shall be used in the making of hats."

The hatters desired only the soft, barbed fur of the beaver's undercoat. Because the coarse guard hair that lay above this was difficult and expensive to remove, and was of no use in making the waterproof felt, Native trappers often made a rough coat out of several pelts which would be worn with the fur side down for several seasons. Once the guard hair fell out, the pelt was a "coat beaver" or a "castor gras" and was significantly more valuable than "castor sec" or "parchment."

With the paper currencies of the colonies in a seemingly perpetual state of hyperinflation, beaver pelts were often exchanged between whites as a form of money. A bale of parchments might go from warehouse to warehouse around the colony before someone finally sent it to Europe. But if beaver wasn't available, anything with fur would go; one order in 1751 listed a wildcat, otters, wolves, foxes, fishers, minks, martens, raccoons, and muskrats.

For all its complexity, though, the English fur trade remained rather paltry compared to that of the far-flung voyageurs of New France. By 1700 the French were trading with native nations in the Rocky Mountains, and the Iroquois were spread too thin to try to do much about it. Their fearsome reputation was intact, but the attrition of the continual wars and raids and new European diseases took its toll on the Iroquois' ability to protect their vast sphere of influence.

Meanwhile, the French had launched several large-scale attacks on individual nations of the Iroquois Confederacy. The home turf was also increasingly under pressure from the Susquehanna and other tribes that were being pushed out of the lands to the south and east by European colonists and their African slaves. In short, the Iroquois were overextended and threatened by the pace of English expansion to their south. They began to make deals with their former enemies the French that preserved the Iroquois right to hunt in lands they had previously conquered, but required them to desist from molesting French traders moving up and down the Saint Lawrence River.

In the end, perhaps inevitably, the Iroquois attempt to control the fur trade was reduced to an effort to ensure their own independence between the growing spheres of French and English influence. In 1701, at a big conference in Montreal, they made peace with the Ottawa, the Miami, the Illinois, the Winnebago, the Potawatomi. They promised to remain neutral in any coming war between England and France, and gave permission for Jesuits to come into their territory. As the center of the balance of power in North America, the Iroquois did not want to be perceived as too strongly wedded to one side or the other. For a short time gifts poured in from both great powers.

There was another ongoing development that made this new policy amenable to the Haudenosaunee, one that brought the Adirondack region squarely back into the fur trade picture. With every passing decade, English industry further outpaced its French competition. French gunpowder was still preferable, but virtually everything else was better and cheaper from England. English manufactures—and as the new century progressed, New England rum—drew furs to New York regardless of where or by whom they were caught. After King William's War ended in 1685 more furs were actually smuggled through the park to Albany from Canada than were brought in legally from the west.

Canadians typically hired Iroquois to carry the pelts to New York. Many of these were Mohawks who moved from their home valley to Sault Saint Louis, near Montreal, where they were converted by the Jesuits. They became known as Caughnawagas—Praying Indians— and their descendants still live on the Caughnawaga Reservation in Quebec.

Once again, the preferred route was up and down Lakes Champlain and George, though French patrols on Champlain presented a problem. To avoid them, some smugglers made the trip over the ice in winter, or went directly through the park along the Sacandaga River. Another winter route used by smugglers from the end of the 1700s up until the War of 1812—when it was rebellious Americans who wanted contraband English goods from Canada—was on snowshoes up the Grass River, which originates in the northwest corner of the park. One way or another, the furs usually got through, if only because whenever the French authorities clamped down too hard on the trade the Praying Indians would mention to their powerful Jesuit confessors that they were thinking of heading back to New York. The priests would pull the necessary strings to keep the pews full.

It was all very secretive, though more to protect the merchants on the French side than those in Albany. In letters that traveled up the lakes with the Mohawks, Canadian contacts were identified only by code. Robert Sanders, one of the bigger contraband traders on the New York side, never knew the real names of the persons with whom he traded. The most notorious smugglers of all, however, were two women who for years ran their operation right under the noses of the French authorities. Ultimately even the Jesuits couldn't, or wouldn't, prevent the Desaltier sisters' eviction from Sault Saint Louis.

In little over a century, the pressures of the international fur trade had largely transformed the relationship of the Iroquois to the wilderness in which they lived. Some had gone so far as to be converted by the French to a religion that kept its sights not on the care and maintenance of the Great Longhouse of this world, but firmly on the hereafter. And while the majority still followed the old ways and understandings as far as religion and philosophy were concerned, economically they were far more like their European trading partners in Albany than their grandparents were when Henry Hudson first arrived. With beaver in short supply, the Iroquois' exquisite knowledge of the forest and its workings earned them a higher margin as smugglers than as trappers. They too were middlemen now, trying to protect their piece of the trade.

Such was the state of the fur business in upstate New York at the appearance on the scene of one of the most colorful characters in colonial history, a man who perhaps not coincidentally also built one of the first summer pleasure homes in what is now the Adirondack Park. William Johnson was a fur trader, too, but what he represented was the arrival in upstate New York of that third, British, strategy toward wilderness that had first taken root with the Pilgrims in Massachusetts.

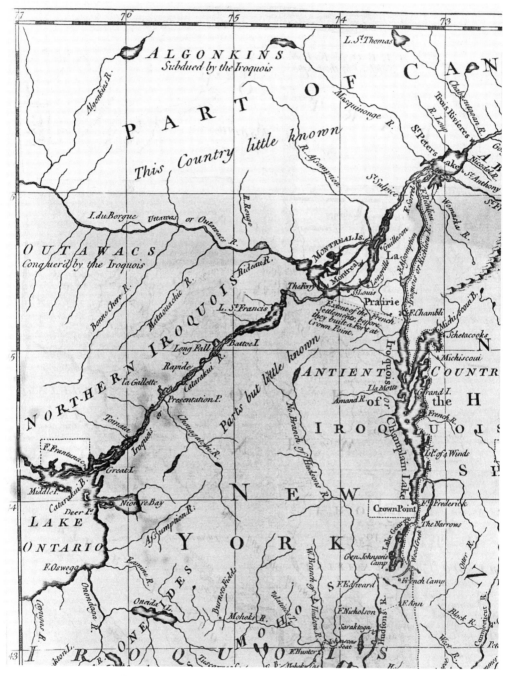

The Adirondacks during the French and Indian War—1757.

3   *Dances of War*

When the man who would become Sir William Johnson, Baronet, his Britannic Majesty's superintendent general of Indian affairs, colonel of the Six Nations, and major general in the British service arrived in the Mohawk Valley in 1734, he was just the poor nineteen-year-old nephew from Ireland sent to develop his rich uncle's new speculative holdings in the wilds of upstate New York. But that soon changed.

To the chagrin of the burghers of Albany, he rapidly made himself very rich off the fur trade. In 1743 the Albany faction forced a law through the Provincial Assembly specifically intended to put a brake on Johnson's trade. But it was too late to enforce it. Johnson was such good friends with the Iroquois and his fellow settlers by that time that he was virtually above the colonial law. He ignored it and carried on making money.

The traditional clique of fur traders and exporters was even more outraged in 1746, when Governor George Clinton put Johnson in charge of New York's Indian affairs. The Assembly refused to fund any ceremonial gifts for Johnson to present to the Native nations. Soon enough, though, Johnson's goodwill with the Mohawks—along with presents paid for out of his own pockets—pro-

duced the result Clinton desired. The Iroquois announced in August
of 1746 at a conference in Albany that "should any French priests now
dare to come among us, we know no use for them but to roast them."

Just the fact that Johnson or his uncle, the British admiral Sir Peter
Warren, owned land in the heart of Iroquois territory was a sign that
things were in flux. As more and more of the fur trade became dominated by the Praying Indians engaged in smuggling French furs down
to New York, the bargaining power of their unredeemed Iroquois
cousins waned. More importantly though, the ending of the Albany
monopoly and the opening of a fort at Oswego in 1725 meant the
Mohawk River was now an important supply route to the English military force on the Great Lakes; New York reversed its old policy of dis-
couraging white settlement above Albany and began to promote the
colonization of Iroquois territory.

Perhaps worst of all for the Haudenosaunee, by the mid-1700s rum
had caught up with and surpassed wool as the primary trade good.
Throughout the 1600s the Iroquois leadership at Onondaga and elsewhere requested that the Europeans control the quantity of alcohol sold
to their people, or ban it outright, but they were turned down. The
markup on New England rum, even before watering down, was often five
times that on woolens. By the time the Iroquois succeeded in getting the
New York legislature to revive an ancient prohibition against selling
rum to Indians, in 1716, it was already too late. Dissent among their own
people drove the Iroquois leadership to ask that it be repealed.

Through legitimate real estate transactions and outright thievery,
the Haudenosaunee began to lose pieces of the Great Longhouse,
including the Adirondacks. But this should not be interpreted to mean
that the confederacy was taken for granted, or that the Iroquois were
powerless. The competition between the French and the English in
North America was lurching toward its midcentury climax in the
French and Indian War, and the Iroquois were more important than
ever. The deference paid to them was such that when their representatives showed up at a conference in 1710 with all the hatchets, mus-
kets, and other items they had purchased over the decades that had
broken or worn out, Governor Robert Hunter agreed that, of course,
they should all be repaired free of charge.

For William Johnson, this meant his power and influence among
whites in the colony grew in proportion to his ability to sway the Iro-

quois, and especially the Mohawks, back in the direction of the English at a time when they were increasingly inclined to trust the French. The source of his influence among the Haudenosaunee, on the other hand, was simply that he always dealt with them relatively fairly, and on their own terms.

Johnson lived in the wilderness of upstate New York as if it were a foreign country, which of course at the time it was, but which remarkably few of his countrymen understood. He learned the Mohawk language, a feat previously attempted only by Jogues and a few other missionaries. "The style abounds with noble images, strong metaphors, and equal in allegory to many of the eastern languages," he wrote. By "eastern," he presumably meant European.

And when circumstances warranted it, Johnson shed his powdered wig and knickers and donned a breechcloth. More than once he led delegations of Iroquois to Albany fully decked out, as were they, in traditional war dress and paint. Francis Parkman wrote that Johnson "joined in their games and dances, sometimes borrowed their dress and their paint, and whooped, yelped, and stamped like one of themselves."

A later biographer, James Thomas Flexner, wrote of Johnson that "whole areas of his mind remained unencumbered with those seemingly revealed preconceptions, based on early training, that make most people unreceptive to exotic thought. Add to this that, although transcendentally able, he was the least introspective of men, that he never tried to codify his ideas and was thus unaware of theoretical inconsistencies, and that his instinctive human sympathies were warm."

Johnson became the Haudenosaunee's advocate before the colonial and royal governments. He regularly begged the Lords of Trade in London for more money for gifts for them. He railed against the Livingstons and other crooked land speculators. He repeatedly implored the Assembly to outlaw the sale of alcohol to Natives.

In a letter to Governor Clinton on May 7, 1747, he mentions that a man named Clement had set up a booze joint twenty yards from Johnson's own house. Clement was getting all the government bounty money that Johnson was paying out to Iroquois for French and Huron scalps, he complained, "which leaves them as poor as ratts."

Scalp bounties were standard practice for both European powers, though authorities had to be vigilant against the skillful warrior who could carve two scalps off a single human head. In the 1750s the New

York Assembly paid ten pounds for hair and skin off the heads of adult males and twenty pounds for live prisoners. Male children brought ten pounds dead or alive. There was no bounty in New York on female scalps, but if one had enough inventory to justify a trip across the Berkshires, Massachusetts would buy them.

Not that Johnson, who would eventually die of sclerosis of the liver, had any problem with *giving* drinks to Indians. He regularly threw huge parties at his mansion, at which whole oxen were roasted and the rum punch—he bought his limes by the thousand—and beer flowed plentifully and free of charge. One of Johnson's contemporaries, a man who clearly had less appreciation for cultural diversity than his host, wrote in his journal: "July 2nd. Dined with Sir Wm. at Johnson Hall. The office of Superintendent very troublesome. Sir Wm. continually plagued with Indians about him—generally from 300 to 900 in number—spoil his garden, and keep his house always dirty."

It was only the time-honored practice of taking advantage of the Native appetite for alcohol that offended Johnson. "There is another grand villain, George Clock," Johnson went on in his letter to Governor Clinton, "who lives by Canajoharie Castle [the second Mohawk town] and robs the Indians of all their clothes." It's unclear from the letter whether Johnson was more concerned for the well-being of his

"Sir William Johnson Hall," by E. L. Henry, 1903. COURTESY OF THE ALBANY INSTITUTE OF HISTORY AND ART.

friends, or for their diminished ability to kill the French and their allies. "It is impossible to do anything with them while there is such a plenty [of liquor] to be had all round the neighborhood, being forever drunk," he wrote.

Johnson was one of the very few white men ever to be officially made an honorary member of the Mohawk nation. They called him "Warraghiyagey," which he happily translated for anyone who asked as "Man Who Undertakes Great Things." He always kept a council fire burning in his backyard, except for a brief period when he quit representing New York to the Iroquois out of disgust at colonial indifference to Indian affairs.

He did not, however, go native the way more than a few assimilated prisoners and other Europeans did. Though he enjoyed behaving like a Roman while in Rome he wasn't a tourist. Johnson was collecting land, in the park and elsewhere. One story goes that his great friend Tiyanoga, who was also known as Hendrick and was one of the most important Mohawk sachems of the time, mentioned that he had dreamed recently that Johnson had given him a nice new military jacket of the sort Johnson himself wore. The jacket was promptly presented to a grateful Hendrick.

A few months later, though, Johnson told Hendrick that he, too, had recently had a good dream. In it the wise and generous Mohawk chief had given him, William Johnson, the triangle of land lying between the two branches of the Moose River. Johnson duly received the sizable tract, which is now in the park. Henceforth the two friends agreed to discontinue dreaming.

This story is almost certainly apocryphal; the savvy white who out-dreams the Native was a stock myth on the frontier from New York to Georgia. But Johnson usually did get his lands for a very good price. And he intended to fill them with Europeans. After the French and Indian War he proudly pointed out that even though his lands were considered in the line of fire "I nevertheless, at considerable expense, established over 100 families thereon during the heat of the war, furnishing them with cattle, provisions, and money to encourage them to remain thereon, at a time when all the neighborhood were abandoning their settlements. . . ."

Johnson respected the Mohawks, and loved them, but he was both a proud product and an agent of the advancing white frontier. Besides, his tastes and ambitions were far too feudal ever to take up full-time living in the forest.

The gardens at his manor house just south of the park in Johnstown were tended by a man he called "Old Daddy Savage,"[1] but the serious farm work was handled by a harvest manager and ten or fifteen African slaves. Most of these had been confiscated from Spanish ships during the War of Jenkins's Ear by Johnson's uncle, the British admiral. The slaves were generally outfitted like locals in loincloths or deerskin leggings, except that Johnson had special jackets sewn for them and the rest of the staff by his full-time tailor.

In addition to the tailor, he employed a secretary, a doctor, a blacksmith, and various cooks and scullery maids. A uniformed Mohawk boy gave out tobacco. Two white-skinned dwarfs, both of them apparently named Bartholomew, waited at table while another short person, Billy, entertained the guests with his violin. Billy got his job after the blind Irish harpist who had it before him moved to Philadelphia. Johnson's valet was a large man of African and Native American descent, whom he called Pontioch.[2] His bodyguards were Mohawk.

Pontioch invariably accompanied Johnson on trips to his summer houses in what is now the park, and Billy went along as well whenever the boss was in the mood for music. The first house was about fourteen miles from Johnstown on the Sacandaga River. It was a handsome one-story white cottage with green trim and doors, and a fieldstone foundation. A columned porch went all the way around the house and was constructed with a promenade on the top. Two slaves, whose first names were Nicholas and Flora, lived there all summer tending to the large garden, pruning the fruit trees, milking the cows, and brushing the two horses that Johnson kept there. It was called, appropriately, Summer House, though the best hunting and fishing was in the spring and fall.

The second house was about four miles downstream on a knoll at a bend in the river. There was an enormous wetland on the east side

---

[1] Johnson Hall is still a lovely building, with manicured grounds. But trying to imagine the dignitaries of the Iroquois Confederacy arriving by dense forest path for wild, ox-roasting Baccanals is made difficult today by the man on the sit-down lawn mower and the chubby boy with the remote-control miniature off-road vehicle.

[2] Johnson once negotiated with the real Pontiac, which is doubtless where he got the nickname for his trusty valet.

of the river where tens of thousands of waterfowl nested and wild cranberries grew in abundance. Pontioch would row from one house to the other as required while Billy fiddled in the bow and Johnson sat in the stern steering, fishing, or shooting at ducks with his double-barreled gun.

Clearly William Johnson wasn't seeking a "wilderness" experience in the untamed way it would now be defined. The riverbanks between the two houses were always kept trim and clear of swamp willows and other obstacles to his angling. Still, choosing to go even farther from "civilization" than his day-to-day life on the frontier for purposes of recreation was something that no one in America would have dreamed of doing a century before. Wild land was not just inaccessible and frightening to the European at the beginning of the seventeenth century, it was actually considered downright unattractive. As Roderick Nash points out in his classic *Wilderness and the American Mind,* mountains, in particular, were regarded as "warts, pimples, blisters, and other ugly deformities on the earth's surface."

At the time of Johnson's mid-eighteenth-century fishing adventures in the park, the Romanticism that would ultimately change attitudes toward wilderness was just beginning to appear back in Europe. Among Europeans in America, where the wilderness was still populated by occasionally hostile people with differently colored skin, such ideas were as yet unthinkable. So if Johnson was fashion-forward in his appreciation of the out-of-doors it was most likely by accident, though he was clearly someone who cared little for the sensibilities of more refined circles. He had large dinner parties almost every night that lasted until two or three in the morning. He loved dirty jokes. He went to the Sacandaga simply because he had fun there.

The river was his playground, his Eden, and he named various landmarks along the way after things that happened to him, names that in some cases have stuck. A stream where his fishing buddy Doc Daly fell out of the boat became Daly's Creek; one where the same thing happened to another crony named Hans became, of course, Hans's Creek. He didn't strive for originality. He called the second house simply Fish House.

Fish House was not nearly as well appointed as Summer House, having only two rooms, no permanent staff, and no furniture. But that didn't prevent it from serving as a pleasure palace of the first order.

Near the mouth of Hans's Creek lived a farmer Johnson knew named Wormwood. And Farmer Wormwood, very conveniently, had two unmarried farmer's daughters.

Johnson would often bring a bed down with him from the summer house, and as he passed the farm if he were in a lively mood he would fire off his double-barreled gun in quick succession. Hearing the signal, one of the Wormwood girls—usually the black-haired, dark-eyed, "well-formed" Susannah, but occasionally her apparently less attractive but still willing younger sister, Elizabeth—would run down a little path to Fish House. When Sir William and Pontioch finished fishing their way down the stream to the house, one or the other Wormwood daughters, or maybe even both, would invariably be waiting with open arms.

Once in a while, their parents would come along for fun and spend the night on the floor in the next room. At least once Susannah, her parents, and Johnson all slept together in one bed. "Sir William told us how to lay," old man Wormwood is remembered to have said one morning to a neighbor, Mrs. Shew, who lived with her husband a quarter of a mile farther down the river from Fish House.

"He first directed the women to get in the middle, 'and now', said he to me, 'you get on that side and take care of your old woman next to you, and I'll get in on this side and try to take care of Susannah.' " Everyone was apparently happy with the arrangement except Mrs. Shew, who was appalled.

Johnson loved women, and they seemed to have appreciated him. He was six feet tall, which was big for the time. He had dark hair and green eyes that looked gray in a certain light and were either slightly crossed or slightly walleyed, depending on the describer. He must have been attractive; the English press reported that he had fathered seven hundred children. At least one of these was with Susannah Wormwood.

His primary love during the first half of his life, however, was a woman named Catherine Weisenberg. She, according to the nineteenth-century historian Jeptha Simms, was an "uncommonly fair and whole-some looking maid." As with the Wormwood sisters, she seems to have come to Johnson as a result of his vaguely seignorial relationship with the mostly German settlers who lived around him.

Some of her many descendants later claimed otherwise, but Weisenberg most likely arrived in America as an indentured servant in the 1740s. She apparently spent some time in Madagascar before winding up in New York City where she was "bought" on the wharf by a pair of brothers who lived near Johnson at Warrensburg.

They didn't have her for long because, as the lore has one brother explaining: "That damned Irishman came the other day and offered me five pounds for her, threatening to horsewhip me and steal her if I would not sell her. I thought five pounds was better than a flogging and took it, and he's got the gal." Johnson may have married Weisenberg at some point, though there is no record of it. Her children, at any rate, were raised as heirs to the estate.

After Weisenberg's death in 1759, Johnson's primary relationship was with the formidable Christian Mohawk woman Molly Brant, with whom he eventually had nine children. She virtually ran the household, ordering supplies and organizing the staff. But more importantly, she cemented and influenced Johnson's links to the matriarchal Iroquois, a culture in which the male chiefs and sachems were elected by and served at the pleasure of the women of the nation. Her brother was Joseph Brant, who fought with the British in the American Revolution, and then helped the new United States secure "peace" with the Native nations once the war was over.

It was, in fact, Johnson's Iroquois connections that had first drawn him to the park. Long before he ever built Fish House, he was tapped by Governor William Shirley of Massachusetts to round up as many Iroquois fighters as he could, and lead the militia from New England and New York in the king's effort to remove the French from Lakes George and Champlain.

Ever since 1731, when the French built Fort Saint Frédéric at Crown Point, they and their allies had periodically harassed the frontiers of New York and New England. They even called their fort "Scalp Point." The raid of August 1746 was particularly successful but not atypical. Five hundred French soldiers and two hundred Abnaki and converted Iroquois warriors paddled south from the fort along the lakeshore through the Drowned Lands, which are now at the southeast corner of the park. From there they marched over to Massachusetts and took the entire population of Williamstown (twenty-two people) back to Canada to be traded for French prisoners.

On the way back to Scalp Point, the commander, François-Pierre de Rigaud de Vaudreuil, wrote in his journal, "every house was set on fire, and numbers of domestic animals of all sorts were killed. French and Indians vied with each other in pillage. . . . Wherever we went we made the same havoc, laid waste both sides of the river, through twelve leagues of fertile country, burned houses, barns, stables, and even a meeting-house, in all above two hundred establishments, killed all the cattle, and ruined all the crops."

Back at Champlain, Rigaud further "gave leave to the Indians, at their request, to continue their fighting and ravaging, in small parties . . . wherever they pleased, and I even gave them a few officers and cadets to lead them."

The key to success in wilderness battle of this sort was having an adequate supply of native warriors. So when hostilities between France and England once again heated up in the 1750s, sparked this time in North America over who would control the Ohio Valley, Governor William Shirley of Massachusetts enlisted the aid of the one man in British North America with significant influence among the Iroquois.

Johnson responded by inviting eleven hundred Iroquois warriors over to his house to confer. After four days of speeches and consultations, he threw down a war belt and an Oneida chief picked it up. There was an enormous war dance, in which hundreds of warriors danced out retellings of their individual exploits. Then everyone had punch.

But when the time came to actually leave for Albany, where the militia from New England and New York were gathering, only three hundred warriors showed up. There were too many relatives—which is to say Praying Indians—fighting on the French side, they said.

In July of 1755, when all the colonial troops were camped near Albany, Johnson arrived with his Mohawk warriors. Massachusetts and Connecticut had each supplied twelve hundred men, Rhode Island four hundred, New Hampshire five hundred, and New York eight hundred.

The collected farmers and artisan's apprentices were surely glad to have Native assistance, but some of the more pious New Englanders wondered aloud when their commander painted his face with bear grease and soot, initiated another war dance, and with his own sword hacked off the first piece of the whole ox that was roasted in the Mohawk's honor. Since the days of Cotton Mather, New England preachers had warned their flocks against being seduced into a state of wildness by the presence of wilderness. After all, even Jesus himself had been tempted by the devil during his forty days in the wilderness. And here leading them into battle was a whooping Johnson, living proof of the phenomenon.

After months of delay Johnson finally decided in late August to head up to Lake George. His men had to cut trees down all along the way in order for the army to pass. But he wasn't inclined to let the hard work or serious purpose of a war effort spoil the fun. "We went on about four or five miles, then stopped, ate pieces of broken bread and cheese, and drank some fresh lemon-punch and the best of wine with General Johnson and some of the field officers," wrote a gunsmith from Northampton, Massachusetts, named Seth Pomeroy. The same thing happened the next day. They made less than five miles a day.

They ultimately got to Horican, however, and Johnson renamed it Lake George, in part out of hope. "Not only in honor of His majesty," he wrote to the Lords of Trade, "but to ascertain his undoubted dominion here." The men were ordered to begin building Fort William Henry, not far from where Father Jogues and his captors had come ashore 113 years before.

"Lake George," 1856, by John Frederick Kensett. Courtesy of the Adirondack Museum, Blue Mountain Lake.

In contrast to Johnson, who had never been in any army before, his adversary Baron Ludwig August Dieskau was a hero of the last war between the French and the English, the War of Austrian Succession. A German in the employ of the French, his plan had been to assault Oswego until he discovered from documents captured in another battle in Virginia that Johnson's orders were to head up Lake George. Not the type to sit around drinking wine and lemonade, Dieskau drove his army hard down Champlain to Ticonderoga, which the French called Carillon.

Once there, he issued orders to his officers limiting them to one spare shirt, one extra pair of shoes, a blanket, bearskin, and twelve days of provisions. Native American forces were specifically instructed not to take any scalps until after all the fighting was over because, Dieskau pointed out, they could kill ten Englishmen in the time it took to scalp one.

They canoed up Champlain to the Drowned Lands. Their apparent intention was to attack Fort Lyman, at the Hudson end of the Long Carry, but they intercepted an English messenger and learned that the bulk of Johnson's army was already up at Lake George. The six hundred Caughnawaga and Algonquin warriors among them argued strongly that they should turn north and fight the camp rather than attempt to take the already fortified Lyman. Dieskau agreed.

He knew his 216 French regulars, 684 Canadians, and 600 Native warriors would be outnumbered, but he gave the order to head north. "The more there are, the more we will kill," he said. The English colonial militias had earned for themselves a reputation as being among the least effective fighting forces anywhere in the world.

Johnson's army was camped with the lake at its back. A forest of pine lay to its front, a wetland of alders and swamp maples to the right, and there was a hill on the left. They had been there for weeks, ostensibly waiting for boats to be carried up from the Hudson, when Johnson was told by one of his scouts that a body of soldiers was moving from the southern end of Champlain down toward Fort Lyman. It apparently didn't occur to him that this might be Dieskau's main army, or that it might turn and come back up to him at Lake George. So he sent messengers to warn Lyman. It was one of these men that Dieskau captured.

According to Francis Parkman, Johnson was wakened in the middle of the night by an aide who informed him that the main army of the enemy was approaching the unfinished fort. At first light, he sent a thousand of his men out to meet them. Johnson originally wanted to send two groups of five hundred soldiers each; one down to Dieskau directly, and one around to South Bay, at the southern end of Champlain, to head off their expected retreat. But Hendrick, the senior chief among his Mohawk allies, argued against it with a bit of Native American wisdom that James Fenimore Cooper might have been proud to dream up. He picked up a stick and broke it, then he picked up a handful of sticks and showed that together they were unbreakable.

Johnson was sufficiently swayed and decided to send the thousand men out to meet the enemy head-on. Hendrick still thought the mission foolish. "If they are to be killed," he told Johnson, "they are too many. If they are to fight, they are too few." Nevertheless, the three hundred Mohawk warriors were at the head of the column that marched down the brand-new road out of the camp at dawn. At the very front, on horseback because he was too old and rotund to march, was Hendrick himself, Johnson's dearest Mohawk friend after his own wife, Molly Brant. Hendrick was among the first to be killed.

For some inexplicable reason they didn't send out scouts and marched straight into a trap. Dieskau had ordered his Native forces to spread out on either side of the road and hide in the forest so as to attack from behind when the English got all the way back to the French regulars and Canadian forces. But before they were far enough along to encounter the main French force, according to some versions, one of Dieskau's Praying Indians shouted to Hendrick to change sides. The two groups then commenced a discussion that seemed headed toward finding a way to avoid a situation neither side wanted, in which Iroquois cousins would bear the brunt of a white man's battle.

But someone among Hendrick's men fired prematurely. The spray of bullets returned from the woods on either side of the road caused the head of the column to "double up like a pack of cards," Dieskau said later. It quickly became a rout, with Johnson's men only barely managing to cover their backsides as they ran back to the camp with the French in hot pursuit.

In Dieskau's mind, however, the damage had been done. His Praying Indians had not allowed the enemy to be encircled. Worse, they prevented his taking advantage of English confusion by stopping to argue with their supposed allies, the Abnakis, about whether or not to kill several Mohawk prisoners.

Meanwhile, back at the unfinished fort, Johnson and his remaining troops knew that their side was losing the fight because the popping of musket fire kept getting louder. A few reinforcements were sent out, but still the French pushed forward. Johnson ordered that trees be felled as fast as the men could cut them down. These were lined end to end, augmented here and there with a few tipped-over wagons and some upended boats. Behind this rustic imitation of a European fortress, they intended to make their final stand.

Less than an hour and a half after the first shots had been heard, the defeated forces came running back, along with whatever wounded they could carry. Close behind were the French regulars. When they appeared out of the woods and set up in formation about 150 yards away, Johnson and his men found themselves surrounded on three sides. In front were the famous German baron's regular soldiers; to their left and right, his Canadian militia. (After the disastrous fratricide of the morning, most of the Iroquois on both sides of the conflict had decided not to participate further in the battle.) Behind Johnson lay the lake.

Given the disarray in Johnson's camp, Dieskau might have taken the day had he been able to rapidly organize an all-out assault. But his provincial forces on either side had spread themselves too far out for him to control, and Johnson's cannon soon scared them off farther still. So the real action was quickly concentrated in front, where the fight took on the aspects of battle that would become dear to American folklore after the Revolution. Apparently foolish formations of brightly uniformed Europeans arranged themselves into elegant lines while farmers and fur trappers in all manner of rags mowed them down from behind logs.

As evidenced by his almost effective ambush, Dieskau was more in tune to the new reality of forest warfare than many who preceded or followed him. But still, for the baron and so many other European generals, it was as if the wilderness simply didn't exist, at least not to a degree that required a rethinking of the rules of engagement. For the next five hours the French lined up and were mauled.

One Englishman hit in the leg quite early on, however, was Johnson. For most of the battle he was able to make only a few sallies out of his tent to view a fight that was now primarily under the control of his second-in-command, Phineas Lyman. Dieskau was also hit,

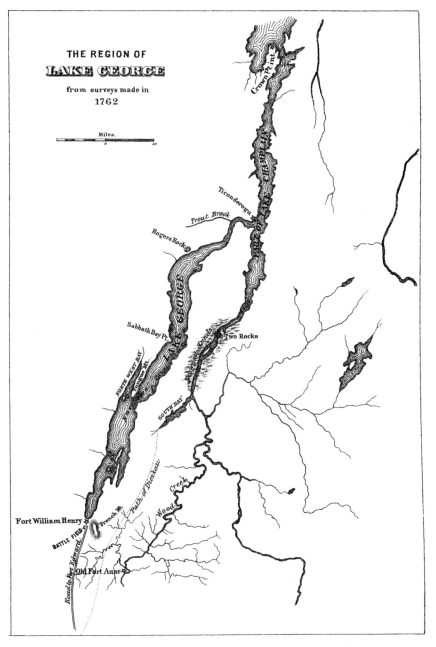

Map showing locations of the forts at Crown Point, Ticonderoga, and Lake George. From 1898 edition of Francis Parkman's Montcalm and Wolfe.

picked off as he ran across the front in his easily identifiable officer's uniform. His adjutant, who was also wounded, was washing the general's wound with brandy when Dieskau was hit two more times in the knee and thigh. At this point they decided it might be wise to move behind a tree, where Dieskau remained for the rest of the battle.

By five in the evening it was the English forces who were chasing the French. One colonial militiaman, finding the famous enemy commander leaning against his tree, drew a bead on him from very close range. According to Dieskau's own account of the battle, he waved his hands at the man hoping to signal him not to shoot, but the soldier shot him in the hip anyway. Dieskau demanded to be carried to Johnson, who ordered his surgeons to look after the enemy general. Dieskau later said, "And though wounded himself, [Johnson] refused all assistance till my wounds were dressed."

Dieskau also wrote that the Iroquois were furious that Johnson would not let them have the enemy general. There was apparently a long argument in Mohawk, and when Dieskau asked what the Iroquois wanted, Johnson answered, "To burn you, by God, eat you, and smoke you in their pipes, in revenge for three or four of their chiefs that were killed." They wanted revenge, Johnson explained, for the death of Hendrick.

It was a bloody day, but not overwhelming even by eighteenth-century standards. The English dead and wounded numbered 262, while the French suffered 228 casualties by their own count and 400 according to the English.

The importance of Johnson's leadership during and after the battle was a matter of debate almost as soon as the shooting stopped and has continued to be so among historians ever since. His detractors, who later included Francis Parkman, point out that he made no effort to follow through on his victory. He didn't try to apprehend Dieskau's canoes and supplies, nor did he head for Ticonderoga, even though the governors who hired him urged him to do so. Johnson was too wounded to go, they concede, but he was too vain to let his deputy Lyman have the glory—glory that some felt Lyman deserved even for the victory at Lake George.

Johnson supporters at the time and in later histories counter that were it not for Johnson's influence with the Iroquois, and their influence in turn with the Caughnawagas, the whole battle might have been lost. Dieskau himself, they point out, complained that he was betrayed by his Praying Indians.

There is no question that Johnson won the public-relations battle of the moment. The British plan for the summer had been to attack all the French fronts at once, but the mission to Niagara under Governor Shirley got no farther than Oswego. Far worse than that, though, was the ignominious defeat in the Ohio Valley of the supreme commander of British forces on the continent, General Edward Braddock. After the disastrous "Battle of the Wilderness," during which Braddock was killed, the routed English forces were led back to Maryland by Lieutenant Colonel George Washington.

It's true Johnson's army hung around Lake George until the end of November, at which point it was decided it was too late to do anything about Ticonderoga or Crown Point. But the Battle of Lake George, as it came to be called, turned out to be the only bright spot for the English in the summer land campaign. Johnson received a hero's welcome in New York City, the English Parliament awarded him five thousand pounds, and the king made him a baronet. Henceforth, he was known as Sir William. His archrival, Governor Shirley of Massachusetts, by contrast, was recalled to England.

The war dragged on. Every summer, in varying amounts and with new commanders, troops gathered in Albany and then headed up to the park to kill or be killed on the shores of Lakes George and Champlain, often as not by disease. Latrines, kitchens, graves, and cattle-slaughtering areas were all on top of each other in the camps.

"[There are] about twenty-five hundred men, five hundred of them sick, the greatest part of them what they call poorly; they bury from five to eight daily; extremely indolent, and dirty to a degree," reported a Colonel Burton to the new British commander-in-chief, the Earl of Loudoun, the summer after Johnson's victory. The only consolation for the troops seems to have been the daily gill of rum that was part of the soldiers' pay. The camp at Lake George, Burton said plainly, "is nastier than anything I could conceive."

Reports from the French down the lake at Ticonderoga during that summer were somewhat better. After the usual complaints about soldier food, Captain Duchat, of the Regiment de Languedoc, wrote home that "luckily the lakes are full of fish, and both officers and soldiers have to turn fishermen." He also mentioned the weekly arrival of trophies brought in by their Native American allies.

"Not a week passes but the French send [the English colonists] a band of hairdressers, whom they would be very glad to dispense with. It is incredible what quantity of scalps they bring us . . . ," he wrote.

On the English side the scalp taking that second summer of the war was primarily accomplished by a band of militiamen, most of whom were from New Hampshire. Organized by Johnson the previous year to provide intelligence when his Mohawk contingent went home after the battle, they were under the command of a tall man with a big nose named Robert Rogers. Before volunteering for service, Rogers had been accused of passing phony currency, and he may have been a smuggler as well.

But he could lead armed men into the forest and bring them back out again, which few other whites could do. With their special woodsy uniforms and their incredible feats of derring-do "Rogers' Rangers" became celebrities on both sides of the Atlantic. Legend has it that Rogers Rock, a hundred-foot sheer granite face rising out of Lake George just south of Ticonderoga, got its name when the fearless leader of the Rangers supposedly slid all the way down it on snowshoes, barely evading the Indians who were chasing him. Another version, only slightly more plausible, has the Rangers fooling their pursuers by running away from the precipice with their snowshoes on backward.

All through the winter of 1756 the Rangers stayed with the small contingent at Fort William Henry. In January, Rogers and seventeen armed men traveled all the way down Lake George on ice skates. At the first narrows they changed to snowshoes and tramped through the forest behind Ticonderoga halfway to Crown Point, where they ambushed a supply sleigh of fresh beef. They took a few prisoners and buried the meat in the snow. A similar excursion in February with fifty men that camped "on a great mountain to the West'rd of Crown Point" managed to burn a few French barns and kill a handful of enemy livestock, for which they were treated as conquering heroes when they got back to Fort William Henry.

The Rangers' favorite haunt was the four-mile valley between Lake George and Ticonderoga, where there was a French camp about every mile. In May, Rogers and eleven men hid in the woods between

Ticonderoga and the first camp. After a column of more than a hundred French soldiers had passed, they took on a group of twenty and escaped with one of them in captivity. On another occasion, by speaking in French, Rogers and five men managed to steal a sentinel from his post within sight of the fort itself.

At the end of June, Rogers and fifty men portaged five whaleboats across from Lake George over to Wood Creek in the Drowned Lands and rowed secretly up Champlain. Under cover of darkness, they passed close enough to Ticonderoga to hear the French sentries. About ten miles from Crown Point they hid out for two days waiting for a night dark enough to sneak by the second fort. During that time hundreds of French boats passed them, traveling in both directions between the forts. One group of French soldiers landed for lunch within earshot of the hidden Rangers.

When they discovered a schooner at anchor fifteen miles farther down the lake they decided they had found a target whose loss would adequately rankle the French. But in their attempt to pirate the ship they were frustrated by two smaller boats of French soldiers. These boats, along with their entire loads of wheat, flour, rice, wine, and brandy were sunk, "excepting some few casks of brandy & wine which we hid in very secure places," Rogers reported when he got back.

The Rangers did not always escape unscathed. In the mountains northwest of Bolton Landing they lost sixteen men when they were ambushed in the rain by a large party of French forces. Rogers himself took a bullet in the wrist, which he calmly tied up with the ribbon from his ponytail. Another time, fifty Rangers under a man named Captain Hodges were surprised by three times their number of the enemy and only six survived. More than once, Rangers returned to Fort William Henry in states of near starvation. One such party survived by eating the hearts of their own dead comrades.

Rogers happened to be out on patrol during the first week of August in 1757 and missed the most infamous battle of the whole war. By spring of that year, circumstances in North America decidedly favored the enemies of England. Half of the Iroquois Confederacy were allied with France and it was all Johnson could do to keep the rest neutral. Warriors from the Far West, meanwhile, were pouring into Ticonderoga to help their trading partners fight the English. By the end of July, the Marquis de Montcalm had eight thousand armed men at Ticonderoga.

Two thousand of them were Native Americans in what was doubt-less one of the greatest collections of different Native nations ever. At the grand war council called by Montcalm on the twenty-ninth of July there were in attendance representatives of forty-one nations and subtribes. Among the eight hundred "mission savages," which is to say those converted to Christianity by the Jesuits, were the Praying Indians of Caughnawaga, Two Mountains, and La Presentation; the Hurons of Lorette and Detroit; the Nipissings of Lake Nipissing; the Abnakis of Saint Francis, Bécancour, Missisquoi, and the Penobscot River area; Algonquins from Three Rivers and Two Mountains; Mic-macs and Malecites from Acadia.

Among the 979 unconverted members of western nations were seven different groups of Ottawas. There were Ojibwas from Lake Superior, Mississagas from Lakes Erie and Huron, and Potawatomis and Menominees from Lake Michigan. From Wisconsin there were Sacs, Foxes, and Winnebagos. There were even Plains Indians: Miamis from the Illinois prairie and Kiowas from the banks of the Des Moines River. There were a few warriors that the French were unable to identify.

"Imagine a great assembly of savages adorned with every orna-ment most suited to disfigure them in European eyes, painted with vermilion, white, green, yellow, and black made of soot and the scrap-ings of pots," wrote a descriptive Jesuit missionary named Roubaud who came to the camp with his flock of Christian warriors. "A single savage face combines all these different colors, methodically laid on with the help of a little tallow, which serves for pomatum. The head is shaved except at the top, where there is a small tuft, to which are fas-tened feathers, a few beads of wampum, or some such trinket. Every part of the head has its ornament. Pendants hang from the nose and also from the ears, which are split in infancy and drawn down by weights till they flap at last against the shoulders.

"The rest of the equipment answers to this fantastic decoration: a shirt bedaubed with vermilion, wampum collars, silver bracelets, a large knife hanging on the breast, moose-skin moccasins, and a belt of various colors always absurdly combined. The sachems and war-chiefs are distinguished from the rest: the latter by a gorget, and the former by a medal, with the King's portrait on one side, and on the other Mars and Bellona joining hands, with the device, Virtus et Honor."

There were many speeches. Montcalm produced an enormous wampum belt of some six thousand beads and presented it to an Ottawa named Pennahouel, the oldest chief present. There was a feast. Oxen were roasted. Then the war dances commenced.

European commanders were generally expected to participate in such ceremonies, dancing their own "war song." It was essentially an improvisational effort.

"I sang the war song in the name of M. de Montcalm, and was much applauded," Montcalm's aide-de-camp, Louis-Antoine de Bougainville, said of a war dance he had performed in order to convince the remaining Catholic Wyandots to come down to Lake George. "It was nothing but these words, 'let us trample the English under our feet,' chanted over and over again, in cadence with the movements of the savages."

At dawn on the thirtieth of July, 1757, twenty-five hundred Canadians, regulars, and Praying Indians left Ticonderoga and marched south along the ancient Mohawk trail that went through the woods on the Adirondack side of the lake. They were to meet the rest of the party at what is now Bolton Landing. Two days later, again at dawn, sixteen hundred Native warriors set off down the exquisite lake in canoes followed by 250 boats—some of them rowed, others under sail—loaded with the regular French troops. Montcalm's cannon were on double bateaux, tied together catamaran-style. There was martial music. Voyageurs sang. It was a brilliant morning.

That evening, in a moment that Buster Keaton could have scripted, two small English boats out for a patrol from Fort William Henry rounded a point and saw coming toward them twelve hundred hostile Indians in war canoes. They rowed hard for shore, hotly pursued, and amazingly a few made it back to camp. Montcalm wasn't intending a surprise anyway. When his flotilla rounded the point the next morning they fired off their cannon just in case the English needed more of a wake-up call.

Inside the fort were twelve hundred defenders under the command of Lieutenant Colonel George Monro. Major General Daniel Webb was only fourteen miles away on the Hudson at Fort Edward with access to another thirty-five hundred men, but he would not be persuaded to assist his countrymen at Lake George. On the third of August he received not one but two notes from Monro, one saying simply, "I believe you will think it proper to send a reinforcement as soon as possible." On the fourth, Monro wrote again, saying he was out-numbered and the French appeared to be very heavily armed. Webb didn't bother to reply.

At some point William Johnson showed up at Fort Edward in full Mohawk war regalia and with a small band of warriors that through his personal influence he was able to convince to go to the defense of Monro. When Webb refused to be convinced to march with them to the northern fort they began slowly stripping off garments. One piece at a time they threw at Webb's feet, tauntingly asking him with each article of clothing if he still refused to go. Finally all of them, includ-ing Sir William, were left only in breechcloths, and still Webb would not go. They gave up and marched out in disgust, though they later sent someone back for their clothes.

The afternoon of August fourth, Montcalm's Indians complained that they were not being adequately consulted about strategy and the French general sent a message to Monro saying he might not be able to restrain the natives after a fierce fight.

"I owe it to humanity," he wrote, "to summon you to surrender." Monro refused.

That evening Montcalm set his heavy artillery in trenches and on the morning of the fifth, eight heavy cannon opened up on the fort at sunrise from the left. By the morning of the sixth, another eleven can-nons were in place firing from the right. The fort fired back all day long. Fourteen miles away, General Webb could hear the explosions, and though he finally sent a small reinforcement he did not bring his main army to the rescue of his countrymen at Lake George.

By the seventh, three hundred people inside the fort had been killed. Many more were dying of smallpox, which had broken out and was spreading rapidly in the crowded conditions. Efforts by small par-ties to get out were unsuccessful. Most of their cannon were burst from overheating, or disabled by explosions from shots fired by the French. The walls were breached. All night, they fought on, but on the morning of the eighth Monro raised a white flag. He agreed to sur-render if his people were allowed to march out with the Union Jack flying, and were escorted as far as Fort Edward. The French could have the fort and all its arms except for a single symbolic cannon.

The fight had been a traditional European siege of an armed fort, and the terms were honorable according to the set of rules governing

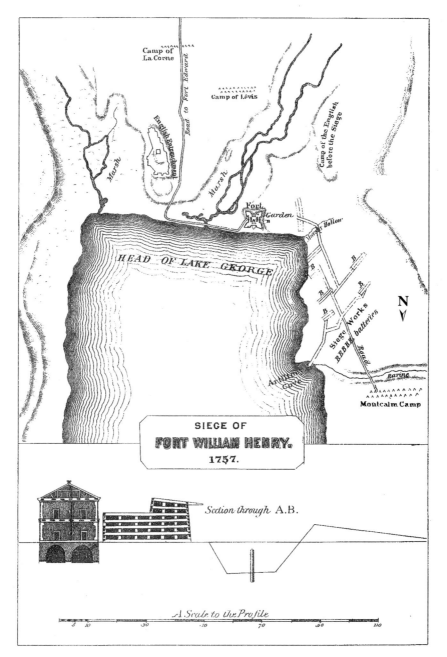

Diagram of 1857 battlefield at head of Lake George. From 1898 edition of Francis Parkman's Montcalm and Wolfe.

the way Europeans killed each other. But as anyone who has read the opening chapters of *The Last of the Mohicans* knows, Montcalm was unable to enforce the terms on those of his allies for whom the rules did not apply. Genteel principles that allowed an English army to retreat unharmed, in fact, probably fueled the suspicion among the Iroquois and other Native nations that the true aim of both the French and the English was to get the original inhabitants of the land to kill as many of each other as possible.

At any rate, the reality under which the Marquis de Montcalm and Monro negotiated was only tenuously maintained even in the fort itself. As soon as the defeated forces were out of William Henry, hundreds of Montcalm's warriors stormed in and killed the sick who had been left behind. The priest Roubaud wrote: "I saw one of these barbarians come out of the casements with a human head in his hand, from which the blood ran in streams, and which he paraded as if he had got the finest prize in the world." But by the evening, Montcalm was able to restore some order.

"We shall be but too happy if we can prevent a massacre," wrote Bougainville in his journal. "Detestable position! of which nobody who has not been in it can have any idea, and which makes victory itself a sorrow to the victors. The Marquis spared no efforts to prevent the rapacity of the savages and, I must say, of certain persons associated with them, from resulting in something worse than plunder."

Outside the square mile or so of charred logs and stumps surrounding the fort—the primary achievement of the previous summer's English army—Montcalm's rules of engagement collapsed altogether. The defeated column marching for Fort Edward the next morning was soon mobbed by native troops, grabbing hats and clothing from them. Resisters were killed with hatchets. Women and children were dragged off. Pandemonium reigned. At the back of the column, the Abnaki Christians from Maine let out a war whoop and quickly killed or captured eighty New Hampshire soldiers. Montcalm rushed to the scene but did not succeed in stopping the riot.

Meanwhile, at the front of the column the regular French troops who were supposed to be guarding the prisoners refused to do so. Some suggested glibly that the English take to the woods. One man, Jonathan Carver, said later that while he was being dragged off by two warriors toward the swamp he begged protection from a French sentinel who responded by shoving him back to his captors. He escaped only when his captors abandoned him to chase an English officer who was running by with nothing but a beautiful pair of government-issue scarlet boxers on.

Carver was joined in flight for a while by a boy of twelve or thirteen, but the youngster was soon caught. Carver assumed from the aborted screams he heard coming from behind him that the boy was killed.

French estimates were that fifty or sixty English prisoners were slaughtered in the melee. Another six or seven hundred were carried off or beaten up, of which Montcalm was able to get four hundred back over the course of the day. Many more fugitives, including most of the women and children, managed to make it back to the defeated Fort William Henry. Monro was there too, having come in early on to demand better protection for his people.

For the next few days cannon were fired from the fort on a regular basis to help those lost in the forest find their way back through the woods to Lake George. Other stragglers, the majority almost naked, trickled into Fort Edward over the next three or four days. And on the fifteenth of August, this time under significantly stronger guard, the prisoners were finally marched south. The main perpetrators of the massacre by that time were on their way to Montreal with around two hundred prisoners that Montcalm was unable to ransom.

Once the prisoners were gone, Fort William Henry was completely demolished and the assembled corpses were thrown on an enormous pyre. The French left on the sixteenth. Lake George was deserted. Until, that is, the following June, that of 1758, when yet another army of English regulars and colonial militia began to gather at the southeastern corner of the park.

The French and Indian War was more than half over, but there was more blood to be spilled at Ticonderoga. The new commander of the English forces was Major General James Abercromby, but the real leader was General George Howe. And this time it was Montcalm who was outnumbered four to one. The English set off down Lake George in boats on a glorious dawn—900 bateaux, 135 whaleboats, and several dozen flatboats with artillery. The men sang as they rowed through the sunshine between the green hills rising on either side of Horicon, just as the French had done as they rowed in the opposite direction the year before. They played bugles, bagpipes, and drums.

At around ten in the morning, when the boats arranged themselves into single file to maximize distance from either shore at the first narrows, the line was six miles long. Rogers' Rangers were out in front. From up on Rogers Rock, French outposts watched their progress. And at noon, the vast army landed at precisely the point where Montcalm's forces had put in on their opposite voyage a year before.

They began what was supposed to be a short trek through the forest to surround the fort at Ticonderoga. Rogers' Rangers were sent to flush out advanced enemy positions, and the main army started making the four-mile march at 2 P.M. But after going less than a mile, the seemingly inexplicable happened. Fifteen thousand armed men got lost in the woods. The advance party of French, roughly three hundred men who had been chased off the landing place when the English arrived, became lost as well. And soon enough, since both groups were wandering around trying to get to the same place, they ran into each other.

General Howe had spent the winter studying the wilderness. After a few reconnaissance trips with Rogers' Rangers, he introduced some reforms into the army that were intended to improve its ability to fight in the forest. Musket barrels were blackened, coats were cut short. There were none of the usual laundry women along while the troops were on maneuvers. Despite these indignities, however, Howe was immensely popular with the 6,300 regular troops and 9,000 colonial militiamen. He was the driving force of the entire army. But in the first bullets of the day, Howe was shot.

"I was about six yards from him," wrote one of his soldiers later. "He fell on his back and never moved, only his hands quivered an instant."

The Rangers soon gained control of the small party of French, capturing most of them with few losses. But the morale of the English was destroyed by the death of Howe. "In Lord Howe," said a contemporary, Major Thomas Mante, "the soul of General Abercromby's army seemed to expire. From the unhappy moment the General was deprived of his advice, neither order nor discipline was observed, and a strange kind of infatuation usurped the place of resolution." Parkman wrote, "The death of one man was the ruin of fifteen thousand."

Ticonderoga is a small peninsula that juts out into Lake Champlain from the western shore. Seen from the Adirondack side, the land at first rises to a point about a mile from where the fort stood and then it declines gently. On both sides, the land falls steeply to the water. While Abercromby's men were regrouping at the landing place on Lake George, Montcalm's troops frantically finished a zigzagging wall of logs along the ridge above the fort.

Just as William Johnson's men had done before, they cut down and lopped off thousands of trees. This time, instead of simply laying them end to end, they built the logs into a substantial fortification between six and eight feet tall, with places for soldiers to stand and fire with only their heads exposed. Notches were cut, like loopholes in a castle, to further protect the defenders from the English.

The bows from the trees used to make the wall were piled in an overlapping pattern out in front of the wall, close enough so that anyone who made it that far would be under crossfire from the zigzagging main defensive line. The sticks and branches that faced the expected assault were sharpened to points, making the mess into something like a line of pine-scented barbed wire. And finally, just to make things even more difficult for the advancing English, all the remaining trees within a musket shot of the wall were cut so that they pointed toward the attacking army and formed a tangled mass where they fell.

Abercromby had several choices. From the top of nearby Mount Defiance his artillery could endlessly fire grapeshot into the breastwork. The other side of the peninsula could be secured and the French starved out. He could wait for his cannon to be brought up, and blast through the wooden wall. But he chose what would seem to be the least effective strategy of all. He ordered his troops to storm the line.

Sometime on the morning of the eighth, Sir William Johnson arrived with a party of Iroquois intending to reinforce the English effort. But since they once been on the winning side of a similar situation, they decided to spend the day up on Mount Defiance watching the bloodbath.

It began around noon. As the first wave of English worked their way forward through the tangled mass of trees, toward the sharpened bows, they could see the wall ahead of them but not the three-deep formations of French regulars behind it waiting for them to come into range. When Montcalm, standing in the hot sun in his shirtsleeves, gave the order to fire the whole wall disappeared into the smoke of gunpowder.

"The scene was frightful," wrote Parkman in a sentence typical for both its exquisite length and style: "masses of infuriated men who could not go forward and would not go back; straining for an enemy they could not reach, and firing on an enemy they could not see; caught in the entanglement of fallen trees; tripped by briers, stumbling over logs; tearing through boughs; shouting, yelling, cursing, and pelted all the while with bullets that killed them by the scores, stretched them on the ground, or hung them on jagged branches in strange attitudes of death."

Word went back to Abercromby a mile and a half behind the battle that the French defenses were impregnable. He ordered another wave forward. And another, and another. The next to the last rush was the most furious of all. Over and over again two columns of Highlanders rushed the line and were forced back, only to rush forward into the spray of bullets again. Montcalm even sent out a sortie to fire on them from the sides, but that didn't stop them. Not until half the soldiers in the unit were dead did they fall back permanently. Abercromby ordered another wave.

Only darkness stopped the carnage. Of the English, 1,944 had been killed; Montcalm's forces counted 377 dead.

Abercromby still had 13,000 men, more than enough to pursue one of the other strategies available to him. But when the French scouts went out the next morning there were no English soldiers to be found anywhere near Ticonderoga. The army had fled in such haste that they had left behind hundreds of barrels of provisions and piles of equipment. English boots were found sticking out of a marsh that had been crossed, apparently left there by soldiers in too much of a hurry to pull them out. Needless to say, the 3,500 French and Canadians left in Ticonderoga were pleasantly surprised.

Abercromby, whom his troops now derisively called Mrs. Nabbie Cromby, went directly to New York City. The army was put to work rebuilding Fort William Henry, and the remainder of the summer dragged out in the usual manner, with minor skirmishes up and down the Adirondack side. Most of the fighting, once again, was led by Rogers' Rangers.

During one of these encounters, Captain Israel Putnam of Connecticut, who would later become a major general for the Americans in the Revolution, was captured by a party of French Canadians. He was tied to a tree and one warrior amused himself by a carnival-like exhibition of tomahawk throwing, repeatedly sending the hatchet into the tree just above Putnam's head. Then, he later told his biographer, a French soldier stuck the barrel of a musket to his chest and pretended to fire. At this point Putnam's comrades drove the enemy back a few hundred yards, and he spent the next few hours in the middle of fierce crossfire unhappily tied to his tree.

Which is precisely where the French forces found him when they recovered the lost ground. That night in camp they stripped him naked and piled brush around his feet as if to burn him alive. If Putnam was praying for rain, his God heard him, and the roasting was postponed. Only temporarily, however. When the downpour let up, the pyre was lit, but a French officer finally doused the fire and returned him to the Praying Indian to whom he belonged. He spent that night staked flat on the ground with a generous collection of brush piled up on top of him for good measure. After the obligatory trip to Montreal, he was eventually traded back to English America in a prisoner exchange.

The year of 1758 went better for the English than the events on Lake George would suggest. In other battles, the French lost Fort Frontenac, which controlled passage from the Saint Lawrence to Lake Ontario and the West. Louisbourg, Nova Scotia, fell to Lord Jeffrey Amherst. And in the west, Fort Duquesne, where Braddock had been so trounced, was renamed by its English conquerors Fort Pitt.

The war had finally turned in England's favor. The following summer, when it was Amherst's turn to lead the English up Lake George, they found the French had blown up Carillon and fled. Eleven thousand men went right past Ticonderoga and spent the winter at Crown Point. For those who had been a part of any of the five previous campaigns, it was a welcome anticlimax. Quebec and Niagara also fell to the English that year. And in 1760, at Montreal, the two-hundred-year-old entity called New France ceased to exist when Canada was ceded to the king of England.

In a way, the end of the French and Indian War symbolically cemented an ongoing shift away from the fur trade, and thus a change in the relationship of white Americans to the wilderness around them. Furs had fallen from their position of dominance in the English colonies at the end of the 1600s to a mere 20 percent of the exports to England by 1750. Henceforth the ever more agrarian economies to the south would be free from competing for land with the far-flung fur-trading operation of the French in Canada. Even more than the American Revolution fifteen years later, which saw its own battles in the Champlain Valley, the French and Indian War ensured that the now seemingly inevitable filling in of the land with farmers and proto-industrialists would continue.

The experiment in a wilderness-based economy in North America as typified by the Dutch and French approaches was over. For the Iroquois owners of the Adirondacks it meant, with the brief exception of the American Revolution and its aftermath, the evaporation of a middle ground on which to stake their survival diplomacy. Only a decade after the war's end a pair of land speculators, using the good offices of the Mohawks' great friend William Johnson, bought more than a million Adirondack acres in a single purchase.

Not that the fur trade ceased to exist. It was poised to enter the mythic heyday of Jim Bridger and the other nineteenth-century mountain men of the Rockies and beyond. But the nature of the business changed. It was bigger and more organized. Wampum, the ceremonial beads traditionally made by coastal Indians, was being manufactured by European immigrants in factories in Albany. Equally important was the change in the demographics of the trappers and middlemen. More and more of them were white—"company men." They loved their wilderness existence; they were at home in the forest. But it was not their home, not the Great Longhouse. They took for granted that they would soon be followed by "civilization," and they acted accordingly.

4   *The Price of Otter*
in China

A couple of times a year a large, friendly trapper named Toby Edwards gets in his pickup truck and makes the rounds of his fellow trappers, not only in the Adirondacks but all over northern New York. He doesn't actually buy furs outright but collects them and delivers them to Montreal where they are graded and auctioned off in large lots to international buyers from as far away as China. Then, a few weeks later, the trappers receive a computer-generated check for their share of the take.

Edwards, who's in his thirties, lives in a handsome log house he built for his family in the southern end of the park, just across the Great Sacandaga Lake and up a ways from Fish House.[1] "My uncle had a camp here," he explained one afternoon on his porch swing in the off-season. "It was my dad's land but my uncle didn't

---

[1] "Sacandaga Lake," as opposed to river, because in the 1920s the state built a dam at Conklingville. There's a small brass plaque where Fish House Road hits Route 7, a place still identified as Fish House on some maps. It informs anyone interested enough to stop and find it in the weeds that Johnson had a house straight ahead in what is now the middle of the lake.

Sir William Johnson died suddenly in 1774, supposedly undecided about which way to go on the impending revolution. His wife and his heirs, on the other hand, were active loyalists, and fled to Canada when war broke out. Robert Rogers of the Rangers, after a stint in the service of the Dey of Algiers,

want to actually own it because he was about to get married and if he ever got divorced he didn't want his wife to get it. He was thinking ahead I guess, in case he needed to live on it." Edwards laughed. "He got divorced all right, but he never did build a proper house here, so I got it."

Edwards had just returned from the spring auction in Montreal, and when talk turned to trapping he pulled from his pocket a fax he'd picked up earlier in the day at the hardware store. "Let's see," he said peering at it, "of twenty-six thousand beaver, they ended up selling twenty-two thousand for an average price of $22.31 a skin. They sold a hundred percent of the 1,063 otter they had, and the top price for a single otter was $105." He lay the fax on his lap and thought for a moment. "That's the highest I've ever seen otter sell for.

"We knew this year and last year that otter were the hot item, so a lot of guys went out and trapped 'em hard. The reason they're high right now is China's buying them. And they're shearing them real short, like"—he held up two fingers pinched almost together—"a quarter inch. They look like the damnedest thing. They had a couple up in Montreal that were sheared already. It doesn't even look like fur anymore, but man is it soft.

"But you never know, otter could be back to thirty dollars apiece next year." He looked back at the fax.

"Wild mink were cheap, but hey, they're out of season. You always try to sell the wild ones in December, because in January the ranch mink come on the market and depress the prices. The thing that helps wild mink sell is they're smaller. And ours up here are lighter leather, which makes for a lighter-weight coat. When you make fur into a coat for a woman to wear it can get heavy. That's why female fisher has for years been more expensive than the males, because they were lighter leather.

---

also aligned with the losing side in the American Revolution. He was banished from New Hampshire in 1778.

Summer House and Fish House were used for a while by American soldiers to defend against the possibility of an attack down the Sacandaga from the north. Both houses burned to the ground around 1781, on the orders, Jeptha Simms surmised, of Johnson's son, who realized that he would never get them back.

Most of Johnson's staff went to Canada as well, with the exception of Billy the violinist, who went to Manhattan. Whether he did so out of love for the cause of liberty, or because he felt there would be more demand there for physically challenged violinists is unknown.

"For years the price for fisher was a hundred fifty for females, seventy-five for males. There was a guy in New York City named Max Bass and he bought just about every fisher on the market. There's probably only twenty or thirty thousand fisher caught in New York, Vermont, and Massachusetts. But now, Max Bass is out of it, and fisher are right down to nothing now. They're now fourteen or twenty dollars. But one year in the eighties they were over two hundred dollars apiece.

"Get this," Edwards said when it was suggested that there is much that a trapper needs to know. "On the mink it's the opposite of fisher and the males are worth more, even though the leather on the females is lighter. Now years ago it was the other way and they said the female mink were worth more. But not now. A lot of it is a gimmick. I know a lot of fur buyers when they go to sell what they've bought from individual trappers out in the country, they sell it counting noses. You know, a one-shot price for either sex. But in the country, if they can buy one for ten dollars less a skin because of the sex, they'll do it. So there's a lot of different gimmicks.

"Like you used to have to sell your fisher skins skin-out, now it's fur-out. Some species you have to skin the animal and dry it on a board and leave it leather side out. Mink are leather-out, rats are leather-out, coon are leather-out. Others, like foxes and coyotes, after it's dried for a day you have to turn it inside out like you would a T-shirt and sell it with the fur side out. It's just the way the buyers want things.

"Only with beaver and badger there's no fur in or out because they're sold flat." Pause. "You can't hide anything with them, because the buyer can see both sides.

"Like with foxes or coyotes, sometimes if they're all shot up, I'll sew 'em up. And since you sell 'em fur-out, if you clean 'em up just right, and if there's not too much fur missing, they go into the sale as 'goods.' But if it was skin-out, the buyer could see the hole.

"With fox they look for color, so they want to see the fur. Coyote, too. But with coon, they can pretty much tell whether it's a dark or light coon from what's visible, and they want to see the primeness of the hide. And that's all they need to know.

"I would say of trappers, compared to years ago"—he picked up an earlier thread—"that there's a lot more information."

In February of 1990, the New York Department of Environmental Conservation and Cornell University did a survey of trappers in the state and found that 48 percent of them lost money chasing skins. Twenty-one percent said they broke even, which was 1 percent more than said they made any money. Almost 99 percent of the trappers are male, most with a high school diploma and a third with some college education. They usually learned to trap from their fathers or uncles or older brothers.

But not all. "I learned from books," Edwards said. "Years ago there would be a lot of families. A father, a couple sons, then the father would die and the sons would keep going, maybe bringing their sons. The Cummings in Blue Mountain Lake were like that." Edwards himself began trapping when he was ten, with some traps that had belonged to his uncle.

"There's a lot of guys trapping in the Adirondacks," he said at one point, "but they don't live here so much anymore, and I'm not sure why. I picked up furs south of Syracuse for instance from a couple who caught them up at Tupper. Some trappers come here for vacation, some are construction guys who work all summer and then come here and trap in the winter when they're laid off. They might drive in with

Unidentified Adirondack trapper with foxes and deer head (photographer unknown).
COURTESY OF THE ADIRONDACK MUSEUM, BLUE MOUNTAIN LAKE.

a snowmobile for a day or two. Almost all winter trapping is done on snowmobiles now.

"Very few guys have an old-style trapline camp anymore. That's tough going and you can't build a permanent camp on state land, so unless they have a camp on private property somewhere. . . . Plus, it's not worth it to ski or snowshoe in. There's probably a lot of furs back in the wilderness areas, but there's so many beaver elsewhere, right by the side of the road, that it's just not worth it.

"There's a few guys around who are really good trappers, but some are outlaws. I picked up a hundred sixty beaver from one guy and he had another forty on the drying racks. They say when he goes into an area you want to go the other way. He does stuff like hunt coyote from snowmobile. Another guy I know in Glens Falls trapped over two hundred beaver last year."

Like most successful trappers, Edwards was somewhat circumspect about revealing his own favorite trapping locations. "Once people find out you catch a lot of fur, they start trapping around your house," he said with a chuckle. "I've had guys trap right around my house. A guy just had traps there, I guess he figured that's where I got my fur.

"You can see thinking that way, but it's more about how much time the guy spends before the season even starts. If you know each place you're going to set—maybe if you're setting for otter, you've moved some rocks around the crick so the spot is just ready—then opening day you're there first thing, and boom you're down the road. Boom, down the road. Boom. Boom. Boom.

"That, and knowing your animal of course," he said after a moment's thought. "You don't catch muskrats in the mountains. You don't look for fisher in western New York.

"Also you have to know how to manage your line. With coon for instance, you can't trap an area for two weeks. You're going to get all you're going to get in the first couple days. Unless the weather plays hell with you. Real cold isn't good, real wet isn't good. But a light misty or damp night is good for coon, and you'll get all you're going to get.

"Bad rain isn't good for getting fox. A wet packy snow, a couple of inches, is real good for fisher. They'll move on a wet damp night. That, and the fact that your lure stays more to the ground instead of dispersing all over the place.

"I personally use skunk essence for a calling lure; that goes a long way. Believe it or not a lot of things like to eat skunk, especially in winter. I generally catch the skunk unintentionally when I'm trapping coon, but when I do, I'll squeeze the scent sack on that skunk into a jar of warm baking grease. Melted Vaseline works real well, too. Let it cool off, and you got a nice skunk paste that you can put on a tree a couple feet from your trap.

"Then right on the trap itself you put your beaver bait, some beaver meat and a dab of castor, maybe. Everything likes to eat beaver.

"I do it all at the fur shed," he said in response to a question about his wife's attitude toward skunk essence. "It's bad enough the smell of my clothes. I'd never skin an animal in the house."

Trappers have long had something of a public-relations problem. Ben Franklin called them "the most vicious and abandoned wretches of our nation." Most worrisome to trappers in recent years are the efforts of various animal rights groups. The State of New York, which relies on trappers to control the burgeoning population of beaver, is trying to do what it can to help trappers improve their image. At "Advanced Trapper Training Seminars," which applicants for new trapping licenses are required to attend, in addition to information on methods, markets, trap types, and animal diseases, participants are given tips on "How to Be an Advocate."

Toby Edwards has had a few encounters with what he calls "anti-fur types," but not too many. "You see the anti-fur people on television in the cities mostly. If somebody stands up and lies every night on the news and no one contradicts them, people start to believe the lies. The manufacturers have occasionally tried to counter some of it. But trappers themselves are cheap. I like 'em, but just try to get a buck out of 'em."

The 1990 survey found that most New York trappers had annual incomes of less than forty thousand dollars, and a third made less than twenty thousand a year. Today, there are less than ten thousand licensed trappers, down from more than thirty thousand during the Reagan years when wearing fur was hot fashion. If prices drop too low, the study concluded, wild trapping could disappear.

"And we're up against the Humane Society—we're up against big bucks," Edwards added.

In an odd way, the public-relations battle going on in urban America and in Europe between those who are wealthy enough to wear furs

and those who are wealthy enough to spend time and money defending defenseless furry animals, recalls the ancient clash between the
French and English responses to wilderness. The anti-fur logic, by
necessity, imparts a moral superiority to the products of human industry and agriculture over those "harvested" from the wild. The condition of wildness is not considered "hideous and desolate" by the
opponents of trapping, to be sure, but it is, in effect, just as segregated
from the rightful boundaries of human endeavor as it was for William
Bradford and the Separatists.

For most trappers of the Adirondacks and elsewhere, on the other
hand, the ability to go into the woods day after day and year after year
to collect furs for fun and profit gives them a greater stake in preserving the land around them than they might otherwise have. Like many
year-round residents of the Adirondacks, Edwards is generally predis-
posed to resent the regulatory structure of the park. When he is not
trapping, he and his brother and father run a small logging operation.
But Edwards himself volunteered that there are places he knows just
outside the Blue Line that used to be prime trapping habitat and are
now the province of malls and subdivisions. "So I guess the park is
okay in that respect," he said.

To biologists and wildlife managers like Bob Inslerman, who,
granted, is a trapper himself, Edwards's observation points to a crucial
flaw in what they call the "emotional arguments" of the anti-trapping
lobby. The ecological truth is that the threat to terrestrial species
worldwide, cute and furry or otherwise, comes more often from loss of
habitat rather than from hunting or trapping. Second homes, agriculture, acid rain, clear-cutting, erosion: these and other products of the
nonwild world are forces to fear. Few places on the globe are as devoid
of animal life as conventionally grown cotton fields.

To be fair, of course, most anti-fur advocates also support the whole
range of environmental issues, from organic farming to wilderness
preservation to the reintroduction of wolves. Unlike the trappers, they
do so without a direct pecuniary interest in the outcome. But practically
speaking, in the Adirondacks at least, conservationists have never won
a major battle without the support of the trappers and their far more
plentiful brethren, the hunters and anglers. It is only the blurring of the
line between the human and the "protected," say some in the Adirondack conservation community, that makes the park politically feasible.

For his part, Toby Edwards generally tries to avoid getting into philosophical arguments with people who disapprove of his trapping. "At the county fairs you might have somebody come up to your table and say 'I hate fur blah blah blah,' " he said. "And a lot just walk by and don't even want to talk, and I say 'well, okay.'

"If you're feeling like picking 'em apart you can say nice leather shoes there, or nice purse, or do you like chicken, that kind of thing. But we usually don't. Some do want to talk though, and you ask, 'why don't you like trappers,' and they say, 'well, you don't ever check your traps.' And we say, 'wait a minute, we have laws we have to check them every day, or every forty-eight hours in some cases.'

" 'Well,' they say, 'you have big teeth on your traps.' No ma'am, teeth have been outlawed for sixty years. This is the size of our traps. . . ." He let his voice trail off. He sometimes explains to questioners that if the trap is set correctly it usually doesn't catch the wrong animal, and if it does the animal can often be released unharmed.

"And sometimes after we talk they say, 'oh, well, oh.' And sometimes they say, 'I still don't like fur.' " Edwards shrugged.

There are a dozen small-type pages of regulations regarding when and where and how and for what animal a person can trap in New York State. The seasons vary from wildlife management region to region, but the main difference between the park and the rest of the state is that in the park there is a season for trapping pine marten.

The largest trap allowable for use on land is five and three-quarters inches from the insides of the jaws. The largest in water is seven and one-quarter inches. The regulations are so exact that when the measurement was changed a few years back from the outside of the jaws to the inside of the jaws, the limits were adjusted accordingly by a quarter of an inch.

5   *The End of an Era*

Nick Stoner owned a trap with jaws that were four feet long, endowed with five-inch interlocking spikes. It weighed in the neighborhood of forty-five pounds, was powered by two immense springs, and required a minor crew to set.

One man opened one jaw with a log wedged under a rock. A second man opened the other jaw the same way. And a third, presumably a particularly brave and trusting person, went between the two and set the pan. By the time Stoner died sometime around 1870, he had used it to trap thirty Adirondack black bears. One that got away left behind a paw. His colleague Nat Foster had an identical trap that he used to trap ninety-six bears in three seasons.

Professional trapping sputtered along in the Adirondacks for a half century or more after the American Revolution, before gradually giving way to deer hunting and guiding. Some of the trappers, like Stoner and Foster, came as close as any Adirondackers to the mythic image of the western mountain man, or the wilderness scout. When Foster was later put on trial for murder, the man defending him claimed that James Fenimore Cooper had actually modeled Natty Bumppo after his client. And the historian Jeptha Simms, in his hagiographic *Trappers of New York,* couldn't resist calling Stoner "my Leatherstocking," even though he acknowledged that Cooper always insisted his swashbuckling protagonist was entirely fictional.

And there were others. There was William Wood, who became something of a local celebrity after he froze his feet off one winter on Raquette Lake. They froze so solid while tending his trapline that, Donaldson reports in his classic two-volume *History of the Adirondacks,* "they gradually sloughed off." But Wood, who was found by Nat Foster in a snowdrift near the Independence River, contrived a way to attach snowshoes to his stumps and kept right on trapping.

There was the colorfully named Green White, whose arrival at a trading post was always memorable. A blacksmith by trade who made his own knives, White was probably the most successful trapper of the early nineteenth century. But he had a common frontier weakness. In the fall of 1815, he came out of the woods with three hundred dollars' worth of furs. The fact that many Adirondack families didn't make as much in two years didn't stop him from getting falling-down drunk and staying that way until the last penny was gone. Then, as he always did, Green White blearily headed back to the woods for more furs.

A trapper named Uncle Jock made a specialty of hunting without a gun. He had a dog to run down deer, which he then used to bait his traps for "wanpurnockers," as pine marten were then called. Uncle Jock was a tough dude; he and his sidekick Crookneck Simmons once killed a moose with a knife tied to the end of a pole. Another time out in the woods Jock got sick with pleurisy and used the same knife to cut open his leg in order to bleed himself. Crookneck passed out from the sight of it, but Uncle Jock calmly sutured himself back up, using his own hair for thread. When old Crookneck came to, he was ordered to make a big pot of hemlock tea. This Jock drank. And after a long nap, the story goes, he awoke entirely cured.

There was Joseph Benchley, who carried a violin with him into the woods to play from the tops of mountains. And there was his brother George, who mysteriously froze to death near Raquette Lake in the winter of 1820.

There was Elisha Belden, who lived around Ticonderoga in the 1790s and perfected a method of catching rattlesnakes from a large den near Rogers Rock, which he sold as curiosities in more settled parts of the world. When sales were slow he made up the difference by going to taverns and getting drinkers to pay him to let the snakes bite him. One time when he was bitten badly while collecting snakes on a Sunday, he was remembered to have said, "it was because the varmints did not know [me], as [I] was dressed up and had on white stockings—they thought [I] was Judge Kellog."

They were all large characters. Nick Stoner, who wore gold earrings, had been the kind of fife boy in the American Revolution who periodically guided his commanding officers on late-night visits to particularly patriotic Johnstown widows. Nat Foster, a big double-jointed man who had nothing but molars all the way around both jaws, carried musket balls between the bases of his fingers for so long that pouches formed there; if he held up his palms the bullets were invisible. They were the colorful, freedom-loving, manly American men of the type that wilderness is supposed to create.

But the Revolution had been more than fife playing and midnight lovemaking; Nick Stoner was badly wounded by a flying fragment of skull when the boy next to him was hit in the face with a cannonball. And there was a meaner reality as well behind the nostalgic images of the trappers in the decades after independence. The Adirondacks at the beginning of the nineteenth century were sort of an eddy in the frontier, forgotten in the rush to better lands in the west. To a large extent, it was a drunken and violent backwater at that, where neither the former owners of the territory nor the game were given much of a chance by the conquering heroes.

When Nick Stoner concluded that a Native trapper had stolen his furs, the man was expected to consider himself lucky to escape with a glass of whiskey smashed against the side of his head. At least he hadn't been killed with a red-hot andiron like the man at the Union House Bar.

Stoner, who lived just south of the park in a village called Fonda's Bush, was already drunk when he showed up at the kitchen of the Union House. The Union House was a popular watering hole and fur trading locale in nearby Johnstown, and seven Native American trappers were already there eating and drinking. They had presumably trapped and hunted their way down through the park from Canada. For reasons not remembered, the six-foot-tall Stoner was soon throwing one of these patrons across a table, smashing bottles every which way.

He next tossed the man into the fireplace, where he was seriously burned. On his way out of the kitchen, Stoner stopped long enough to put his foot on the neck of another passed-out Native and rip an earring he fancied from the man's ear. In the barroom next door he tried to calm down, which probably meant having another drink.

Meanwhile, one of the burned man's companions heard that the crazed white trapper's name was Stoner and pulled out his knife. On it were nine notches for nine American scalps taken in the Revolution. One of them, he imprudently bragged, was for "Old Stoner."

Stoner's father had, in fact, been killed in his field by a raiding party and it was the braggart's misfortune that the younger Stoner stumbled back into the kitchen just in time to hear the boast. He grabbed a glowing andiron from the fire and brained the man, though not without burning his own hand in the process.

Stoner's friends at this point decided it might be wise to get him out of the bar. And those of the Native trappers who were not too drunk or injured to move carried those who were back into the park. They had left their canoes, gear, and wives at Fish House. Later that night Stoner was put in jail until a mob of fellow Revolutionary War veterans broke down the door and carried him on their shoulders to another tavern. He was never tried.

There were still quite a few Native Americans using the park in the first half of the nineteenth century. Most of them were "Saint Regis Indians," or Mohawks who had been removed from their "castles" along the river that bears their name to the Saint Regis Reservation on the Saint Lawrence. There were also Praying Indians from the reservation at Caughnawaga, and some Abnakis from New England. Occasionally Stoner trapped with Saint Regis Indians. One known as Flag was remembered for his loon-skin hat; one named Dr. Gill was especially good at spearing beaver. But if he decided that Indians he encountered in the woods had molested his traps, Stoner shot them without bothering to ask questions.

Nevertheless Stoner was relatively mild compared to "Uncle Nat" Foster, for whom killing Natives was something of a hobby. Foster shot them fairly regularly for their pelts, which of course he was always certain were stolen from his traps. He shot a man because he thought he had done too well for the British during the war. He killed another after a long shoot-out by faking his own death and waiting for the man to come out from behind his tree to scalp him. His hatred for the original inhabitants of the place, he said, stemmed from the time his sister had been taken captive by them in the 1780s and had to be rescued.

Near Old Forge, Foster shot a man in the back while a bunch of town fathers watched. The story given out later was that a Native had come up and asked the group, which included Foster, if anyone knew where to find Nat Foster. He said he was going to go kill Foster if he found him, which seems an unlikely thing to say to a group of white men in the town where Foster lived.

Without revealing his true identity, Foster challenged him to a shooting contest. As agreed, the Native trapper shot first and then handed his gun to Foster for him to use. Foster complimented the man on his aim and told him to go plug the bullet hole to eliminate the possibility of any confusion over who fired which shot. He then put a bullet in the visitor's back with the man's own gun.

The affair was investigated by the authorities, but all those who survived the incident agreed it was an accident. It must have occurred because Foster was unused to the poor dead man's weapon, they said.

Foster killed so many people that he developed a crude storytelling style that apparently passed for humor. The punchline was always the same: the "red devils," as he called them, were never actually shot by Foster, they just seemed to die mysteriously when he was around.

"I watched 'em as they came toward the bridge and felt sure they were the ones who had been stealing from my traps," Jeptha Simms quoted him as saying. "They were Injuns anyhow, I was sure of that. They came onto the bridge over the flowing stream and I raised my rifle and covered 'em with the sight, and thought—'how easy it would be to shoot both on 'em at once.' But as I was thinking thus they both had got to the middle of the log, where they appeared to get dizzy, for they both fell into the stream below. And"—here he would probably shake his head in a way meant to tell you that he wasn't telling you everything—"they didn't bother my traps after that."

Or: "I was walking in the woods when I saw an Injun lay down to drink; something was the matter with him for he dropped his face into the water and drowned. I thought I might as well take his gun, blanket, and stuff as to leave them there to spoil." Like Cooper's Natty Bumppo, when Nat Foster laughed he reportedly made no noise.

Foster's first trapping trip to the Fulton Chain was an occasion to kill two men who happened to be Natives interested in taking game from the same area. They may have been hunting there for decades, or even generations, and very well might have considered the newcomer's traps to be an encroachment on their turf. Or they may, as Foster said, have been thieves who were going to kill him when he shot them instead. Anyway, they wound up dead and he didn't. Such events were usually described by his various biographers in terms like "grim necessity."

Foster moved full-time to the Old Forge area from the neighborhood of Fish House in 1832, primarily because there was nothing much left to trap along the Sacandaga River. The process of moving deeper and deeper into the Adirondacks as the game gave way had been going on for some time. As early as 1796, one trapper moved to Norway, New York, because, he said, the game was already gone from around Lakes George and Champlain. Nick Stoner, too, had begun his career along the Sacandaga and had gradually moved deeper into the future park as the game gave out. Stoner, in fact, wandered all the way up to the headwaters of the Grass River, in the northwest corner of the park.

The usual time to head into the bush for an extended trapping excursion was late September through November, and then again right after the breakup of ice. The trapper's outfit typically included gun and ammunition, hatchet, knife, flint, steel, tinder, and compass—Foster supposedly never carried one and could tell the direction by the way the tips of the hemlocks were bent by the prevailing west wind—a teapot and tea, frying pan, salt, and cornmeal. And, of course, rum. On top of this, each trapper could reasonably carry three beaver traps if on foot or on snowshoes, more if a packhorse or canoe were brought along. A dog was useful.

Both Foster and Stoner owned custom-made guns called double shotters. Unlike a double-barreled gun, these had two hammers on the same barrel and were loaded with two balls and two shots of powder, the first resting on the second. Foster's was made light at the muzzle and heavy at the breech, which he said helped in shooting game on the move.

When shooting in a hurry, Foster would pour in the powder, roll the ball down the barrel, slam the butt of the gun with his hand, and it was ready to go. He was able to aim, load, and fire six bullets within a minute, though a ball so loaded wouldn't go nearly as far as one that was properly tamped down. He would always load two balls for bear.

Unidentified Adirondack trapper (photographer unknown). COURTESY OF THE
ADIRONDACK MUSEUM, BLUE MOUNTAIN LAKE.

Presumably he did the same for wolves, if he happened to be shooting
them one at a time, which didn't always turn out to be the case.

The beginning of his usual line of traps was at the intersection of
the Limekiln Creek and the Moose River, where he would often camp
for a night. From there his traps went up the creek to Limekiln Lake,
and then north to Fourth Lake on the Fulton Chain, then northeast-
erly to Raquette Lake.

There is a falls on the Limekiln Creek, and near there one morning he took from his various traps and snares several beavers, a fisher,
a red fox, and a couple of mink. As every hiker who reads the signs at
Adirondack trailheads knows, the final minutes of the day are supposed to be spent artfully suspending one's food from the trees, but
after the skinning was done that day Foster simply went to sleep, leaving the pile of meat at the outskirts of his camp. A few hours later he
was surrounded by a large pack of hungry wolves.

As soon as the remains of his trapping were gone, the pack became
interested in Foster himself, who had taken up a position on a nearby
rock with his gun. His fingers were loaded up with musket balls. He

shot as many of the dogs as he could until the pack dispersed and he went back to bed. But only briefly. Twice more that night he was awakened by the howling and snarling of the pack, and each time he got up and shot at them. In the morning there were thirteen dead or wounded wolves.

It was a good night for Foster, who was something of a wolf specialist. As the traditional furbearing animals began to give way, better money could be made chasing bigger game. The government in Albany considered it in the interests of all the residents of New York to eliminate the top (nonhuman) predators from the remaining wilderness. Panthers, as mountain lions were called in the Adirondacks, and wolves both brought fairly hefty state bounties. The local farm towns were also expected to pitch in some money for the heads of wolves taken in the vicinity. When one town balked at paying up, Foster even organized a strike among wolf trappers.

Money could also be made from moose and deer. Unlike virtually every other marketable species, the white-tailed deer population of the Adirondacks was probably rising rapidly during the 1800s because the activity of miners, farmers, and loggers vastly expanded their favored mixture of clearing and forest. Moose and especially deer were taken in great numbers for the urban meat markets to the south, and to feed the lumber and mining camps that were beginning to appear all over the more accessible parts of the region.

One of the stories Foster liked to tell his children was of leaving a dead deer to chase another that got away and then returning to find the first one gone. He found it a few feet away hidden under some leaves, which he knew was the work of a panther. He replaced the carcass with a log and sure enough, the big cat soon returned with two small kittens. He shot all three. "I did a pretty good afternoon's work," he said, "getting a deer and the three panther heads, which brought me a good bounty."

But perhaps the most prodigious amount of game Nat Foster ever took happened up near Panther Lake. He was working his way through the forest when a deer ran by him, obviously pursued by some predator. Knowing the current bounty for wolves was thirty dollars a head, he let the deer pass in order to see what followed.

What followed were two large wolves, which he promptly shot. As he was skinning the dogs, a mother panther and two kittens approached, apparently attracted by the smell of blood. He shot them all. Then two more panthers approached, a large male, which Foster presumed was the mate of the first, and another half-grown male. They too were soon dead.

Something about all this made Foster hungry, and as he didn't care for dog or cat meat, he remembered the deer that had started it all. So he left the two dead wolves and five dead panthers in a heap and headed for the lake, where he figured—correctly it turned out—that the buck would be resting from the ordeal with the wolves it thought it had escaped. Another ball of lead, another puff of smoke, and Foster was eating venison.

The shooting of kittens and fawns and pretty much anything else that moved was fairly standard practice in what was a particularly gluttonous period of wildlife removal. In the Champlain Valley bounties would not be paid on wolf puppies whose eyes were not yet open, but only because the towns figured pups that young wouldn't survive long without their mother anyway. There were bounties on crows and blackbirds in some towns, and along the immense wetland that is now Great Sacandaga Lake, waterfowl were netted or shot by the thousands for urban markets. On the Fourth of July in 1810, Stoner and a group of men surveying a road celebrated by catching a large turtle and making eggnog from the 172 eggs they found in it.

Nor were the trappers of the period noticeably encumbered by notions of humane treatment. Stoner's pet, until he shot it, was a large muzzled wolf that dragged a ball and chain around his yard. Another time he kept a moose locked in his barn.

But most trappers and hunters did have various personal taboos. Foster, for instance, wouldn't kill eagles. This provided him with another reason to hate Native Americans, all of whom, he believed, did hunt the national bird. And everyone had an opinion on the great issue of how best to hunt deer. Those who chased deer into the lakes with dogs and then rowed out to them and cut their necks accused those who waited for them quietly with guns of being sneaky. The chasers, meanwhile, were held in contempt for letting the dogs do the hunting. Jacking deer at night with lanterns from boats was either cowardly or efficient, depending on whether it was your personal method. The debate, which would ultimately be settled at a later date by the Legislature, was more often about manliness than environmental responsibility or humanitarian concern.

The fact that Peter Waters, another trapper on the Fulton Chain, occasionally jacked deer was supposedly one of the reasons Foster didn't like him. There was also a matter of a borrowed boat. And Waters, whom everyone called Drid, had threatened on several occasions to kill Foster. The main problem, however, was no doubt the color of Drid's skin. He may have been the last Native American killed by Foster, and was almost certainly the only one for which Uncle Nat was ever tried for murder.

By the time in 1832 that Foster had moved to Old Forge, at the foot of the Fulton Chain, and taken over the lease of the abandoned Herreshoff Manor, the deadly farming and mining saga of the prominent Brown family of Providence, Rhode Island, had already largely played itself out. The place was something of a trappers' colony, where the vanguard of the hordes of urban rusticators to come were just beginning to appear. Indeed, Foster had been hired to guide four gentlemen hunters from Connecticut on the morning of the shooting in 1833. Drid planned to accompany them for part of the trip and then go on to Raquette Lake alone.

The day Drid died started with another of what were apparently many arguments between the two men, and Foster received a cut on the arm. He told the others to go ahead up the lake without him. But instead of staying home and nursing his wound, he took his gun and ran up through the woods three miles from the dam at Old Forge to the place where the river opened into First Lake. There he hid in the bushes on a point of land and waited for the canoes.

When they appeared, Foster stepped out and shot Drid out of his boat. He then went back home and got in bed, where the hunters found him when they returned to Old Forge.[1]

To the surprise of no one, when Nat Foster's case went to trial the summer after the killing he was quickly acquitted by his peers. But the process seems to have spoiled the fun of the Adirondacks for old Uncle Nat. It was like the proverbial glimpse of the neighbors' smoke, and he went west, though he got only as far as Pennsylvania.

---

[1] Where Drid died became known as Indian Point, and there is now a nice camp at the spot with those two words on a sign hanging over the doors of its three-boat garage. Twenty-five yards farther into the lake there is a stop sign, of the red hexagonal sort usually found on roads. It is apparently meant to prevent collisions between boats and Jet Skis coming up the channel from Old Forge and those already going around in circles on the lake. A mile farther around the lake to the right, someone has erected in their yard a twelve-foot-tall cement and plaster statue of a loinclothed brave. His solemn gaze across the lake is, as expected, full of dignity.

For his part, Nick Stoner ended up running a boardinghouse with his third wife in a town called Newkirk near the southern border of the park. Gangrene got Green White. He died of it in 1830 after a tree fell on his wilderness shanty one night, breaking his leg. Belden was finally found bloated and dead by Rogers Rock, killed by his snakes. Uncle Jock passed away rather suddenly at the dinner table.

At any rate, by the middle of the 1800s much of the game the trappers were after was either going fast or already gone. Wolves, moose, and panthers were extremely scarce by midcentury. A trapper couldn't make a decent full-time living off of lynx, fisher, marten, and most of the other furbearers. That deer were more plentiful than ever was a consolation, to be sure. But even that was evidence that the long era when the fur trade was the dominant human activity in the Adirondacks, an era culminating in the end of the French and Indian War, was now truly over. The deer, after all, were living on clearings made by people who had a very different idea of the uses of wilderness.

As for *Castor canadensis,* the industrious beaver, which drove the fur economy for centuries and which, according to both Toby Edwards and Bob Inslerman, is now overrunning parts of the park, it too was gone. In the 1840s James DeKay, who led the first official attempt by the state of New York to gather data on wildlife in the Adirondacks, found no beaver. Thirty years later, after a similar survey, biologist C. Hart Merriam concluded that beaver "have, excepting a few isolated individuals, been exterminated."

6   *Squires and Speculators*

The traditional explanation of how John Brown—the merchant of Providence, Rhode Island, not the abolitionist of Harpers Ferry—came to own a great piece of the Adirondacks that included the place where Nat Foster would shoot Drid is that he acquired it through the bad judgment of a good-for-nothing son-in-law.

In the summer of 1794 John Francis, who was both Brown's business partner and the husband of his eldest daughter, Abby, went to New York City to sell "one thousand and fifty whole chests of merchantable Bohea tea" that had just arrived from Asia on one of their ships, the *George Washington*. But instead of the expected $150,000, the younger man returned to Providence with a second mortgage on a vast expanse of wilderness in upstate New York. "When Brown was informed of the utterly foolish and incomprehensible thing his trusted son-in-law had done—presumably under the influence of wine," wrote the historian Donaldson a century later, "he dropped his head into his hands and wept bitter tears of mortification and disappointment."

John Brown was a daring and successful international merchant, one of the first Americans to send trading ships to China, and one of the last to take part in the slave trade. He was a rabble-rouser in the war for independence who rowed out on Narragansett Bay in a small boat in the dead of night and set fire to King George's revenue cutter the HMS *Gaspee* more than a year before the more often remembered Boston Tea Party. He was a friend and correspondent of George Washington. His house in Providence was declared by John Quincy Adams to be the "most magnificent and elegant mansion I have seen on this continent." An Ivy League university is named for his clan.

That three generations of this first family of the Ocean State spent their fortunes in an obsessive and ultimately humiliating attempt to make good out of a piece of wilderness gotten through a drunken gamble by a playboy son-in-law is a very good story. The tale is even better when the death of another family member, Charles Frederick Herreshoff, is added to the Adirondack ledger. But Brown family correspondence, unearthed in recent years by a descendant on a mission to clear John Francis's name, reveals that Abby Brown's maligned husband was not a wayward lush but a well-loved and sickly member of the family. He did have a weakness for "laudanum or liquors," which may have been the source of the rumors about his seemingly poor judgment regarding the Adirondack purchase. But his addiction was short-lived.

As he returned home from selling the cargo of tea, Francis was met by friends at a tavern outside Providence and informed that in his short absence his two-year-old daughter had died unexpectedly. He was rarely seen sober again, occasionally turning up in the most fashionable coffee houses of Providence in a decidedly boorish mood. But the binge lasted for less than a year; nine months later he was dead. He was thirty-three years old.

By that time it was already beginning to look as if James Greenleaf, the man to whom he sold the cargo of the *George Washington,* was not likely to pay for it. There was nothing particularly unwise about Francis's decision to sell the tea on credit; Greenleaf's partner at the time was Robert Morris, a principal financier of the American effort in the Revolution and the "superintendent of finance" of the new nation in the years between independence and the adoption of the Constitution. Furthermore, personal letters of credit were often passed around as legal tender in the absence of a national currency. Brown and Francis never expected to need to call in the mortgages.

But Greenleaf was bankrupt. So was his partner, Morris, and a whole slew of other formerly reputable American businessmen who, after helping to finance the war to throw off the yoke of British tyranny, turned voraciously to the equally all-American pastime of land speculation and subdivision. With the end of the war with England, all territory formally belonging to the Crown, or to loyalist sympathizers, reverted to the state governments. The new states were simultaneously strapped for revenues and interested in attracting settlers, so they eagerly sold vast parcels of land at cut rates to anyone with the political and economic leverage to put a deal together.[1]

Not that this was any different than it had been before the Revolution. The first truly sizable purchase of park land from the Mohawks took place in 1771 at the home of Sir William Johnson. The location was no coincidence as Johnson was the critical link in any deal that involved both the Iroquois and the king of England. In January of that year two shipwrights from Manhattan named William Totten and Stephen Crossfield acted as front men for Johnson's cronies, the Jessup brothers, and purchased from the Mohawks a vast triangle of land with corners near Keene Valley in the northeast, Cranberry Lake in the northwest, and Lake Pleasant in the south.

The Totten and Crossfield Purchase, as it became known, included within its 1.1 million acres Raquette Lake, Blue Mountain Lake, Indian Lake, Long Lake, and Lake Pleasant. The terms were typical of the transactions of the time; the Mohawks received a little over a thousand pounds sterling and the king collected eight times that amount in taxes and fees. Like Johnson's heirs, the Jessups sided with the English in the Revolution, and their land reverted to the state of New York.

The land that ultimately became Brown's Tract came not from the Totten and Crossfield Purchase but from an even bigger land grab that took place during the feeding frenzy in the first decades of the

[1] Iroquois territory in upstate New York was one of the particularly hot places for investment, in part because as early as 1724 Cadwallader Colden, who was then the surveyor general of the colony, had floated the idea of a canal to the Great Lakes. More recently, George Washington had traveled upstate and pronounced that "vast inland navigation" was possible. The Erie Canal, of course, would ultimately not go through the park, but as the route was uncertain, all land remotely in the area was considered a sound bet. The other smart picks were "Federal City," where Washington, D.C., was to be built, and the Ohio Valley, where the Browns also owned a tract.

new republic. In 1792 a speculator named Alexander Macomb bought from the State of New York roughly an eighth of its total territory—an astounding four million acres, half of it within the park—for around eight cents an acre.

It was a real estate deal so sweet, and so quietly executed, that the Legislature simply assumed that something unethical involving then-Governor George Clinton must have taken place. Exhaustive legislative hearings were held, during which senatorial oratory on the right of the people to know ran high. Nothing came of it, though, and Clinton was exonerated.

Alexander Macomb, meanwhile, found himself unable to digest the enormous helping he had taken and landed in debtors' prison within six months of the great purchase. From there he transferred most of his land to his principal backers in the deal, William Constable and Daniel McCormick. They, in turn, immediately began the process of subdividing and reselling.

Constable, in particular, was gifted at finding buyers; the high sheriff of London bought 26,000 acres for a shilling an acre. Another large parcel went to a group of bankers from Holland who had a scheme to break the sugar and slave economy of the Caribbean by flooding the market with maple syrup. But Constable's biggest profit came only a half year after buying 1.9 million acres from Macomb for fifty thousand pounds when he sold 1.3 million of them to a Samuel Ward for a hundred thousand. Ward then sold 210,000 acres to James Greenleaf, who in turn quickly mortgaged them to a New York merchant named John Livingston, and then a second time to John Francis against the purchase of the tea.

At the peak of the fever in 1795, Greenleaf and Morris's firm, the North American Land Company, controlled over six million acres of land in all parts of the new country. But by then it was all becoming a game of hot potato, in which huge parcels of territory changed hands as rapidly as prominent men could be hauled in and out of debtors' prison. Contracts were hardly dry on purchases before new deals were made to sell. They simply drew lines around vast pieces of property that no one really had any idea about and sold them to each other.

To top-tier speculators like Constable and Morris, the forests and lakes and peaks that are now the park were as intangible as the individual bedrooms and kitchen sinks of middle-class homes are to modern traders of mortgage-backed securities. Just as bales of beaver skins occasionally stood in for hard currency in the 1600s, so wilderness, in parcels of hundreds of thousands of acres at a time and generally unseen by its owners, was a relatively liquid asset in the 1700s. It was one of the benefits of wilderness that it could, in a pinch, be traded for tea.

The whole phenomenon was based on the bedrock faith that the development of the new nation's vast inland wilderness holdings would inevitably resemble the experience of the seaboard. The forests, of course, would be replaced by farms, with a concomitant rise in the value of the land. The trick—one that eluded the Browns—was to unload your holdings without becoming bogged down in the details of building roads and retailing your particular section of wilderness to settlers.

This was a very different conception of the relationship between an owner and his land from the baronial vision of William Gilliland, who in the same decades built and lost a minor empire just inside the park's eastern boundary. Like William Johnson, Gilliland was an Irish immigrant with large ambitions. In the 1750s he was run out of the old country by the family of a woman with whom he was in love but with whom he was not of equal station, and wound up in New York City, where he soon became a rich merchant.

Gilliland was not inclined toward the new and distinctly American habit of land speculation, however. His imagined future of the wilderness was also agricultural, but along feudal rather than capitalistic lines. To a once poor man who had been spurned by the landed, a large estate was the essence of status. After marrying his partner's daughter and adding her dowry to his own money, he bought a tract on Lake Champlain's western shore in 1765 and moved from Manhattan to the mouth of the Boquet River. With him were thirteen men and three women, the first of what he hoped would become scores of tenant farmers.

For a short time Gilliland succeeded. The Champlain Valley is far more fertile than most of the rest of the park, and the lake itself was a generous resource; on his first angling trip Gilliland caught sixty fish. By 1775 several hundred people lived on the estate, which by then stretched for several miles along Champlain's western shore. There were twenty-eight houses, a school, two gristmills, two sawmills, forty

"The Adirondack Mountains, Near Elizabethtown, Essex Co., N.Y.," 1866, by John Henry Dolph. COURTESY OF THE ADIRONDACK MUSEUM, BLUE MOUNTAIN LAKE.

barns or other outbuildings, and all the various livestock and farm implements that went along with them. He named the village of Willsboro after himself, and Elizabethtown after his wife. Just as he had imagined, Gilliland was general lord of the realm.

But it all crumbled in the Revolution, though not for the usual reason of siding with the king. Quite the opposite. He was such a fervent advocate of independence that the English put a price of five hundred pounds on his head, inducing some of his own employees into an attempt to abduct him and spirit him to Canada. That plot was foiled, but Gilliland's slide from manorial greatness was not far off. In 1778 he was accused of being a traitor to the cause of liberty by, of all people, Benedict Arnold, and while he was in prison on that charge the British sacked his holdings. He ultimately lost everything he had, including his title to the land. From 1786 to 1791 he, too, was in debtors' prison.

When he got out he returned to Willsboro, broken in spirit, and earned a meager living surveying tracts for others who were still in a position to speculate on Adirondack wilderness. In February of 1796, during a surveying mission in the wilderness, something went wrong with his legs. Gilliland crawled through the icy forest until the flesh was completely worn off of his frostbitten palms and knees. He was lost. And when he was found a few days later with the bones of his hands and legs exposed, he was frozen solid.

That same year, the land bubble burst and the new nation slipped into its first national recession. It was the "Panic of 1796." By April of

1797, both James Greenleaf and his partner were broke and in debtors' prison, primarily to protect them from potentially violent creditors. The only way to salvage anything from the tea sale, John Brown ultimately decided, was to take possession of the land in the Adirondacks. But at that time he, too, was strapped for cash. So he made a blatantly emotional appeal to his dead son-in-law's brother, Tom Francis.

"Pray remember that my securing the 210,000 acres of land will be fixing a certain and handsome fortune to your dear nephew John B. Francis who is a fine fellar . . ." he wrote in a letter in 1798. He wanted thirty thousand dollars to pay off the holder of the first mortgage on the property.

Tom Francis had already been burned twice by Brown's dealings with Greenleaf, so he was understandably reluctant to get in deeper, but Old Thunder, as the family called John Brown, prevailed. The land would easily be worth half a million dollars by the time the little fatherless boy was of age, Brown predicted. He was wrong. The land cost Brown the approximately ninety thousand dollars unpaid balance on the cargo of tea, around thirty thousand to other Greenleaf creditors, and whatever he paid Aaron Burr for legal services. For three generations, various Brown relatives poured money, sweat, and blood into the project. When they finally divested themselves of their park holdings, the family had recouped only thirty-three thousand dollars.

But in that December of 1798, when John Brown at last became the sole owner of 210,000 acres of land surrounding the Fulton Chain Lakes, he was certain he was about to build an empire in the wilderness. As soon as the deeds were signed, he set off for the Adirondacks.

He never did get onto his tract that winter, but he got close. In February of 1799, Brown showed up in Boon's Settlement, which is now the town of Boonville just to the west of the park. Boon's was the nearest thing to a village in the vicinity of his purchase, which is to say there was a store there. He hired surveyors, from whom he expected to learn everything about his land, which began twelve miles to the east.

"You'll be sure to note every mill place, every good place for a compact town, the ore, the salt springs if aney, the kind of timber, the lay of the ground weither good or bad or indifferent, weither broken, or even or weither large or small hills and every other observation you think worthey of my knowing," he wrote to them in March from back in Providence.

He had no intention of proceeding incrementally. "I shall be on the ground in all April," he told his surveyors, and together they would continue working "till the Whole Tract is layd out into four rod rhodes within one mile of each [other] in every town & the rhodes at right angles within two miles [of each other] and every farm to be laid half mile squair & fronting one of said rhodes. . . ."

There were to be eight townships in all, which Brown optimistically named Industry, Enterprise, Perseverance, Unanimity, Frugality, Sobriety, Economy, and Regularity. At the confluence of the North and Middle Branches of the Moose River—land that William Johnson supposedly dreamed Hendrick into giving him—he envisioned a good-sized village with three hundred lots of ten acres apiece.

Brown was talking about laying five hundred miles of roads in all, with nice clean right angles at every intersection. The surveyors were encouraging, perhaps sensing that they had a good client on the line. They were certain, they told him, that there were copper and lead deposits on his land.

Despite the preliminary talk of mining and logging, Brown believed that the backbone of the society that would bloom on his wild lands would be farmers. In the nineteenth century in America the progress of agriculture, in all interpretations of the word "progress," was something of a given; of course the Adirondacks would support farmers. Brown's plan was the same one that underlay all of the speculators and developers of the period and that ultimately accompanied the removal of Native Americans and marketable wild animals from across most of the American continent. By strategically positioning himself within the flow of what everyone knew to be an inevitable process of spreading out and filling in, John Brown believed he would become rich. Or, more to the point, he believed he would become richer than he already was.

Thus, from the moment it occurred to him that he must actually obtain title to the land to the day he died, John Brown was convinced that if he funded a few more improvements—another road here, a gristmill there—and offered reasonable terms of credit, it would naturally follow that masses of righteous hardworking homesteaders would flow onto his land and transform it from its current degraded state into a profitable land of milk and honey. The wilderness was lying there, waiting to give itself up to him.

"I therefore contemplate . . . receiving many thousands [of] bushels of wheat at Albany from my 210,000 acres of land in a few years," he wrote to his foreman on the site in 1799.

Gilliland and Brown both used the biblical imagery of Isaac Jogues, Cotton Mather, and William Bradford when they described their pieces of the park as "howling wilderness."[2] And when Gilliland further called the forested shores of Lake Champlain a "wasteland," he was merely using the standard term in eighteenth-century contracts to describe places that were not yet under cultivation; in 1784 the New York State Legislature passed a measure calling for the speedy sale and settlement "of the waste and unappropriated lands within the State." Until he arrived to improve it, Gilliland explained in his journal, the land served "no other purpose but to accommodate the savages and beasts of the forest."

What was beautiful to Gilliland and Brown and other Americans was not towering pines or lonely lakes. It wasn't range after range of blanketed mountains stretching away from the summit of Algonquin, sometimes protruding from heavy fog, sometimes separated by azure lakes. It wasn't a dead muskrat in the trap, or a herd of easily harvested deer yarded up in the middle of a circle of high snowdrifts. Or a moose poked with a knife on a stick. What pleased them, what had been beautiful to Western culture since the ancient Greeks and Hebrews, was the pastoral. Eden had been a garden, after all. Wilderness was outside the wall.

In the spring of 1799, as promised, John Brown arrived in the Adirondacks, ready to oversee the laying out of his future breadbasket. Conditions on the tract were rustic to say the least. His bark-roofed cabin, the first building in the town of Industry, was just about as far from his graceful mansion in Providence as a person could get. There were the usual ungodly hordes of spring insects. And rain. But Brown only figured to stay a few weeks at the most. He endured without complaint.

Some things, however, even a reasonable man should not be made to do without. In his first letter from the tract Brown requested that a cow be sent in "and some meal so that I may have some Hasterpudding." Though not unusually tall, Old Thunder weighed in the neigh-

---

[2] As Thoreau wrote in *The Maine Woods:* "Generally speaking, a howling wilderness does not howl: it is the imagination of the traveller that does the howling."

borhood of three hundred pounds. The cow and pudding were apparently sent right out.

Toward the end of that summer Brown began to get reports that farther into the forest on his land the ground got progressively rockier. "I confess [the surveyors] give accts of more stones that I wish to have had," he wrote from Providence. But optimism, or perhaps vision, prevailed. "A large proportion of Stones Would in time be an Advantage rather than a Disadvantage to the Land," he went on, "as no fence in the World is Equilly Valuable to a Good Stone wall . . ."

Robert Frost might have agreed, but potential settlers with a choice between Brown's land and the flat, deep soils of the far side of the Alleghenies were less impressed. They were, after all, moving *from* rocky New England. Even Brown's trusty foreman, James Sheldon, could not be convinced to move to the tract permanently.

The essential problem with all the expectations of a pastoral future for Brown's Tract and the rest of the Adirondack wilderness was that the land simply was not as fertile as the relatively flat lands to the west, where the Brown family was also speculating. The soil in the Adirondacks is thin and rocky; only 10 percent of it is now considered arable. The growing season in many parts of the park is less than a hundred days a year. Frost in July is unusual, to be sure, but even snow in that month is not unheard of. Average snowfall in the winter in the higher parts of the park is over a hundred inches, and on the western flank, where Brown's Tract lies, storms moving east from the Great Lakes regularly dump well over two hundred inches a winter.

When John Brown died in 1803, he had spent in the neighborhood of $25,000 on "improvements" to the tract. He had paid for the construction of a road from Boonville to what would become Old Forge in Township 7, Economy. He built a gristmill, a sawmill, and a few houses and outbuildings. Yet, there were probably fewer than a dozen people living on the tract. The lines were drawn and for the most part surveyed, the towns were named, but the place was still, by almost any definition past or present, a howling wilderness.

7   *Love and Sweat*

There were a few homesteaders who built their little houses in the big woods of the Adirondacks, both on Brown's Tract and elsewhere. There was at least one farm in Keene Valley by 1797, and farms in Newcomb and North Elba by 1816. And of course it was these men and women, the footsoldiers of agricultural progress, who actually did the hard and mostly futile work of attempting to transform the park's wild expanses into fields of waving grain.

Most came from New England. "New York fever," as the first craze for lands to the west was called, took hold almost as soon as the Iroquois were divested of their territory. It was the first stage in the process of "westering" that would eventually populate the continent with European Americans, but it did not happen quite as spontaneously as the folklore of westward expansion usually suggests. In order to attract a critical mass of settlers to a new tract, some developers, including Brown and his offspring, offered free land to the first few families to arrive and stay for a few years. Sales agents of some of the largest landholders in New York prowled the northeast trolling for prospective buyers, advertising in newspapers, holding informational meetings.

"Blue Ridge from Root's. Adirondacks." Circa 1880, by Seneca Ray Stoddard.
COURTESY OF THE ADIRONDACK MUSEUM, BLUE MOUNTAIN LAKE.

"We had heard that Ti[conderoga] was a Paradise, that we should find pigs and fowls ready cooked running about with knives and forks stuck in their backs, crying, 'Eat us!' But when we got there it was all bushes," complained one woman who moved to the park from Vermont in the 1790s.

Vermont was hit with the fever more than its neighbors, and often a farmer from that state would put in his crops in the spring and then take off for New York. While the plants back home were being watered, hopefully, by God, and the animals were being tended, in all likelihood, by his wife, he would tour around New York looking for a promising spot for a new home. The idea was to return to New England in time to bring in the harvest. The following summer he might return alone to the chosen land to begin the process of clearing. Other families chose to make a clean move to the Adirondacks bringing with them, they hoped, enough supplies to last them through that first year without crops.

The first step was to chop down as many trees as possible. By the second half of the 1800s, when timber supplies grew thin in New England, trees would become the most valuable resource in the Adirondacks. By the end of the same century trees would be protected by the state's constitution. But to the farmers at the beginning of the century the immense three- and four-hundred-year-old hemlocks, pines, spruces, and maples were worse than valueless. They were simply in the way. They were weeds. The preferred term was not "trees" or "forest" but "bush," which to modern ears, at least, has a certain ring of disdain.

Day after day after day would-be farmers chopped down giants, allowing them to fall as they might. Then in autumn, on a sufficiently breezy and dry day, the whole tangled mess was set on fire. The hotter the blaze the better, and if any of the surrounding forest caught fire, it was chalked up to good luck. Logs that didn't burn sufficiently were piled up and lit again. Crops were simply planted around the charred stumps.

It was a difficult life of dirt floors and greased paper windows and nearly constant labor. For homesteaders who had nothing to sell, nothing could be bought. As Flavius Cook, the town historian of Ticonderoga, rhapsodized in his 1858 *Home Sketches of Essex County*, "Men scraped their own axe-helves; and bent their own ox-bows; and smoothed their own whip-stocks; and braided their own whip-lashes; and put handles to their own jack-knives; and peeled their own brooms out of white birch or sweet walnut, or braided them out of hemlock; and shaved their own barrel staves; and hooped their own beer-casks; and sewed up their own harnesses; and shaped their own horse-shoes; and run their own bullets; and tapped their own boots; and swingled their own flax; and hollowed their own wooden dishes; and ironed their own ox-carts; and mended their own bob-sleds."

The women, meanwhile, "picked their own wool, and carded their own rolls, and spun their own yarn, and drove their own looms, and made their own cloth, and cut their own garments, and did their own making and mending . . . and dipped their own candles, and tried their own soap, and bottomed their own chairs, and braided their own baskets, and wove their own carpets, and quilted their own coverlids, and picked their own geese feathers, and milked their own cows, and tended their own calves and pig-pens, and went a visiting on their own feet, or rode to meeting or wedding on ox-sleds with a bundle of straw for a seat, and at their backs two hickory stakes and a long chain."

It was called "toughing it."

"After I married we moved across the valley westward where we had to tough it," a seventy-four-year-old Mrs. Adolphus Sheldon recounted in one of the few existing accounts of life on a park homestead. "I had toughed it at my father's and now I had to tough it here. Only a half acre was cleared. There we lived for five years without a stove or fireplace. We absolutely had no chimney. We burned wood right against the logs of the cabin and when they got afire we put it out."

Sheldon was fortunate enough to live near a gristmill. She remembered "once going to a mill and dusting up flour from behind the bolt that had worms in it, picking them out and so making bread." But those who lived twenty, thirty, or sixty miles into the woods ground their corn in a hollowed-out stump with a rock that was suspended from the top of a nearby sapling. The rest of the typical winter diet was made up primarily of salt pork, beans, potatoes, and occasionally wild turkey or venison.

"You could have no sheep," Sheldon explained. "The wolves would tear you right down. You could hear them away off in the night. One would howl, then another answer—howl, howl, howl, then another way off, howl, howl, howl, till they got up such a roar that it would almost tear you down." She and her husband once went out to their cornfield in the middle of the night; she held a torch so that he could shoot the bear that fed there every night. Another time she brought in the crops by herself while her husband recovered from a nearly fatal scything accident.

"We lived, you might say, on work and love," she concluded.

Not all the wolves had fur. In 1794 speculators from New York hired two inhabitants of a settlement just south of the park to stage a phony Indian attack to try and scare off the other villagers, so that their land would be vacant and thus available for resale. According to Jeptha Simms, the plot was undone when someone noticed that the footprints leading up the Sacandaga River didn't turn inward at the toes, as Native American feet supposedly did, but outward, like whites. The perpetrators, a pair of brothers named Olmstead, were promptly run out of town by a mob. The two faux Indians had enough time, though, to convince the wife of one of the townsmen to run away with them.

As for entertainment, early homesteaders took it wherever they got it. "On the north side of Black Mountain is a cluster of some half-dozen houses, in a vale called the bosom, but from what I do not know," reported the wandering angler Charles Lanman in 1848. "The presiding geniuses of the place are a band of girls, weighing two hundred pounds a piece, who farm it with their father for a liv-

Early Adirondack Farmstead. Courtesy of the Adirondack Museum, Blue Mountain Lake.

ing, but whose principal amusement is rattlesnake hunting. Their favorite playground is the notorious cliff on Tongue mountain, where they go with naked feet (rowing their own boats across the Lake), and pull out by their tails from the rocks the pretty playthings, and, snapping them to death, they lay them away in a basket as trophies of their skill."

Most of those park homesteaders who survived and stuck it out did so not so much by farming as by dabbling in as many different forest industries as possible. Nick Stoner, Nat Foster, and no doubt numerous other trappers lived on farms that were primarily tended by their wives. Virtually every homesteader tapped maples in the early spring and boiled the sap down to make syrup. Maple sugar was occasionally even distilled into rum, though homemade whiskey was preferable.

An even more important source of income for many was potash, which could bring a family from sixty to eighty dollars a ton. Potash was used as a raw material by the makers of glass, soap, dyes, explosives, and various other products. In 1822 it was one of New York's primary exports, mostly to England where it was used to clean wool. But to make a ton of the stuff required cutting, curing, and burning thirty cords of firewood, gathering up the ashes, leaching them with water, and boiling down the resulting lye. Then you had to haul the finished product to the nearest market, which could be tens of miles away.

Potash pots were among the endless stream of goods sent out to Brown's Tract by the succession of relatives of John Brown who inherited Old Thunder's great development project. One thought orchards might be the solution and sent out two hundred apple trees, but then lost interest. Another arranged for two hundred fancy Merino sheep to be herded overland all the way from Rhode Island out to the tract, which took six weeks, but they eventually died. Grindstones were shipped, along with mill saws, crosscut saws, bellows leather. On and on. And of course, for the hired men working on the seemingly endless task of keeping a road open from the tract to the rest of the world, wages, whiskey, gin, and hard cider were shipped out.

The work was endless, but some days were more fun than others. One night after working all day on the road, instead of collecting firewood a crew led by John Brown Francis, the son of the John Francis who originally sold the boatload of tea, simply "set fire to an old dead tree which burns majestically." What the hell, they no doubt thought. "The blaze reaching 80 or one hundred feet & the whole surrounding wilderness illuminated," Francis raved in his diary.

On June 27, 1817, John Brown Francis wrote that he went to the North Branch of the Moose River "to be bit by mosquitoes for we caught no fish." That particular day got even worse. Captain James Gould, who had been the chief roadbuilder since 1799 and was one of only two families who had lived on the tract for any length of time, and who was in fact the most committed employee the Browns ever had, got kicked in the crotch by an ox and died.

Anecdotal evidence from persons who actually tried to farm in the Adirondacks slowly mounted, making it all the harder to attract settlers to the region. One local described the land on Brown's Tract as "so poor it would make a crow shed tears of blood to fly over it." And in the 1830s, yet another member of the Brown family lamented that locals were telling jokes about "a judge who threatened to banish a criminal to John Brown's Tract, which so frightened the poor fellow that he cleared out and has not been heard of since."

But blind faith in the agricultural potential of the Adirondacks persisted. At the end of the 1830s the state geologist, Ebenezer Emmons, reported to the Legislature that the Adirondacks "will be found an excellent country for grazing, raising stock, and producing butter and cheese." A few years later, in 1843, the Reverend John Todd visited the small community of pioneers at Long Lake, which lies to the north and east of Brown's Tract, and predicted confidently that "the day shall arrive in which these forests shall be cut down, and along the lakes and valleys and around the base of these glorious mountains there shall be a virtuous, industrious and Christian population. . . ."

Another preacher and writer who visited the Long Lake colony a few years later was less impressed. "Say what men will, it is an awfully rough, cold, and forbidding country to the farmer," wrote the Reverend Joel T. Headley, in the *New York Observer.* "Crowding may drive farmers here," he said, "but no gentler means."

Headley, whom Edgar Allan Poe called "the autocrat of all quacks," was an early proselytizer for saving the forest. "Cut down the trees and two thirds of all the beauty of this region would depart," he wrote. "And how solemn it is to move all day through a majestic colonnade of trees and feel that you are in a boundless cathedral whose organ notes swell and die away with the passing wind like some grand requiem. Still more exciting is it to lie at midnight by your camp fire and watch the moon sailing up amid the trees or listen to the cry of the loon, wild and lonely, on the wild and lonely lake, or the hoot of the owl in the deep recesses of the forest."

He was clearly on the cusp of a new understanding. Yet even Headley could not, or dared not, fully divest himself of his belief in the ultimate goodness of agricultural development in the Adirondacks. He was not that radical. His pessimism about the future of farming in the region was strictly the result of a loss of faith and hope, but not the abandonment of basic American values.

"I would like to see this desolate country settled," Headley wrote, "but it never will be till the West is all occupied."

8 *Death of a Zealot*

The Browns of Rhode Island were not the only ones who made rather grand agrarian plans for the wilds of the future park from the comfort of rooms far from the Adirondacks. In 1792 William Constable agreed to sell roughly 600,000 acres of the Macomb Purchase to a French nobleman named Pierre Chassanis. Chassanis hoped to create an agricultural community called Castorland, where members of the French aristocracy could find refuge from the deadly excesses of the revolution. Owing to lack of interest from potential buyers, the purchase was soon reduced to 200,000 acres. Part of that was inside the northwest corner of the park.

Most of what is known of Castorland comes from an official journal of the corporation that was rescued by a young American on a college graduation tour of Europe in 1862. It was among a pile of papers along the Seine that were to be sold for rag content. According to the journal, in June of 1793 forty-one shareholders met in an apartment in Paris to organize the society they intended to found in the northern wilds of New York State.

They agreed on a seal for the Castorland corporation and a design for commemorative coins, which were later made. On one side of the coin was the head of the goddess Cybele, "who personified the earth as inhabited or cultivated"; on the other side Ceres was shown tapping a maple tree over the image of a beaver. Two great cities were planned, each with fourteen thousand lots. Two thousand lots in each were set aside for churches and markets. As in Brown's earnestly named towns to the south, right angles abounded in the plans for Castorland.

Two commissaries of the corporation, Simon Desjardins and Pierre Pharoux, left for America almost immediately. Whether this was because Desjardins had been a chamberlain to the now headless king, Louis XVI, and was therefore not anxious to linger in Paris while the guillotine was in such good repair is not known. But the journal does report that the two sailed on the eighth of July in 1793, and brought with them, among other things, a two-thousand-volume library and a generous supply of wine.

They were not as impressed with their new home as their country-man de Tocqueville later would be. On the road from Albany to Sche-nectady they noted that "to escape the expense of hospitality, every good American puts a tavern sign on his door, if located on the public road; and in their inns we sometimes can find neither bread, nor meat, nor a bed."

Like the Browns, they struggled year after year to build roads and keep bridges open. They watched crops take hold, and then be killed by frost. At one point twenty families did come to Castorland from France, including Louis XVI's royal forester. But interest among the members of the old regime was never as great as its founders hoped it might be, and it flagged entirely once Napoleon invited all the exiles to return to France. Castorland foundered, and in 1814 the corporate charter was not renewed. Some of the land subsequently became the summer home of Napoleon's brother, Joseph Bonaparte, after he was removed from the throne of Spain.

The prospect of displaced Parisian courtiers building an agricul-tural society on land that was too rocky and cold for most Vermonters was surely the strangest outcome of the mix of fervent speculation and unquestioned faith in the pastoral future of the Adirondack wilderness. But only moderately more realistic in hindsight was an attempt during the 1840s to settle newly freed and fugitive southern slaves in the North Elba–Lake Placid[1] area. This took place under the

[1] The park is famous, among other things, for its plethora of confusing place-names. The prob-lem usually stems from the fact that the underlying town names are not always the same as the more well-known hamlets that lie in them. Nor do the hamlets named after lakes always lie on

guidance of another, significantly more famous man with the name John Brown.

Not a whole lot is known about North Elba before the militant abolitionist John Brown and his family moved there in 1849. The most notable thing that may or may not have happened in the area was the bloody destruction during the French and Indian War of a small seasonal community of Native Americans. While the village warriors were away harvesting scalps for the French, it was assumed, Robert Rogers and his Rangers stole in and collected the scalps of their families for the English. But the story is not well documented.

In 1809 an ironworks was founded in North Elba by William McIntyre. But the mine failed in 1815, and most of the homesteaders who had made their way up the Ausable River to the area wandered off for the usual reasons. By 1840 only six families lived there.

Most of the land in North Elba, along with hundreds of thousands of acres elsewhere in the state, belonged to the prominent New York abolitionist Gerrit Smith. He had inherited the land from his father, Peter Smith, who made a fortune as a fur-trading partner of John Jacob Astor. In 1846, the younger Smith began giving forty-acre plots around the state to fugitive slaves and other African Americans. Most of the men and women who took him up on the offer wisely chose lands in more fertile areas of the state. But a handful wound up in the park.

Through his work in the abolition movement, John Brown was aware of the program, and he had met Smith once. So in 1848 when Brown, who had tried and failed at a half-dozen business ventures over the years, found himself bankrupt once more, he went to the wealthy idealist at his large white-columned house in Peterboro, New York, with a proposal.

"I am something of a pioneer," Brown said. "I grew up among the woods and wild Indians of Ohio, and am used to the climate and the way of life that your colony find so trying. I will take one of your farms myself, clear it up and plant it, and show my colored neighbors how much work should be done; will give them work as I have occasion, look after them in all needful ways, and be a kind of father to them."

---

their namesake bodies of water. Thus, the large and popular village (or hamlet, to use the APA's term) of Lake Placid lies within the town of North Elba. Moreover, the lake in the center of Lake Placid is called Mirror Lake. Lake Placid the lake is just outside of the hamlet, though it is in the town of North Elba.

"The Adirondacks—View at North Elba," circa 1880, by Seneca Ray Stoddard.
COURTESY OF THE ADIRONDACK MUSEUM, BLUE MOUNTAIN LAKE.

Smith agreed on the spot, and offered to sell Brown 240 acres in North Elba at a dollar an acre. Brown went immediately to the Adirondacks to look around, and liked what he saw. In May of 1848 he and his large family—over the course of his life with two wives he had nineteen children, nine of whom died in childhood—moved from Springfield, Massachusetts, to a rented house in North Elba.

The few black families that were already in the area were struggling. The land had not been properly surveyed, so none were sure if they were on the right plots, and title was not yet cleared. In the years after the 1850 fugitive slave law allowing bounty hunters to prowl the free states in search of runaways, most of North Elba's African Americans seemed to prefer to live together rather than out on isolated farms anyway. There was a small community of about ten modest, square log houses with flat roofs along the Elba River. Flying over the settlement, some sources report, was a large red flag with the name "Timbuctoo" written on it.

For a while, John Brown attempted to live up to his side of the bargain. He spent some of his first months surveying farms belonging to African Americans and some of it clearing his own land. He hired as many black helpers as he could afford, including at least one who was a fugitive slave. He imported some fine Devonshire cattle from England, which he hoped would be the beginning of a local dairy industry, and showed them at an Essex County Fair in September of 1848.

According to Richard Henry Dana Jr., the Browns practiced their preaching in those years. Dana, the author of the classic sea memoir *Two Years before the Mast,* was opposed to slavery himself, but there is a hint of surprise in his description of the egalitarianism at the dinner he shared with the Brown family. "We were all ranged at a long table, some dozen of us more or less, and these two Negroes and one other had their places with us," he wrote later. "These two Negroes," Dana had implied earlier in his memoir, were fugitive slaves. "Mr. Brown said a solemn grace. I observed that he called the Negroes by their surnames, with the prefixes of Mr. and Mrs. The man was 'Mr. Jefferson,' and the woman 'Mrs. Wait.' He introduced us to them in due form, 'Mr. Dana, Mr. Jefferson,' 'Mr. Metcalf, Mrs. Wait.' " Brown was, Dana concluded, "a kind of king" among the blacks of North Elba.

Dana was on the Brown farm quite by accident. In the summer of 1849 he journeyed up the Connecticut Valley and across Champlain to the Adirondacks, becoming one of the earliest tourists to travel there. He and two companions traveled up the Boquet River to Elizabethtown and from there to Keene, where they slept on the floor of a place called Ford's Tavern. Going west, "we began to meet signs of frontier life—log cabins, little clearings, bad roads overshadowed by forests, mountain torrents, and the refreshing odor of balsam firs and hemlocks."

At one of these log cabins they hired a local to lead them over the Indian Pass to Newcomb, where they spent a few days in the woods with the legendary guide John Cheney. After an education like that, they were convinced they could find their own way back over the pass. They took no camping equipment with them as they expected to be back at the log cabins for dinner.

Instead, that evening they each had a bite of the single, four-inch trout one of them caught and then spent the night sleeping rather fitfully on the ground. They were lost. But the next day they stumbled out of the woods onto a road about a half mile from John Brown's cabin.

"Three more worn, wearied, black-fly-bitten travelers seldom came to this humble, hospitable door," Dana wrote, apparently forgetting that two of his dinner companions, and perhaps a third, had probably found their way to this farmhouse in the middle of the

Adirondacks from somewhere south of the Mason-Dixon Line via the Underground Railroad.

"The farm was a mere recent clearing. The stumps of trees stood out, blackened by burning, and crops were growing among them, and there was a plenty of felled timber," Dana said. Brown was not there when they arrived, but he appeared a few hours later. "Late in the afternoon, a long buckboard wagon came in sight and on it were seated a Negro man and a woman, with bundles; while a tall gaunt, dark complexioned man walked before."

John Brown loved the Adirondacks. "Every thing you see reminds one of Omnipotence," he said of the mountains, and "if you do get your crops cut off once in a while, you will feel your dependence." Another time he said, "Nothing but the strong sense of duty, obligation, & propriety, would keep me from laying my bones to rest there."

But a slew of lawsuits growing out of the failure of his wool business kept him away from the Adirondacks from 1851 to 1855. After that, it was his leadership in the Free-Soil border uprisings in Kansas that kept drawing him away from the future park. In 1854 five of his sons went to Kansas to fight "the slave power," and Brown joined them the following year. In 1856 he orchestrated the "Pottawatomie massacre," killing five proslavery men at a place called Osawatomie. "Old Brown of Osawatomie" became the rallying cry of the abolitionists in the east. In 1857 there was another fight at the same place, in which Brown's son Frederick was killed.

On his way home one year John Brown stopped along the way at Canton, Connecticut, and picked up his grandfather's tombstone.[2] On the face of the slab read the words "In Memory of Capt. John Brown, who died at New York, Sept. ye 3, 1776, in the 48 year of his Age."

Back in North Elba, Brown set it up facing the front door of his house, about twenty yards away, near an immense boulder. On the back of it he inscribed an epitaph for the son he had just lost: "In memory of Frederick, son of John and Dianthe [his first wife] Brown, born Dec. 21 1830 and murdered at Osawatomie Kansas August 30, 1856 for his adherence to the cause of freedom." On the boulder he carved the letters "J.B.," indicating where he wanted his own body to be buried one day.

---

[2] This was a spare stone, so to speak, having been replaced with a stone that had Brown's grandmother's name on it as well. Some accounts suggest that Brown did not himself pick up the stone but had it sent.

On the sixteenth of October in 1859, John Brown and twenty-one other men took over the federal arsenal at Harpers Ferry, Virginia (now West Virginia). In the fight that followed, one of his sons died and another was mortally wounded. Members of several other North Elba families were also among the dead. Brown himself was captured, and after refusing his lawyers' suggestion that he plead not guilty by reason of insanity, he was convicted of treason and hanged.

"How mysterious is the touch of Fate which gives a man immortality on earth!" wrote Dana later. "It would have been past belief had we been told that this quiet frontier farmer, already at or beyond middle life, with no noticeable past, would within ten years be the central figure of a great tragic scene, gazed upon with wonder, pity, admiration, or execration by half a continent! That this man should be thought to have imperiled the slave empire in America and added a new danger to the stability of the Union! That his almost undistinguishable name of John Brown should be whispered among four millions of slaves, and sung wherever the English tongue is spoken, and incorporated into an anthem to whose solemn cadence men should march to battle by tens of thousands! That he should have done something toward changing the face of civilization itself!

"All is now become a region of peculiar sacredness. That plain, bare farm amid the blackened stumps, the attempts at scientific agriculture under such disadvantages, the simple dwelling, the surveyor's tools, the setting of the little scene amid the grand, awful mountain ranges, the Negro colony and inmates, the family bred to duty and principle, and held to them by a power recognized as being from above—all these now come back on my memory with a character nowise changed, indeed, in substance but as it were, illuminated."

John Brown's body now lies where he hoped it would, by the boulder in North Elba. His widow, Mary, was allowed to bring it there immediately following his execution on December 2, 1859. During the journey north from Virginia, however, she was not allowed to stop with it in Philadelphia overnight, for fear that its presence would incite a riot. A decoy coffin was used to draw off the crowd from the train station while the real body was spirited out a side door.

The burial took place on the eighth of December. There was no snow on the ground. The presiding minister made the journey to North Elba specifically to attend Brown's funeral, but had not planned to perform the ceremony. There was no one else around with the proper credentials, though, so he agreed to pray for the ultimate salvation of the dead. It seemed the only charitable thing to do, but when his parishioners back in Burlington found this out, most of the wealthiest members quit his congregation in protest; John Brown was martyred, but he was not yet a generally recognized hero.

One of Brown's final requests before his execution was that three names be added to the old gravestone in North Elba. His own name went directly below his grandfather's: "JOHN BROWN, born May 9, 1800, was executed at Charleton, Va. Dec. 2, 1859." Below that, almost running out of space, were added the words "OLIVER BROWN, born Mar. 9, 1839, was killed at Harper's Ferry on October 17, 1859." On the back of the stone, beneath Frederick's name, was added "WATSON BROWN born Oct. 7, 1835 was wounded at Harper's Ferry Oct. 17 and died Oct. 19, 1859." In 1866, a stonecutter was hired by a Civil War veteran from Boston to add JOHN BROWN, 1859, in foot-high letters on the back of the boulder.

The bodies of Brown's sons weren't returned to North Elba to be buried beneath the stone for several decades. Watson's arrived in 1882, after having been used for medical research at the Virginia Medical College. And in 1899, the last eight bodies from the Harpers Ferry raid were found in a mass grave beside the Shenandoah River and brought secretly to North Elba in ordinary traveling trunks.

The John Brown farm is a state historical site now, located just behind the giant ski jumps that were built for the 1980 Winter Olympics in Lake Placid. All of the various additions to the little two-room farmhouse made over the years by farmers who came after the Browns have been removed. There's a barn up behind the house, in good repair, set in a small field of mostly goldenrod. A tall wrought-iron fence surrounds the boulder and the graves, and the stone that Brown brought from Connecticut is encased in glass.

Just outside the fence is a bench with a good view to the southeast, toward the High Peaks. In the near distance, a thin line of hay fields and a barn are visible along Heart Lake Road. But even closer is what looks to be a larger stretch of land that is covered with young poplar and birch and various scraggly bushes. Poplar and birch, favorites of the beaver, are the vanguard species of a returning forest. There are groves like this outside of Willsboro as well, and in Keene Valley, Newcomb, and elsewhere in the park. They are farm-

Rededication of John Brown's Grave, 1896, by Seneca Ray Stoddard. COURTESY OF
THE ADIRONDACK MUSEUM, BLUE MOUNTAIN LAKE.

ers' fields abandoned—not quite "wilderness," as it's usually defined
these days, but nature is in firm control of the succession of things.
Plant life is running riot. Farmers used to call such places "dead
clearings."

The old Brown place is a monument to the righteous fight of a
middle-aged zealot who in quieter times took his family and his prized
cattle over to the Essex County Fair. It is a monument to Gerrit Smith
and all the other abolitionists, and to the soldiers who died in the war
to come. It commemorates the millions of slaves, of course, and the
newly free men and women of Timbuctoo.

Lying there beneath the massive boulder and his grandfather's
stone, surrounded by the puny fields, the little farmhouse, the advancing forest, and the distant great range of the Adirondacks, John
Brown's body is also testament of sorts to the whole idea of a pastoral
nation of free-soilers. It's moldering there in memory of the notion of
a new republic peopled by independent and righteous landholders,
each on his or her own small family farm, hard-wrested from the
unbounded wilderness.

9 *A Farewell to Farms*

Janice Allen is the Willsboro town librarian. The library is just up the Boquet River a half mile or so from where William Gilliland's original farm was most likely located. The center of Willsboro today is tired. Like the majority of towns in the Adirondacks today, it has seen better days.

"My father was born on a farm around here," Allen said from behind the checkout desk. "This whole area was farms then." The Champlain Valley is the one part of the park where agriculture took hold with some success. But even here, Allen went on to say, it is withering.

"Just about the only ones around who are still really making a go of it are the West brothers, up in a neighborhood we call Riber," she said.

A few more names of active farmers eventually came to her, especially once her attention moved south from Willsboro along the lake toward the neighboring town of Essex where agriculture is still holding its own. But the names of farmers who have quit trying to make a living from the land seemed to flow much easier. "Friend Cross, also up in Riber, he's gotten out of it," she said. "The Soapers, up a little farther, are out of it I think."

Allen's associate at the library, Janet Tucker, mentioned the Trench family, and for a while the two women discussed whether or not the Trenches were still, or were no longer, making a living from farming. Then they traded names.

"The Smiths used to have an orchard up the hill there, didn't they?" said one. Gone, they agreed.

"The Owens," said one, and the other nodded.

"The Sheehans," said the other, "what about them?"

"Gone, I think."

Singletons, Bigelows, Owens again, names kept coming. The Saywards. "There were seven or eight Sayward brothers. All of them had big farms. One did corn. Another did something else. But most of them are out of it now. Only Bud and Steve are still in it I think." Janet Tucker's shift at the library was over and she put on her coat, said good-bye, and left.

"But there are a lot of farm family characteristics still around, however," Allen continued. "People canning their own goods, that kind of thing. Being in 4-H maybe, or the Grange, though neither of those organizations are nearly as big as they once were. For a long, long time in this town, even after the farms started to give way, in my growing-up years, a lot of families had their own pig. And maybe a cow. And absolutely everyone had chickens."

She paused and then said, "Things that you've done for generations don't disappear so rapidly.

"But even that's pretty much dying out now. Very few people even have a vegetable garden now. I was born in 1933 and here it is by the time my children are grown up and people hardly have a garden. With my grandchildren, forget it. 'Go to the market. It's a lot easier.'

"There are a few specialty farms starting to happen around here. Bees and goats. They're not always natives. People from away from here coming in to try and make it. It's kind of a dream of some people, I guess. The natives—the people who have struggled through and seen it all lost—look at them like they're crazy.

"The farm my Dad grew up on was down on what we call the Middle Road. That whole area used to be farms. The kids' job was to follow along and pick up the stones from behind the tractor. They picked up stones every single year. And they would pile them into stone walls or throw them down beside the lake."

She was beginning to explain why none of her father's thirteen siblings wanted the farm after her grandfather died, when a woman and her husband came into the library in search of information about how to help a housecat adjust to moving away for the winter.

"Good-bye," she said before crossing the room to look for cat books, "and good luck."

Willsboro Point is now what Allen called the "resort area" of town. There are small rustic cottages and fine summer homes looking across Lake Champlain to the Green Mountains of Vermont, from which many of the first farmers in the Champlain Valley came. There is nothing on the point that can really be called wilderness, and there are no more farms either. But occasionally, along the beach, are great piles of fieldstones.

10 In the Township of Industry

Charles Frederick Herreshoff may or may not have attempted to have himself buried alive. But whether he did or not, being sealed up in a hole blasted into the side of an Adirondack mountain might have been a somewhat appropriate end to his sad and unlucky life. For it wasn't the impossibility of farming in the park that ultimately killed Herreshoff, it was mining that eroded his will to live.

In many ways he was an unlikely candidate to spend his final years poking around with a pick in a wet tunnel in the middle of nowhere, looking for paydirt. Born in Prussia in 1763 and raised by a friend of Emperor Frederick the Great, Herreshoff received the finest education Europe had to offer. He spoke seven languages fluently, was an expert flute player and trained singer. He stood an aristocratic six feet four inches tall, which was even more unusual in those days than it is today. He married into one of New England's wealthiest families, the Browns of Providence, Rhode Island, and his offspring would become the most famous designers and builders of sailboats in American history. His grandsons' yachts, though, were not to be paid for out of a fortune derived from iron mined in the Adirondacks.

When Herreshoff first arrived on Brown's Tract in 1811, along with his nephew John Brown Francis, the family development project was in serious disrepair. Roads were rutted almost beyond use. The bridge over the Black River had washed away. The dam at the foot of the Fulton Chain was breached. The grist and saw mills were inoperable. Only eight years had passed since the death of his father-in-law, Old Thunder, but only "one real settler" still lived on the tract. That was James Gould, who would later get fatally close to the back end of his ox.

Nevertheless Herreshoff, who was married to John Brown's daughter Sarah, caught the speculative fever. He promptly built himself a large house for that time in the park, with six rooms and a wide porch. It became known as Herreshoff Manor. "I will settle the tract or settle myself," he is remembered for saying in his first year there, mostly because he eventually succeeded in achieving the latter.

Not much of interest is known about his first years on the tract, other than that he nearly drowned once in Fourth Lake when he somehow managed to ignite the island he was standing on. (He almost always smoked a pipe, which was the source of the flames that soon forced him first out onto a branch over the lake and then into the cold water.) Mostly, Herreshoff and Francis came to the tract each summer to oversee the endless work on the roads, the fields, the bridges, and the dams. And in 1815, it was Herreshoff who came up with the idea that sheep ranching would work on the rocky soil where crops would not.

In the summer of 1816, Herreshoff's fourth on the tract, it snowed heavily during the second week of June, and there was ice on the edges of the millpond in both July and August.[1] John Brown Francis, who would eventually become the governor of Rhode Island, apparently let the "year of no summer" convince him to begin pulling back from the project altogether.

But at fifty years old, Herreshoff felt he had fewer options than his nephew. He had already failed as a merchant in New York during his first few years after immigrating to the United States in the 1780s. A later attempt to get into the insurance business foundered when the first ship he underwrote was struck by lightning and destroyed. Other

---

[1] Unbeknownst to the Browns, "the year of no summer" was an almost global phenomenon that was caused by the eruption in 1815 of Tambora, in the Indian Ocean. It was the greatest volcanic explosion in ten thousand years.

careers fizzled. He was deeply in debt. So while Francis slowly distanced himself from day-to-day involvement in his Adirondack inheritance, Charles Herreshoff did not.

The summer ice may have destroyed any lingering hope Herreshoff held that there might be a predominantly agricultural future for the tract. This didn't require entirely giving up the faith in a prosperous transformation of the wilderness, though. Great fortunes were beginning to be made in new ways back home in New England where the industrial revolution was just beginning to pick up steam.

It was a perfectly sensible extension of the pastoral ideal to hope that the application of science and capital was the answer to the riddle of what to do with such stubborn and remote land as the Adirondacks. Many others luckier than Herreshoff entertained the same idea, and the notion has never really left the region. At different times mines, railroads, steamships, canals, hydroelectric dams, and even hypothetical high-tech manufacturers have all held out promise as the technology of the moment that was going to succeed in wrenching wealth from the Adirondacks.

Herreshoff, with his extensive education, may have pondered the philosophical implications of the transfer of his ambition from the ancient ideal of agriculture to the new fad of industry. But it seems more likely he hit upon mining out of desperation. Surely this cursed wilderness could still be made to pay.

"Once more I wish to live through one day not owing one cent, my wife & children secured from penury, the most grating most unhappy of all feelings, next to a guilty conscience," he wrote to some Brown cousins in Providence in August of 1816. "For the enjoyment of that day I would cheerfully assign the remaining." But the real purpose of the letter was to ask for yet another five-thousand-dollar loan. He wanted to build a nail factory on the tract, and he waxed on about the quality of the site for manufacturing. "I will only add that I look for your answer with an anxiety of suspense, I may truly say, never felt before," he said.

The cousins, who had funded him repeatedly in the past, declined the opportunity. In letters to his wife back in Providence around the same time, ominous phrases began appearing. "The only thing hopeful that one can think of in these gloomy times," he wrote, "is the end of all things."

The end, however, had not quite arrived. Just as his hopes had progressed from crops to sheep to nails, in 1817 Herreshoff turned his efforts to mining. He built a forge,[2] one of the hammers from which still sits in the center of the hamlet of Old Forge, and wrote home that "ores are now beyond all doubt inexhaustible and of the richest quality."

Once again, he hadn't found the motherlode after all. Nor did he find it the following year, though he spent more of his cousins' money prospecting. All through the fall of 1818 he and his men blasted their little tunnels farther into the side of a ridge not far from Herreshoff Manor. One day's effort would expose what he described in his journal as "some very pure ore . . . a large and solid body of red rock!" But the next day the deposit would prove neither large nor solid and his tone would turn bitter.

He concocted several ingenious ways to attempt to clean what ore he did find; one with a cylinder of magnets, and another using the force of the waterfall to winnow out the heavier ore from the lighter rock. But successful iron manufacturers of the period generally worked with ore that was pure enough to forge virtually straight from the ground. Most of the iron that Herreshoff was able to produce, only about a ton in all, he ended up making with black grains that he separated with magnets from the sand on the shores of the Fulton Chain.

His mining dreams were not entirely preposterous. There was and is ore in the park, lots of it. In 1777, when Benedict Arnold needed to outfit the first American navy, which he constructed at the southern end of Lake Champlain, he noted in his journal that he "sent a boat with Skene's Negroes to dig ore" at a mine near Port Henry. Over the course of the 1800s more than two hundred forges were in operation in the Adirondack region. There were iron operations at Keeseville, Ausable Forks, Lake Placid, Clintonville, Crown Point, Hammond Corners, Ironville, Dannemora, Lyon Mountain, Ticonderoga, New Russia. On and on.

Up and down the Saranac, Salmon, Ausable, Boquet, and Schroon Rivers there were forges, blast furnaces, and mines. The iron on the sides of the Civil War ship *Monitor* came from the park, as did the first wires used to suspend the Brooklyn Bridge. The first steel produced in the United States was made from ore dug at the McIntyre mine in

[2] As early as 1799 there was talk of iron ore on their property, and John Brown mentioned in a letter in 1802 plans for a forge that was never built.

Newcomb, just south of the High Peaks. During the second half of the 1800s iron manufacturing was probably the largest employer in the Adirondacks.

Herreshoff could also take heart that the earliest finds were often serendipitous. The first ore at Crown Point was discovered in the 1770s by a farmer named Timothy Hunter who was following bees around the hills hoping to find where they kept their honey; a hundred years later more than seven hundred men were daily producing 125 tons of pig iron there. Another outcropping of ore in the Champlain area was found by a boy out shooting partridges. And to the north of Brown's Tract, the huge Benson ore body at Star Lake was discovered by U.S. Army engineers surveying a road between Ogdensburg and Albany in 1810. Whenever they got near the ore, their compasses ceased pointing north.

Nor was Herreshoff the only unlucky prospector in the park. In 1824 James Duane of Manhattan, a son-in-law of the great speculator John Constable, moved his family to thirty miles north of Saranac Lake, where he hoped to build a great iron industry. After four years of looking he found what promised to be a good vein of ore and built a forge. But, as his daughter said later: "just then came the freshet which destroyed so many lives and so much property in Vermont and Northern New York and carried off the forge. He built another forge; it burned; another: it was carried off by another freshet. . . ." But at least Duane had ore.

Ore! Over and over Herreshoff wrote the same flip-flopping story in his journal; *Found ore! . . . Maybe tomorrow.* His sheep, meanwhile, were dying, and once again settlers were moving off the tract faster than they could be convinced to move on. At the end of 1818 his cousins requested that he desist from his habit of writing checks on their accounts without prior permission. He stayed at Herreshoff Manor that winter rather than go home to face his family, and his letters grew less frequent. Herreshoff was beginning to crack. Nevertheless, he remained on the tract, blasting and sifting all the following summer and fall.

Still there was no high-quality ore. Finally, according to one version of the story, on December 18, 1819, he told his men he was returning to Providence that night. He wanted them all to come to work the next day as usual, he said, but instead of looking for red rocks they were to begin filling the hole back in. "If you're paying, Mr. Herreshoff," the men no doubt thought, "we'll fill it in."

When the crew arrived the next morning to follow the strange orders, a man was sent to the bottom of the mine to make sure that no tools had been left there. What he found there was Herreshoff himself. The boss had hidden himself in the mine, apparently hoping to be entombed alive. Another version of the same story has Herreshoff walking into the bottom of the pit in full view of his employees and demanding they close him in; the men sensibly decided to take the rest of the day off.

Whether it happened that way or not, what took place the following morning is not in doubt, though some of the specifics are fuzzy. According to a third-hand report that reached the Brown family in Providence a week later, Herreshoff "put an end to his life by discharging the contents of a pistol through his heart on Sunday at his place." Jeptha Simms says the suicide took place in the yard of Herreshoff Manor, and that the bullet entered not his heart, but "the right side of his temple and exited the left."

Yet another account places the shooting in the bedroom. Donaldson reports that workers interrupted Herreshoff while he was putting on his best clothes, as he did every Sunday even though there was no church on the tract. The mine was flooding and caving in, they told him. Herreshoff went to see for himself, stood quietly by the mine for a while watching it fill in, and then returned home and calmly shot himself.

Whatever the actual details, Herreshoff was most definitely dead, and his body was carried to Boonville and buried. After his death, the family never took quite the same level of interest in the tract. Herreshoff's son lived for several years in the vicinity, but the efforts of both him and John Brown Francis over the next three decades were primarily directed at getting the tax assessments lowered on the property or selling it off in large chunks at ever lower prices.

Bit by bit, much of Brown's Tract fell back into the hands of the state in lieu of taxes. The entire Township 6, which John Brown had named Frugality, was lost in this manner. In 1849 the Browns sold their last piece of the park for $18,500, and considered themselves lucky to have done so.

Today, the little rise where Herreshoff Manor sat overlooking the Moose River no longer exists in quite the same fashion. The house was occupied for a while shortly after Herreshoff's death by the trapper Nat Foster, who was living there when he shot Drid. Later it belonged to an innkeeper named Otis Arnold and became a well-known sportsman's way station. But in 1895 it was gutted by fire and razed. Since then, the sandy hill itself has been substantially cut away and carted over to make the Old Forge town beach. In its place are piles of salt and sand, and the vehicles used by the hamlets of Thendara and Old Forge to tend their roads in winter.

Not far away is a minor gash in the land. It's down a dirt road about a quarter mile, and then a few dozen yards up into thick, third-growth woods, behind a tidy little house with silhouettes of snowmobiles hanging over the door. The fallen limbs and healthy moss make the mine hard to recognize as the work of human beings at first, and then for a moment it is sobering to find that a man's final effort could be so small. Less than fifty feet in any direction from the puny collapsed entrance the ground is entirely undisturbed. In this machine age Herreshoff's hole seems almost comical. Or perhaps, tragic. It is a popular spot among mosquitoes, though, for it is full of water.

11   *The State of Science*

A billion and a half years before Herreshoff decided that his life was inconsequential, a shallow sea covered what is now the Adirondack Park. Modern geologists refer to it as the pre-Grenville ocean, and just to the west of it lay a continent they call Proto-America. At the bottom of that sea, the rocks that Herreshoff and hundreds of other speculators blasted into in search of iron and other minerals were laid down as sand, mud, and lime. Where the sand came from is still unclear, though some of its grains were already over a billion and a half years old, suggesting that they washed off of some other already long gone continent.

Then, as now, the swirling currents of the earth's molten core moved the plates that make up the surface, and for 200 million years the pre-Grenville ocean shrank. As the dense bedrock floor of the ocean began to slip beneath the lighter land of Proto-America an arc of enormous volcanoes was pushed up and erupted in the land. For 100 million years what is now New York looked like the Andes of Peru.

But the mountains would get higher still. Behind the shrinking ocean lay another continent of dry land, called Grenville. When it collided with Proto-America roughly

1.1 billion years ago the peaks that were created probably equaled in stature those now found only in the Himalayas of Tibet. They rose out of a great plateau of land that stretched from Labrador to Mexico. New York now lay thousands of miles inland, in the middle of an immense body of land called the Grenville Supercontinent.

At the very bottom, almost eighteen miles underground, at temperatures anywhere from 600 to 800°C, and under pressure eight thousand times greater than on the surface, the sands and limestones of the old ocean floor were transformed into the marbles, quartzites, and gneisses that are now prevalent in the northwestern parts of the park.

Also at that depth, plutonic rocks—rocks that were originally formed within the earth rather than laid down as sandstones or spewed out by volcanoes—became the granitic gneisses and metanorthosite that make up most of the park's High Peaks. Metanorthosite, a relatively rare stone, is almost identical to the rocks on the bright areas of the moon. Here and there garnets formed.

For hundreds of millions of years the towering mountains and their accompanying plateau eroded away under the relentless pressure of rain and wind. The altitude remained high, however; as the weight of the mountains was removed, the land floated back up on the underlying magma. Finally though, 600 million years ago, a layer of rock and debris fifteen miles thick had washed away. What is now New York was once again at sea level; the Grenville rocks that would become the Adirondacks were again relatively near the surface.

They would not soon become the mountains they are today, however. Geologists believe another ocean, this one called Iapetus, opened along the old line between Proto-America and the Grenville continent and then slowly closed again. An arm of that new ocean, the Potsdam Sea, covered most of what is now New York, and a new layer of sandstone formed over the Grenville rocks.

Not one but two ranges of Himalayan-sized peaks rose and fell during the Iapetus period. The Taconic Mountains, which were formed in a collision with a group of volcanic islands, are all that remain in New York of the first great range. When these were gone yet another group of high jagged peaks, the Acadians, rose when a small continent called Avalon attached itself to New England. These too were broken into sand by the wind and rain, and washed away; the Catskill Mountains to the south of the park are an eroded outwash plain from the Acadians.

Underground, the Grenville rock was stretched until it cracked, mostly along the northeast-southwest axis that is today the primary orientation of valleys, lakes, rivers, and mountain passes in the park.

When Africa glanced off of America roughly 350 million years ago, raising the Appalachians along the entire east coast of the now finally non–proto North American continent, the park's bedrock lay as it had for almost a billion years, just to the west of all the action, buried beneath the detritus of former ranges. The exposed summits of the High Peaks, Herreshoff's red rocks, and all the rest are part of a huge mass of rocks geologists call the Grenville basement.

Dig deep enough anywhere in New York except Long Island, or, for that matter, anywhere in a wide band that stretches all the way from Labrador to Mexico, and you will eventually find these metamorphic rocks that were created during the Grenville orogeny. They are exposed only in the Adirondacks, the Thousand Islands of the Saint Lawrence River, and the mountains of the Canadian Shield. As rocks go, they are extremely old.

As mountains go, however, the Adirondacks are almost brand-new. Between ten and twenty million years ago, just as mammals were beginning their global ascendancy, the Adirondacks began to rise. There was no great collision of continents involved, no cataclysmic spewing of volcanoes. For reasons that are still unknown, a hot spot

Summit of Mount Haystack looking west, circa 1900, by Norman S. Foote. COURTESY OF THE ADIRONDACK MUSEUM, BLUE MOUNTAIN LAKE.

developed in the magma beneath the northeast corner of New York, causing the crust over it to expand. The land began to rise like a round blister, as if the old rocks were simply weary of their long interment.

The Adirondack region has risen perhaps ten thousand feet since the uplift began, though over the eons water and ice have removed thousands of feet of the sedimentary rock that was left behind by the erosion of the previous ranges. Finally, on the tops of some of the Adirondacks, the ancient Grenville rocks were exposed for the first time to air.

In all this geological wisdom, there is no consensus as to how the park's iron ore deposits came to be. They may be sedimentary deposits laid down in the pre-Grenville ocean that were later metamorphosed. It may be that an iron- and oxygen-rich liquid solidified along with molten rock during the Grenville period. Or hot solutions that flowed around and through the granitic gneisses at some point may have dissolved magnetite from a large area and then somehow concentrated it.

What geologists do agree on is that the Adirondack dome is still rising, as much as thirty times more rapidly than the tough Grenville rocks are wearing down. In the early 1980s the tallest Adirondack peak, Mount Marcy, was measured to be growing at the geologically extreme rate of three millimeters a year. Its official height today is 5,344 feet.

As it happened, the first recorded ascent of Mount Marcy was instigated by geologists on a scientific mission. Herreshoff's bad luck notwithstanding, the state government during the first half of the nineteenth century considered the possibility that other New Yorkers might strike it rich in the wilderness upstate to be very real. The era of haphazard growth through the efforts of homesteaders was considered over for the eastern states, and the prudent state government did what it could to foster the industries that were going to generate future growth. With that in mind, the New York Legislature voted in 1836 to sponsor a great geological survey of the entire state.

"The principal object of the survey," said its main proponent, New York Secretary of State John Dix, was "to procure information that may be applied to useful purposes." First on the wish list in the enabling legislation was a catalog of the state's "mineralogical productions."

Of the Adirondacks in particular Dix said, "This district, still almost entirely unexplored as to its mineralogical character, probably contains a larger amount of valuable metals than all the other counties of the state combined." Like Herreshoff, the bureaucracy believed science would succeed where agriculture had failed.

In addition to its practical aims, the survey was motivated by a sense of scientific competition with Massachusetts, which had completed a statewide survey a few years before. And with Pennsylvania, which had plans to undertake one. And with European science in general. The wilderness that had been so fraught with evil to the Jesuits and Puritans was becoming a source of national and state pride. Wild land was the one thing the United States possessed in quantities that Europe lacked, and as Roderick Nash has argued, Americans grasped onto their primeval landscape as a way to assuage a cultural insecurity about the wealth of art and history on the other side of the Atlantic. The New York State survey was intended to inventory and advertise the natural glories of the still-New World. It was in no small measure a brag.

The man appointed to lead the survey effort in the northeast quarter of the state was Ebenezer Emmons. Born in Middlefield, Massachusetts, in 1800, he graduated from Williams in 1818 and then returned to the college to become its first professor of natural history. His official portrait shows a man with a thin face, strong cheekbones, big ears, long sideburns, high forehead, and a slightly hooded left eye.

As a child Emmons collected bugs, rocks, and plants, but not to the detriment of a deeply religious upbringing that stayed with him throughout his life. After his death in 1865, one of his children said that in the Emmons household "Sunday commenced Saturday evening at sundown and did not end until Monday morning, and it was considered sinful to laugh at any time during this interval." His reputation was as a stern, rather distant man. But he knew his rocks and he worked hard.

Which was good, as there was much to be done. Beginning in 1837 Emmons was given a salary of fifteen hundred dollars a year, a small staff, and a territory of 9,700 square miles of wilderness corresponding roughly to the park of today. It was, he said in 1842, "a region of country as little known and as inadequately explored . . . as the secluded valleys of the Rocky Mountains or the burning plains of Central Africa."

This statement, while grand, was not an egregious exaggeration. Mount Washington, the tallest of the White Mountains of New Hampshire, was climbed by Europeans as early as the 1640s, and Lewis and

Clark were back from the Pacific by 1806, but before Ebenezer Emmons there were no recorded ascents of the highest peaks of the Adirondacks. Until his first report came out the accepted wisdom was that the tallest summits in the state of New York were in the Catskills.

Before the survey, the mountains of the park didn't even have a generally accepted name. They were variously known as the Peru Mountains, the Black Mountains, Macomb's Mountains, or the Essex Peaks. Most often, though, and perhaps most telling, the whole region was simply called the Great Northern Wilderness. It was Emmons who first proposed the name Adirondacks, apparently believing that to be the name of the former masters of the region.

He was one of the brightest lights in American geology of the day, and for four years he and his staff took measurements, collected samples, and attempted to make sense of the sometimes crazily metamorphosed rocks of the Adirondacks. Emmons correctly identified the bedrock as from the Precambrian era. And he made progress at sorting and identifying the various layers of sedimentary rock that lay over the Grenville stone.

But, of course, all of Emmons's hard work and sound observation was done without the aid of the theory of plate tectonics, which wasn't proposed until more than a century later. Even more troubling when it came to actually understanding and explaining the topography of the Adirondacks region, he operated without an appreciation of the role of glaciers.

As a result, there were many features of the land for which Emmons and his colleagues on the New York survey were not adequately able to account: kettle ponds, moraines, eskers, and the like. Most perplexing of all were the erratics—building-sized boulders strewn around the surface of the land and made of all different kinds of rock that have nothing to do with the underlying bedrock. Erratics were so common all over the northern latitudes, and so inexplicable, that they became the primary focal point of the debate over the possibility of an ice age, which erupted in the middle of the New York survey with the publication in Europe of the watershed *Etudes sur les glaciers* by Louis Agassiz in 1840.

There were lots of theories about erratics. James DeKay, who did the zoological portion of the Adirondack survey, decided they must have been extruded up out of the bowels of the earth, into peaks which had since disappeared. Their place of extrusion, too, had somehow been obscured. Benjamin DeWitt, who observed the erratics along the shores of the Great Lakes, suggested that the boulders were thrown there by volcanoes, or somehow came up from the lake. H. H. Hayden thought that the axis of the earth had shifted so that the sun passed directly over the poles and suddenly melted the ice caps, creating a boulder-carrying deluge. Still others postulated that an enormous natural dam once held back an inland sea that included all of the Great Lakes and more, and that when it collapsed the torrent carried all the rocks and outwash south. In 1826 an article in the *American Journal of Science* suggested that the earth's rotation had been momentarily and suddenly checked, causing a global tidal wave and throwing all the boulders around.

The common thread in most of the nonglacial theories was that they involved a flood. Specifically, they involved Noah's flood. And when the time came for the four geologists in charge of the New York survey to write their final reports, like the members of other state surveys of the period, they clung to the biblical deluge. Most made references to the new thinking, but by and large they agreed when one of their contemporaries disparagingly described Agassiz' glacial theory as "the principle of prolonging the harmless and undestructive rate of geological change of today backward into the deep past."

Of course the relentless working of seemingly everyday forces is exactly how modern geologists believe the world got to be the way it is, and how it continues to operate. In the long run, this scientific understanding of the planet as a work in progress, not only geologically but biologically as well, fomented a revolution in our ideas of what wilderness means.

On the one hand, science exposed the nonhuman world as more "other" than ever. We found ourselves on a planet that is coldly finding its own way toward an equilibrium without any necessary condition that human survival be a part of it. And as technology, science's offspring, transformed the humanized environment we drew lines around the fragments of relatively unaffected landscape that still existed in the nostalgic hope of protecting them. In the second half of the twentieth century we officially defined some of these areas as "wilderness" precisely to the degree that they showed no sign of human presence.

On the other hand, science's assertion of the interconnectedness of all things belies the Separatists' idea that a perfect human world can ever be constructed entirely outside of this thing called wilderness. It draws humans back into the world at all levels. The environmental writer Bill McKibbin, who lives in the Adirondacks, has written that the impact of technology is so pervasive—even to the point of changing the weather—that "nature" has ceased to exist as a thing separate from ourselves.

In the 1830s and '40s, though, American geologists looked at the natural world as something closer to a finished product. This isn't to say Emmons was a bad scientist, or that he didn't contribute valuable insights about the geology of the Adirondacks. But whether out of religious inclination, professional conservatism, or just a state of being perpetually behind the times, American scientists usually found evidence of catastrophic creative moments. Thus, though he was the first to describe and identify the Potsdam sandstones that make up the walls of the Ausable Chasm, Emmons could not bring himself to conclude that the "Grand Canyon of the Adirondacks" was created by a slow and steady erosion. Instead, he suggested, it was "opened by some convulsion of nature."

If perchance ice carried the erratics, which Emmons conceded was a possibility, it was most definitely the ice of icebergs floating on the great flood.

But Agassiz, who emigrated to America in 1846 and was one of the leading luminaries at Emerson's Philosophers' Camp in the Adirondacks (1858), had compelling counterarguments to the flood theories. Floods did not explain, for instance, why the erratics appeared only above the thirty-ninth parallel. The only tidal wave that would stop so uniformly, he said, was a frozen one. He also pointed out that the tops of northern mountains like the Adirondacks were scored and polished, while farther south, the peaks remained significantly more jagged, indicating that they stuck out of the ice. Northern erratics, which presumably spent more time in the ice, also tended to be rounder and smoother than those dumped at the southern extremes of the glacier's reach.

It goes almost without saying that, a few modern creationists aside, Agassiz ultimately won the debate. Geologists now believe most of the heavy work of sculpting the park of today was done by ice. Most important was the last phase of the ice age, known as the Wisconsin glaciation, which ended less than ten thousand years ago.

The park before the ice was a place not so much of lakes, as it is today, but of rivers. In some places the mile-high glaciers gouged out the beds of rivers that had been flowing along the fault lines, turning many of them into lakes. The Fulton Chain was such a river. Elsewhere, the ice pushed long mounds of unsorted rubble, or till, to its front and sides, creating moraines that sometimes acted as earthen dams. Lake George was once a river that flowed south into the Hudson until a moraine deposited at its southern end transformed it into a lake that empties north into Champlain.

Where the retreating glaciers abandoned a large chunk of ice within a pile of till, one of the park's countless kettle ponds eventually appeared. Where a river formed on top of, or even inside the glacier, a long snaking pile of rubble known as an esker was left behind, like those at Cranberry Lake and in the Five Ponds Wilderness Area. Long after the main body of ice was gone, smaller glaciers remained behind on mountains like Whiteface to advance and retreat annually until they had gouged out the smooth, rounded scoops in the solid rock that geologists now call cirques. And here and there all around the park, the ice abandoned enormous boulders it had collected on its trip south. These boulders are now called erratics.

There are erratics sitting on the very top of Mount Marcy, and Ebenezer Emmons no doubt noticed them during his historic first recorded ascent of the mountain in 1837. The route to the mountain was most likely similar to the modern trail up the Calamity Brook from the McIntyre iron mine in Upper Works. With him were his son, several fellow geologists from his staff, the owners of the mine, and John Cheney, a legendary guide and hunter.

Though Emmons's reports reveal him to be a careful and by no means overly technical writer, the description of that first trip to the top of the park that has endured was not his. Instead, it is John Cheney's words that are most often remembered in the guidebooks and anthologies, usually with the accurate observation that they still ring quite true today. "It makes a man feel what it is to have all creation placed beneath his feet," Cheney said. "There are woods there which it would take a lifetime to hunt over, mountains that seem shouldering each other to boost the one whereon you stand up and away, heaven knows where. Thousands of little lakes among them so light and clean. Old Champlain, though fifty miles away, glistens below you like a strip of white birch when slicked up by the moon on a

View from summit of Mount Marcy (with erratic), circa 1900, by Norman S. Foote.
COURTESY OF THE ADIRONDACK MUSEUM, BLUE MOUNTAIN LAKE.

frosty night, and the Green Mountains fade and fade away until they disappear as gradually as a cold scent when the dew rises."

What Cheney didn't mention, but the ever observant Emmons noticed and duly noted, was that though it was a glorious August day, here and there around the summit were patches of ice half an inch thick.

12   *The Mother Lode*

Emmons named the mountain Marcy, after the New York governor who had appointed him. A nearby peak was given the name Dix, in honor of the secretary of state who had pushed for the survey. Three more summits he christened Henderson, McIntyre (now Algonquin), and McMartin (now Colden), after the owners of the mine from which his party had started their ascent. This was not simply politeness toward his hosts; Emmons believed that the further development of the McIntyre mine was in the national interest. "Never was a vein so favorably situated . . . where so little capital will be required to obtain the ore," he wrote in his first annual report in 1837. "Now the Adirondack ores, it is believed . . . are the great source from which our most valuable iron is to be drawn. It is here, if any where, it can be made in this country; and the whole Union, if true to herself, will encourage its manufacture." He suggested that a chain gang of convicts might be brought in to build a better road to the mine.

David Henderson and Archibald McIntyre discovered their ore body in a singular way. Their first attempt to make iron, on the other side of the High Peaks near Lake Placid, had failed in 1815 after only six years of operation. Being prospectors, though, they didn't give up, and Henderson went back in the fall of 1826 to look again for better deposits. This time he hoped for silver. But before he could even get started looking he was drawn back into the iron business by an Abnaki trapper named Lewis Elijah.

"A strapping young Indian of a Canadian tribe made his appearance at Darrow's gate, the first which had been seen in the settlement for three years," he relayed in a letter to McIntyre dated October 14, 1826. "The Indian opened his blanket and took out a small piece of iron ore about the size of a nut—'you want see 'em ore?—me know 'em bed, all same'—Whereabouts did you find it? 'Me know—over mountain' (pointing to the southwest). Does any other Indian know of it?—'No—me hunt 'em beaver, all 'lone last spring.' "

The letter goes on that way for a while before turning to an equally dialect-driven account of the discomfort of the party's African American cook during the ordeal of following Lewis Elijah for three days over the Indian Pass to the other side of the High Peaks.

In the lore of the region, Native Americans periodically came out of the woods with lumps of paydirt. Usually they had lead, not iron. One such man appeared regularly to trade lead at the Rainbow Inn, on Rainbow Lake, in the early decades of the 1800s. In a sort of Adirondack version of a Brothers Grimm tale, Donaldson tells of two prospectors who tried to follow this particular unnamed Indian to his mine. As they went along, they dropped small white beans to guide them back to the inn.

For an hour or so, they thought that their Native miner was unaware he was being followed, until suddenly he appeared before them and threatened to kill them if they persisted. But when they turned to follow their clever markers back out of the woods, there stood the Indian's wife, with all of their beans. After an awkward moment, she led them back to the inn and gave them their beans. No white man ever found the lead mine.

Lewis Elijah, on the other hand, took David Henderson and his party straight to what the latter described in his letter as "the *great mother* vein of iron, which throws her little veins and sprinklings all over these mountains." It was a find well worth the plug of tobacco and one dollar Elijah had requested as payment for his services. As soon as the prospecting party had covered over all evidence of their visit, they set off in a rainstorm for their camp and became lost. When they finally arrived the next morning, Henderson reported, "the first thing we did was to drink up all the rum we had raw."

Once he was out of the woods, Henderson set off immediately for Albany, taking Lewis Elijah with him lest he do any more guiding before a proper claim could be staked at the land office. The partners soon bought from the state Townships 46 and 47 of the old Totten and Crossfield Purchase, some 105,000 acres that included most of the High Peaks. Within a year, they were mining ore on the site. They had a small testing forge, but for the first decade of operation most of their product was taken by oxcart fifty miles through the woods to the big forges at Lake Champlain. In 1837 the partners built their first puddling furnace.

It was actually the forges and blast furnaces, as opposed to the mines, that had the largest impact on the future park. Besides the presence of ores, the great attraction of the Adirondacks to iron manufacturers in the early decades of the industry was the trees. You didn't need coal and you didn't need a railroad to get it to your forge if you had an adequate supply of charcoal.

The most common method for making iron in the park was with a Catalan, or bloomery forge. It was a relatively simple operation in which crushed ore was heated with charcoal in an open fire that was constantly stoked by a bellows. The pipe for the air from the bellows was coiled around the twenty-five-foot chimney to preheat it lest it cool the concoction and waste fuel. A master bloomsman periodically added charcoal and ore to the fire, stirring the goopy mixture almost continuously with a long rod. His apprentices, meanwhile, hauled the endless buckets of charcoal; as much as a hundred bushels an hour, two buckets at a time. In the 1880s there were twenty continuously burning fires at Mineville, the largest Catalan operation in the world.

Blooming was an acquired art. If the fire was allowed to get too hot, the ore would burn. Nor should it cool down to the point where the mixture began to harden. About a hundred pounds of pasty iron and slag could be made in an hour, and every three hours this "bloom," or "loupe," would be removed from the fire with tongs, carried to the water-powered hammers, and forged into bars of iron about five inches square.

In a blast furnace, like those that Henderson used, the draft created by a much taller chimney helped stoke a far hotter fire than that achieved in a Catalan forge. Heated air was blown in by water-powered bellows, and pulverized marble or limestone was added to the mix to raise the temperature high enough to liquefy the ore so that it separated completely from the slag. This eliminated the need for the forge hammers, but a blast furnace devoured even more prodigious amounts of charcoal than a Catalan furnace.

Charcoal is hardwood that has been burned in an oxygen-deficient environment, and its production was a large part of every iron operation. In the earliest days great piles of hardwood about twenty feet in diameter would be covered with dirt and kept smoldering for up to two weeks. Later, permanent charcoal kilns made of brick and stone sprouted up in the iron country like mushrooms. At its peak in the 1880s the J & J Rogers Company alone operated over fifty kilns; seventeen in the Black Brook area, six at Taylor Pond, four at Mud Pond, three at Silver Lake, three at Military Pond, seven at Wilmington, four at Jay, two at Keene . . .

The best charcoal woods were maple, birch, and beech, but virtually everything could be and was used. Ancient giants, saplings, underbrush, fallen twigs; it all went into the kiln. During the same decades early loggers selectively removed the prime pines and spruces from parts of the future park, and a necklace of tanneries around the region harvested the bark from hemlocks in accessible quarters. But charcoal production was the first real use made of the hardwood species that make up 60 percent of the Adirondack forest. Charcoal makers were the first to clear-cut in the Adirondacks.

The impact on the surrounding forest was obvious. To make a ton of iron required as much as five hundred bushels of charcoal, or about ten cords' worth. In 1864 the forges in the park consumed 6,658,000 bushels of charcoal. In 1880, the J & J Rogers Company was clearing a thousand acres a year and burning four and a half million bushels of charcoal. The even larger Chateaugay Ore and Iron Company, meanwhile, cut over two thousand acres a year to feed its seventy kilns. Between 1873 and 1903 Chateaugay consumed a million and a half cords of wood.

In all, probably a quarter of a million acres were clear-cut to make charcoal for the iron industry. As Barbara McMartin points out in *The*

Great Forest of the Adirondacks, that is less than a tenth of the park acreage. But, she notes, the cutting was concentrated near the roads and, increasingly, the railroads. To travelers along the main routes, the northern wilderness seemed to be disappearing. And significant logging of hardwoods for timber hadn't even begun yet.

Like the farmers before them, the relationship of the miners to the wildlands of the park was purely utilitarian. "If land in that wilderness is to have any value at all it will only be in consequence of the success of our operation at the Adirondack Works," David Henderson wrote in 1845. "It has no value now except in the prospect of such success."

But there were qualitative differences. Almost by physical necessity, iron and mining became large-scale industrial undertakings long before farming ever became agribusiness. When Henderson made the above comment, almost four hundred people were in his employ digging ore, cutting forest, cooking charcoal, and smelting iron. At the main company village, known as Upper Works, there was a large boardinghouse and sixteen other dwellings, a school, a store, a carpenter shop, a blacksmith shop. Eight miles down the Hudson at Lower Works, or Tahawus, as it was more commonly called, a dam backed up the river so that ore, iron, and charcoal could be moved up and down between the two company towns.

While farmers regularly complained about the difficulty of getting goods to and from the wider market, the entrepreneurs of the iron period talked endlessly of machining the landscape to fit their needs. In accordance with the notion of the Adirondack wilderness as a manufacturing center merely in need of the proper application of capital and technology, they agitated for canals, railroads, dams.

On September 3, 1845, David Henderson and his eleven-year-old son and the company guide, John Cheney, went into the forest to scout out the possibility of combining two branches of the upper Hudson River into one in order to better supply water to the Upper Works. At a pond then called the Duck Hole, Henderson gave his pistol to Cheney and suggested he go after some of the resident birds for their dinner. Oddly enough, Cheney, who was one of the most famous guides and hunters of the century, managed only to scare the ducks away. He returned the pistol to Henderson, who put it back in his belt.

A minute later the gun went off and Henderson keeled over. When Cheney came running up, Henderson is remembered to have said three things. "John, you must have left the pistol cocked," was the first. Then he looked around at the pond for a moment. He was a man who apparently enjoyed life, often playing the violin into the evenings at the mining camp so that his employees and their families could dance. "This is a horrible place for a man to die," he said next.

Henderson's last words were to his young son. "Archy," he said after calling him over, "be a good boy and give my love to your mother."

An eight-foot-tall granite monument, bizarrely incongruous given the wildness of the spot today, was dragged in by oxen a few winters after the accident. It says only, "This monument was erected in filial affection to the memory of our dear father, David Henderson, who accidentally lost his life on this spot by the premature discharge of a pistol, 3rd Sept. 1845."

Cheney held the youngster in his arms until the next morning. A year later, when passing through the same area, Cheney remembered the exact spot. "Here on this log I sat all night," he told Joel T. Headley, "and held Mr. Henderson's little son, eleven years of age, in my arms. Oh, how he cried to be taken in to his mother; but it was impossible to find our way through the woods; and he, at length, cried himself to sleep in my arms. Oh, it was a dreadful night."

Duck Pond was renamed "Calamity," in honor of the accident, as was the stream leading out of it and the trail to Marcy that runs alongside it. The trail, in fact, was first widened by the men who came in to carry the corpse out.

The peak years of production at the McIntyre mine were still to come, but after Henderson's death the operation struggled. Ultimately, it never really overcame the disadvantage of its remote location that even Emmons had recognized when he suggested the state build a new road to the mine. The hope of a railway connection came and went with almost cruel regularity, but it was not to be.

Finally, in 1857, after more than half a million dollars had been sunk into the site, the owners gave up. According to one former employee, "work was dropped just as it was. The last cast from the furnace was still in the sand and the tools were left leaning against the wall of the cast house." The place was not entirely deserted, however. When the naturalist John Burroughs passed by in 1863, he noted that there was a man being paid a dollar a day "to live here and see that things were not wantonly destroyed, but allowed to decay properly and decently."

In all likelihood even the elusive railroad wouldn't have saved the McIntyre mine for long. In the 1890s almost unbelievably large, pure, and easily accessible ore bodies were opened in the Mesabi Range of Minnesota. The effect, along with the transition from iron to steel, was dramatic. The American iron industry grew exponentially but in the Adirondacks it stalled. In the 1880s, the park produced as much as a quarter of the nation's iron; by the turn of the century its share was minuscule.

Ore, which was always described as inexhaustible when an Adirondack mine opened, often turned out not to be. Equally finite was the supply of charcoal. The economics of moving trees to market for lumber was one thing, but for charcoal it was quite another, especially when competitors on the Great Lakes could get cheap coal by barge. In 1896 the Crown Point Iron Company dissolved, and in 1901 the assets of the company were bought by American Steel and Wire Company and shipped off. They even took the rails from the railroad.

Only the operation at Mineville, which opened at the peak of the park's production in the 1880s, managed to stay in business continuously into the twentieth century. And it limped there. Like trappers and farmers before them, the miners went west.

The shell of the last blast furnace ever built by the McIntyre Iron and Steel Company still stands about five miles from the hikers' sign-in station at the Calamity Brook trailhead. More than fifty feet high, it was constructed out of thick granite blocks at a cost of sixty thousand dollars just three years before the operations there ceased. The bridge that connected the top of the furnace with the hillside on the other side of the road, across which the charcoal and ore was carted, is long gone. Gone, too, are the large undershot waterwheels that powered the blowers.

It is possible with some scrounging and imagination to make out where the dam that directed water to the wheels was, however. There's no sign of it in the river proper; more than a hundred spring floods have seen to that. But the ends are discernible, overgrown and moss-covered like a Mayan wall. Growing directly over one end is an immense white pine, its girth too big for a grown person's arms to reach all the way around. And the enormous bellows that for a few years fanned the fires to a rock-melting roar are still there, slowly rusting away, their iron sides flaking inexorably back into the soil. There is no longer a caretaker around the McIntyre mine's Upper Works, and the process of decay continues.

There is a caretaker, however, at the Lower Works. During the Second World War, under the auspices of the federal government's Defense Plant Corporation, some forty million dollars were poured into the Adirondack mining industry. One of the first things the government did was build the long-awaited railroad spur to the old McIntyre mine. "Big government," which is routinely accused in the Adirondacks today of preventing industrial jobs, managed to convince big business to do what the free market had not. In 1935 the park produced fewer than 300,000 long tons of ore; seven years later the annual figure was ten times that.

Republic Steel took over and expanded the old operations at Mineville, eventually sinking main shafts more than 3,500 feet deep, with a virtual honeycomb of side drifts, raises, and stopes tunneled off into swirling veins of ore. The same company also revived and vastly expanded the old giant of the region, Chateaugay. Just west of the park, Jones and Laughlin turned the old Benson mines at Star Lake into the largest open-pit magnetite operation in the world, with a pit that was more than two miles long. And at McIntyre, the National Lead Company began blasting and removing what by 1961 would amount to 27 million tons of ore.

The change in fortunes for mining in the Adirondacks was so swift and so sweeping that the industry magazine, *Mining and Metallurgy,* devoted its entire November 1943 edition to the region. The issue was thick with patriotic advertisements for mining equipment, usually illustrated with photos from the Adirondacks. There were ads for feedometers, crushers, grinders, separators, link belt conveyors, mining cars, tracks, filters, loaders. "Steady and relentless as conquering columns, more than a million tons of iron and ilemite ore will travel yearly from the Adirondack MacIntyre Development over Manhattan conveyor belts," boasted the Manhattan Rubber Manufacturing Company.

It was an application of science and technology on a scale that even the innovative Henderson could not have dreamed. Deep holes were made in the ore body with jackhammers and diamond-tipped blast hole drills, and into them three to four hundred pounds of 60 to 90 percent pure dynamite was packed. With each blast, great faces of rock separated from the wall of the pit and appeared to hang suspended for a tiny fraction of a second before thundering to the ground.

The ore was then loaded onto trucks that could carry fifteen to thirty tons apiece and taken to the crushing plant, where enormous jaw crushers and cone crushers waited. When the ground rock could fit through a screen with quarter-inch openings, it traveled on conveyor belts to titanic magnetic separators that removed the iron ore.

Interestingly, though, what National Lead principally wanted at McIntyre was not the iron but the titanium that Henderson had always considered an impurity; titanium from the Adirondacks is what made Dutch Boy paint so white. So, after the magnetic separators, the titanium-rich tailings were further separated and concentrated in another plant with a complicated series of sizing machines, settling tables, sand pumps, and other devices. Waste went straight into Lake Sanford, and into the Hudson. In 1943 the plant worked around the clock, seven days a week, producing 600 long tons of titanium-rich ilemite and 1,200 long tons of magnetite iron concentrate a day. Only state labor laws made the work stop every other Sunday.

In 1960 ore was discovered under the company village of Tahawus. So the company simply moved the town. Seventy-two single-family houses, fifteen duplexes, five apartment buildings, a dormitory, two churches, and a general store were put on trucks and taken ten miles down the road to Newcomb. But the miners and their families didn't seem to mind. In place of their hometown a deep pit gradually opened, and beside it rose a new mountain composed of the "overburden" and other rubble that contained neither iron nor titanium; "Overburden Mountain," it might be called, the newest Adirondack. Sanford Lake disappeared, and the Hudson was routed through an unsightly canal around the new mine.

On the editorial page of the Adirondack issue of *Mining and Metallurgy*, A. B. Parsons insisted that "it should not be concluded from the foregoing that the new and revamped enterprises are in any sense 'war babies' that will lapse into inactivity when the enemies of the United Nations have been defeated." He then scoffed at those who he said "quite seriously" suggested that plastic and aluminum might make a dent in future steel needs.

"As long as steel is required in large quantities," Parsons concluded, "it is reasonable to expect that Adirondack iron ores, in increasing quantity, will find a profitable market." There were eight million tons of ore to be had, after all. The new age that Herreshoff, Emmons, and others predicted had finally arrived.

But Parsons was wrong. Although the modernized mines didn't close immediately—most ran at capacity pretty much through the Marshall Plan and the Korean War—eventually the momentum of the government boost was dissipated. Chateaugay shut its doors, most likely for good, in 1966. Mineville closed not long after. In the midseventies, Jones and Laughlin shut down the sprawling Benson mine. And in 1982, National Lead stopped production at the McIntyre mine. The only active mine in the park today is the relatively modest garnet mine that has been run by the Barton family at Gore Mountain since the 1870s.

From the top of Overburden Mountain at Tahawus, the single pickup truck parked way down by the enormous dusty concentrating plant looks tiny and lonely. It belongs to the only remaining employee at the McIntyre mine, whose job presumably is to make sure the place is not wantonly destroyed, but allowed to decay properly and decently.

There is more to see from up there than just his truck, however. The place offers a fascinating, if slightly forbidden, view unlike any other in the park. There are the real Adirondack peaks to see, of course, most prominently the imposing McIntyre Range. To the south is an unusual and lovely vista of the upper Hudson Valley.

And there is the mine. The enormity of the scar is such that it's difficult now, with all the big machines and their operators gone, to believe that it could have been made in half a human lifespan. It seems strange that something so big could simply be abandoned by those who lived lives and made money creating it.

Finally there is the hill of rubble itself. Here and there all over it, young birches and poplars, viburnum and laurels are growing on what appears to be no soil at all. They are clinging to the sides of that pile as if there were not millions of acres of cool, moist wilderness surrounding it in which to live. They cling as if the mountain of overburden were not the work of a society of puny scientists and laborers, but was in fact a terminal moraine of unsorted glacial till left there by a mile-high river of Canadian ice that receded only, who knows, a thousand years ago.

It's as if the vertically sided pit in the foreground, which like Herreshoff's mine is now full of water, were an embryonic kettle pond just waiting for its sphagnum moss. A kettle pond some six hundred feet deep.

13 *The Trap Dike*

"Ice in a small valley, or in a depression, is better than ice that sticks out in a knob or a ridge," Don Mellor called out, and high up on the wall a blue plastic helmet nodded solemnly.

Nothing else moved. But for the assorted minor contractions of neck muscles that constituted his entire response to Mellor's coaching, Steve Keyes appeared to be as frozen as the waterfall to which he clung. He was held in place by the merest tips of his boots, and by a single short-handled pick, and he waited for a dozen seconds before Mellor spoke to him again.

"And if you spread your feet apart and lean in, you might get more balance," said Mellor. Another solemn nod of the goofy blue hard hat.

Finally Keyes, a young and healthy executive at a big bank in Manhattan, happily married, thinking of having children soon, took his left boot out of the ice. He tapped the metal spikes of his crampon into what seemed a likely spot. *Chink, chink, chink. Chink . . . chink.* He moved up a half a foot. Then his right boot repeated the exercise. *Chink, chink.* Up another half foot. *Chink.*

And then he fell.

It was nothing serious. He dropped only a few feet before his descent was arrested by a rope that went from the harness around his waist to a tree at the top of the ice wall, and then back down to a friend on the ground. The rope was rated to hold 6,000 pounds and Keyes weighed only 165.

More important, all of the knots were properly tied. They were checked and rechecked, and backed up by safety knots. Mellor is sort of the dean of technical climbers in the park—virtually every rock or ice monkey in the Adirondacks has a copy of his guidebook somewhere in their knapsack. He knows more knots than a fly-fishing sailor, and earlier that same morning he had explained why he liked those that are not just strong but are elegant and symmetrical in appearance.

"It's partly aesthetic," he said in the basement of the Rock and River Guiding outfit in Keene. "I just prefer the way simple knots look." Mellor's philosophical approach to the sport of climbing rock and ice is always lurking in his language. But it is usually tempered by practicality. "Also, you can glance at a symmetrical knot and, in a second, know that it's tied correctly," he added.

Most important of all for Steve Keyes, his friend at the bottom of the wall of ice didn't let go of the other end of the rope. After the fall, Keyes hung suspended there with his crampons stuck into the ice. His body was perpendicular to the nearly vertical wall. He was helpless, laughing. "Thanks for the belay," he said politely after being lowered to the ground.

"I didn't really expect you to be able to make it all the way up with one pick on your first day out," Mellor said sympathetically. "But I wanted you to get a sense of what it's like. It's a relatively simple thing to muscle your way up the ice with two axes, but with only one you have to think more—about your route. You have to think more about the ice, focus on it more. If you had made it up, I would have felt you hadn't been challenged enough."

After a late lunch and then a few more hours of icy ascents, sometimes with one ax other times with two, Mellor took his clients back to Ed Palen's house in Keene. A couple of other guides associated with Rock and River were already there enjoying a beer and talking about the day's adventures. Talk also turned to the legendary Adirondack guides of the nineteenth century and the decades before marked trails and mass-produced lightweight camping gear, when virtually no one went into the woods without professional help.

"What people wanted from their guide back in the old days was a Neanderthalic man who would spew out the quaint little sayings," said Ed Palen at one point as he threw a log into the already roaring woodstove. Palen and his ex-wife Anne originally founded Rock and River about a dozen years ago to provide themselves with outdoor jobs in the Adirondacks. They also wanted to help some of their unemployed climber friends to make some side money.

"But that old-time stuff of the famous Adirondack guides simply doesn't exist at all anymore," he went on. "The view that people have toward the guide now is totally different than back then. It's not quaint. It's not storytelling around the fire.

"And of course back then, the guides did everything for the clients. They made the meals. They did everything. So you paid for someone who was your servant as well as your entertainment. Today's guide is not entertainment, is not your servant. It's just a different thing than it used to be, where the guide would chop down trees and build a lean-to for the night and then pull out the meat and spin yarns over the campfire. No one looks for that. No one expects that. No one even knows that that used to exist.

"We're just a highly specialized offshoot of that tradition, though we try to stay with, or play upon, the traditional role by getting the feel of the place. What we do is teach people climbing so that they can develop inner growth, and confidence. You get that recent divorcee who's living with a cat in the city who says, 'I'm going to do it! What's the wildest thing?' Ice climbing or rock climbing. And you watch them grow over the years from facing the fear," Palen said.

At this point a frequent client of Rock and River, a man in his late twenties or early thirties, spoke up for the first and only time of the evening. "I guess I got into it because I always thought the gear was really neat looking," he said, and all the guides gathered around the woodstove laughed with him. But Palen responded, quite seriously. "That's got to be about thirty percent of the people who get into the climbing sport and come up here and want us to teach them. They just like the equipment."

"Yup."

"Yup."

"Yeah, probably," said the other guides. Conversation turned to the brand-new Pulsar ice-climbing ax that Don Mellor found that morning sticking out of the snow at the base of a climb called Pitch-Off Left. And to other things recently lost or found. "Crampon went dink, dink, dink . . . down the hole . . ." someone else said, and the gathered guides chuckled sympathetically.

"I can't even call myself a guide," Palen said later, returning to the previous subject. "That word to me . . ." his voice trailed off in a way that could have been disdain. Or it could have been nostalgia. Or exhaustion from leading the latest group of novices up some snowy peak. His voice is surprisingly deep and has a somewhat tired quality about it.

"What we do is teach. We instruct. We make sure the client is safe. There are a few guys out there in the park who grow the beards, and try to talk the talk. But most people who just want to camp can get a trail map and do it themselves. They'd rather do it themselves. So unless you get deep into hunting or fishing you can't make really a living at old-time guiding anymore."

Around this time Don Mellor stood, stretched, and said his wife was waiting for him. "See you at the end of the Adirondack Loj road at six tomorrow morning, right?" he said to Steve Keyes. According to the plan, Mellor was to lead Keyes and his friend on cross-country skis through the Avalanche Pass to the base of a great cleft in Mount Colden called the Trap Dike, and from there up through ice and snow to the 4,714-foot summit. There would be a few short spots of steep ice to ascend, but each climber would carry only one ice ax.

"Yup," said Keyes, "see you there."

"Okay, good."

To arrive exhausted at the top of Mount Colden on a clear day in late winter, having climbed the Trap Dike with Don Mellor, is a rare privilege. Below, seemingly straight down two thousand feet below, is the frozen surface of Avalanche Lake. Way off to the north, in the general direction of Lake Placid and John Brown's farm, is the great loner of the High Peaks, Whiteface. Almost as far to the southwest is Santanoni. A hundred other peaks are spread between, behind, and around. Most of them, one suspects, Mellor has climbed more than once.

In other seasons in the Adirondacks, lakes and foliage draw and hold the eye of the climber. But in winter, with the trees naked of leaves and the lakes masked by snow, the profound physicality of the mountains themselves is overpowering. This is presumptuous rock, like proud flesh, forcing itself up into strong winds. And none is prouder than the hulking and symmetrical massif that comes into view only when the very summit of Colden is achieved, but which then looms above all the others. It is Mount Marcy, of course, the sublime neighbor to the east.

The descent back through the cleft is steady and uneventful. And fun; giant steps in deep snow, punctuated by an occasional rappel down the few ice pitches. The frozen lake comes up, larger and larger, and at last is met. The skis wait where they were left and just as Mellor predicted, they are in the last pocket of sun in the valley.

Seven miles sounds like a long way to ski now, after having already done it once and then tramped up and down Mount Colden. But it's mostly downhill on the way out, and only the first mile is steep. It's a long, gliding end to the afternoon. At Marcy Dam, a happy-looking French Canadian woman is collecting water, making camp. Another couple camping there explains they spent the day snowshoeing up to the bowl on Phelps Mountain. But Don Mellor, the guide, observes it's better not to stop and talk for long, what with miles still to go.

14 *The Romantics' Arrival*

Six weeks after guiding Ebenezer Emmons and the owners of the McIntyre Iron Works on the first recorded ascent of Mount Marcy, John Cheney found himself trying to convince a one-legged adventurer from Manhattan not to undertake a similar climb. But Charles Fenno Hoffman, whose right leg was crushed beyond repair between a riverboat and a pier when he was eleven years old, was not dissuaded.

Despite his infirmity, Hoffman was well traveled in places both civilized and wild. Before going to the Adirondacks he'd already been to the western frontier and back. So when he read the news accounts of Emmons and company's inaugural trip up Marcy, his interest was piqued. Already in 1837 it seemed to him "strange to find so wild a district in one of the old thirteeners, the Empire State of New York." He set off north immediately to see the new territory for himself.

Hoffman was the editor of the weekly *New York Mirror,* for which he intended to write a series of travel pieces about his adventures in the Adirondacks. He may have asked Cheney rhetorically how a writer could be expected to leave the state's highest summit out of such a series. Or, as some accounts suggest, he may have simply threatened to take his crutches and set off into the woods alone.

Whatever argument he used, Cheney ultimately agreed to accompany him, and the two set off up the Calamity Brook toward the mountain.

But in the end, Cheney's assessment of things was accurate. The still virtually trailless Marcy was too rugged, and they were forced to quit only partway up. It was a bitter moment on the mountainside, and Hoffman wept.

He didn't hold the failure to find a more moderate route to the summit against Cheney, however. When his travel stories appeared, Hoffman waxed on about his intrepid guide. In the 1839 book version, *Wild Scenes in the Forest and Prairie,* he devoted an entire chapter to John Cheney's character and exploits. "If it didn't involve an anachronism," he wrote, employing what was on its way to becoming a regional cliché, "I could swear that Cooper took the character of Natty Bumppo from my mountaineer friend, John Cheney."

Wild Scenes turned out to be an important book. There were a handful of earlier published accounts of travel in the park, most notably a travelogue of an 1836 visit to the Lake George area by Harriet Martineau, a British writer who was not only deaf but had no sense of smell or taste. And several later writers were more influential with the general public. But it was in Hoffman's descriptions of John Cheney that the iconology of the nineteenth-century Adirondack guide was first fully formulated.

In the half century after *Wild Scenes* appeared, a parade of intelligentsia traveled to the park and added their own pieces to the growing literature of the region. Joel T. Headley wrote *The Adirondack; or, Life in the Woods* in 1849. Charles Lanman's 1848 *Adventures of an Angler in Canada, Nova Scotia, and the United States* is one of the more amusing books of the period. Alfred Billings Street went to the park repeatedly in the 1850s and published *Woods and Waters* in 1860, and *The Indian Pass* in 1869. That same year the Reverend William H. H. "Adirondack" Murray wrote the wildly popular *Adventures in the Wilderness.* Scores of others wrote magazine accounts in the *Atlantic, Scribner's, Saturday Evening Post, Forest and Stream,* and elsewhere. What developed was not just a mythology of the great Adirondack guide but a whole theory of wilderness as a romantic counterbalance to the meaner aspects of "civilized" life.

There were painters, too. The most important among them during the first half of the century was Thomas Cole, the father of the Hudson River school. He wrote in a letter from Schroon Lake in 1835 that

"Schroon Lake," 1846, by Thomas Cole. COURTESY OF THE ADIRONDACK MUSEUM, BLUE MOUNTAIN LAKE.

he had "just returned from an excursion in search of the picturesque towards the head-waters of the Hudson." Arthur Fitzwilliam Tait began visiting the Adirondacks in the 1850s and many of his images of the Adirondacks were distributed nationally by Currier and Ives. Winslow Homer was introduced to the region by John Fitch, and went regularly to the Adirondacks in the 1870s, staying mostly in Minerva. Frederic Remington, meanwhile, went to Cranberry Lake.

Keene Valley, in particular, became a center of romantic landscape painting. Asher B. Durand and John Kensett, both masters of the Hudson River school, began making regular visits to the valley and the nearby Ausable Lakes as early as midcentury. Others soon followed. By 1868 a virtual colony of artists had bloomed. A. H. Wyant, John Fitch, Dwight Tryon, William Hart, James and George Smillie,

Artists on the Ausable River, including Roswell M. Shurtleff (front center) and Winslow Homer (with pipe in second row). COURTESY OF THE ADIRONDACK MUSEUM, BLUE MOUNTAIN LAKE.

Samuel Coleman, Wordsworth Thompson, Alpheus Cole, and Joseph Boston were among the regulars.

On suitably picturesque days their white sun umbrellas dotted the cleared fields of local farms. During one afternoon walk across the valley, Roswell Shurtleff counted forty of his colleagues daubing at easels or sketching studies. In all likelihood there were more artists out of his sight at Upper Ausable Lake, which was known affectionately among the painters in those days as "Paradiso."

Also in the 1870s there was at least one itinerant artist in the park, a man named Cyril Burnell. He made a living wandering from place to place with his brushes and paints stowed in his knapsack. "For lodging, food and drink, mostly drink," he would gladly execute an original, if not universally recognized as masterful, work. His only known surviving opus is a fresco that was discovered beneath several layers of whitewash in the 1930s at the Tahawus Club.

Guides were hired by virtually all of the writers and artists, and by other outsiders inspired by their works to travel to the Adirondacks. But of all the hundreds of people who earned a part of their living taking writers, painters, and plain old tourists into the forest during the course of the nineteenth century, the top tier of the pantheon of great Adirondack guides traditionally includes only four: John Cheney, Mitchell Sabattis, Alvah Dunning, and Orson Phelps. Like a fireside fish story told by an accomplished guide, with every repetition the mythology of the Adirondack guide as high priest of the romantic wilderness grew, until, with Orson "Old Mountain" Phelps at least, it almost imploded into a caricature of itself.

"Mythology" in this case should not imply that the existence of the legendary Adirondack guide was imaginary. Though the more influential journalists and painters were themselves guides of a sort, their word alone was not enough to create a legend. The fact that John Plumbley, Murray's guide in *Adventures in the Wilderness*, typically isn't included in the league with the other four shows that as important as the writers were to creating reputations, they weren't everything.

The great guides were quite real, but their role was at least partly mystical. For the wilderness in which they lived and worked was something altogether different than it had been to their grandparents. Two centuries after Isaac Jogues encountered his Iroquois "demons," the park had become one of the residences of God.

According to historians such as Roderick Nash and Max Oelschlaeger, the romantic conception of untamed places grew out of an earlier, Enlightenment infatuation with physics and astronomy. After Copernicus and Newton, intellectual Europeans imagined the universe as a great clock, or a machine. And if the hand of the clockmaker, which is to say the hand of God, was visible even in the mathematical revolutions of the moon around the earth and the earth around the sun, why would it not also be evident in the formerly unattractive mountains?

The problem was, the realization that God created the woods didn't immediately make them any less scary. In 1757 Edmund Burke explained that the terror wilderness evoked in the hearts and minds of mortals was due not to the presence of the devil, as had earlier been believed, but to awe in the face of God's creative power. "Beauty," he argued, was a pleasurable word best reserved for pastoral scenes. Our attraction to God's power made visible in the untamed quarters of the world was "founded in pain." Such places were better described as "sublime."

"It was not a very long leap from the Enlightenment position that in the grandeur of the sublime view one could sense the vastness of the power of God to the romantic belief that God is omnipresent in nature," writes Philip Terrie in *Forever Wild,* his application of Nash's basic analysis to the literature of the Adirondacks. "The mechanistic rationalism of the eighteenth century, in fact, by which Burke and others dissected the constituents of sublimity and beauty, helped to usher in the mystical pantheism of the nineteenth."

In the blossoming of popular Adirondack literature in the nineteenth century, Burkean "awesomes," "awfuls," "sublimes," and "terrifyings" pepper the descriptions of the place with such frequency as to make the stuff occasionally difficult to read. And no place was better suited to the sensibility of the times than the Indian Pass, where John Cheney offered to take the distraught Charles Fenno Hoffman as a sort of consolation prize for the failed attempt up Marcy.

The protoindustrialists of the McIntyre Iron Works thought of the Indian Pass as a business opportunity. "The territory is getting so much notice that I verily believe were a railroad to be made from the lake and a large public house erected it would become a fashionable resort for the summer months—the notch being the greatest curiosity in the country next to the falls of Niagara," wrote Henderson to McIntyre in 1837. "If Niagara be the prince of waterfalls the other exhibits the prince of precipices."

Ebenezer Emmons, the devout scientist, apologized for even noticing it. "In conclusion I remark, that I should not have occupied so much space for the purpose of describing merely a natural curiosity, were it not for the fact that probably in this country there is no object of the kind on a scale so vast and imposing as this." He, too, thought it rivaled Niagara.

But the romantics positively genuflected at the narrow passage between the thousand-foot vertical cliffs of Wallface Mountain and the forty-five-degree western slope of Algonquin. "At last we reached the point, and paused a moment to inhale full, deep breaths. We knew a sublime and terrible sight awaited us. We turned and looked. A shudder shook my frame. My eyes swam, my brain grew dizzy," wrote Alfred Billings Street.

Unlike most of the other visitors, Street made the extra effort to climb partway up Wallface to view the pass from above. "After a few moments of thus bracing my system and recovering from the first sickening shock, I again looked," he goes on. "What a sight! Horrible and yet sublimely beautiful—no, not beautiful; scarce an element of beauty there—all grandeur and terror."[1]

Headley, whose expectations were already built up by the accounts of previous visitors, complained about the hike. "I had expected, from paintings I had seen of this pass, that I was to walk almost on a level into a huge gap between two mountains, and look up on the precipices that toppled heaven high above me. But here was a world of rocks, overgrown with trees and moss—over and under and between which we were compelled to crawl and dive. . . . A more hideous, toilsome breakneck tramp I never took."

But when he finally got to the pass itself, he too was suitably impressed. "From our feet rose this awful cliff that really oppressed me with its near and frightful presence," he wrote.

Hoffman called the pass "one of the most savage and stupendous among the many wild and imposing scenes at the source of the Hudson."

---

[1] Sometimes it got confusing even for Hoffman. Lake Sanford was warm and pleasant for swimming, but the view was dominated by the "perfect pyramidal top" of Marcy covered in snow. "The effect was equally beautiful and sublime," he was forced to conclude.

"The Great Adirondack [Indian] Pass, Painted on the Spot," 1837, by Charles Cromwell Ingham. COURTESY OF THE ADIRONDACK MUSEUM, BLUE MOUNTAIN LAKE.

John Cheney called it, simply, "Church."

Not that Mount Marcy couldn't hold its own in the awe department for those who made it up to the top. "The impression of the whole, it is impossible to convey—nay, I am myself hardly conscious what it is," wrote Headley of the view from the summit. "It seems as if I had seen vagueness, terror, sublimity, strength, and beauty, all embodied, so that I had a new and more definite knowledge of them. God appears to have wrought in these old mountains with His highest power, and designed to leave a symbol of His omnipotence. Man is nothing here, his very shouts die on his lips."

This last sentence exposes a crucial element of the nineteenth-century response to the divine machinery of the enlightenment. What the romantic tourist sought in the wilds of the Adirondacks was not further evidence of celestial engineering but hints of meaning in a universe that suddenly no longer physically revolved around the human species. Hoffman and the others imagined themselves as if in a painting by Thomas Cole, tiny figures set in vast and indifferent landscapes.

Cole, who originally turned to landscape painting because he couldn't afford to hire the models and teachers necessary for learning to draw the figure, influenced a generation of painters with his nostalgic and pessimistic images of America's wild and pastoral landscapes on the cusp of industrial change. In his most ambitious series, *The Course of Empire,* a great and beautiful urban civilization grows out of the wilderness, only to decay and fall and become wild once more.

At the center of the final painting, leaves and vines cling tenaciously to an immense and crumbling Corinthian column, on top of which nests a pair of black cranes; a pillar of civilization originally designed as an homage to a tree is again a trunk.

Despite their appreciation of the emotional power of the surroundings, most of the earliest visitors to the Adirondacks still clung to the assumption that wilderness, however awesome, must give way to civilization in the long run. Thomas Cole himself said he thought the scenery of the Adirondacks would be improved with a little logging. And in their descriptions of the larger lakes that surround the High Peaks, the romantic writers often imagined a future that looked more like Switzerland than the primordial ooze. The beautiful was still more pleasurable than the sublime.

Once in a while the romantic tourists strayed toward a more modern, ecological view of nature. Hoffman marveled at the biodiversity on one island he visited. "What I have never been wearied with studying," he wrote, was "the manner in which nature effects her work of clothing the barren crags with soil." And Lanman devoted several pages to describing a colony of insects: "I was a 'distinguished stranger' in that city and I must confess that it gratified my ambition to be welcomed with such manifestations of regard as the inhabitants thought proper to bestow."

In general, though, they were not what would today be called eco-tourists. A more typical response was that of Headley's when he climbed Owls Head. "I have gazed on many mountain prospects in this and the old world, but this and the view from Tahawus have awakened an entirely new class of emotions. They are American scenes, constituting one of the distinctive features of our country, where nature seems to have formed everything on such a large model, merely because she had so much room to work in. I wanted to set fire to the trees on the summit of the mountain, so as to present an unobstructed view, but the foliage was too green to burn."

The romantics were on their way toward a more conservation-oriented attitude, but the idea of progress still reigned. In the meantime, the Adirondack guide provided more than just physical access to all this sublimity, terror, and awe. Unlike some of the conceptions of wilderness that would come later, the defining element for the romantics was not a total absence of humanity. However small, impotent, and awestruck in a corner of the cosmic canvas they might be, humans were nevertheless still there—"in the equation," as the more extreme among today's anticonservationists might say.

Very much in the equation, in fact. God's main purpose in creating the summit of Marcy was not to provide habitat for subarctic lichens, Headley and the other romantics believed, but "to leave a symbol." The symbol, presumably, was for human consumption. "Nature," Emerson wrote, "is emblematic."

As full-time residents of the wilderness, the guides lived closer to God. They were priests and seers. "The wilderness has unfolded to them its mysteries, and made them wise with a wisdom nowhere written in books," Reverend Murray said of the good Adirondack guides. "They are not unworthy of the magnificent surrounding amid which they dwell."

Best of all, theirs was a brand of holiness that might rub off on the client. Murray, who was the pastor of the influential Park Street Church in Boston, suggested that every congregation would do well to take up a special collection to send their minister to the Adirondacks for a month each year.

"For when the good dominie came back swarth and tough as an Indian, elasticity in his step, fire in his eye, depth and clearness in his reinvigorated voice, wouldn't there be some preaching!" he wrote.

"The preacher sees God in the original there, and often translates him better from his unwritten works than from his written word. He will get more instructive spiritual material from such a trip than from all the 'Sabbath-school festivals' and 'pastoral tea-parties' with which the poor, smiling creature was ever tormented."[2]

The old fears of Cotton Mather and of Montcalm's aide-de-camp Louis-Antoine de Bougainville were now inverted. What endangered the soul was not the presence of wilderness at all, it turned out, but "the din and struggle" of Broadway and Wall Street. Civilization, especially urban civilization, was the potentially dehumanizing condition. By the end of the century it was the city that was, in Upton Sinclair's words, "the jungle."

Joel T. Headley, in particular, wasn't inclined to pull his punches for his New York City readers. He allowed that once in a while the sea air could make life slightly more bearable in Manhattan—"moist from its long dalliance with the salt waves, its kiss is soft and welcome as that of a—I beg your pardon, I meant to say, as a doctor once remarked to me, 'it is a very pleasant stimulant.' "

But he went on to say, "Yet I know Broadway is looking like a furnace just cooled off; and with all your windows and doors thrown open, you are still languid, while a sultry and oppressive night awaits you. I pity you from my heart; you have been in Wall Street the whole of this scorching day, and have not drawn a breath below your throat, for the air you live on was never made for the lungs.

"You are pale and exhausted, while now and then comes over you a sweet vision of rushing streams and waving tree tops, and cool floods of air. I see you in imagination, flung at full length upon the sofa, and hear that expression of impatience which escapes your lips."

To all of these assaults of the urban world that science and industry had created, the wilderness of the Adirondacks was offered as a tonic. "But here it is delicious—my lungs heave freely and strongly, and every moment refreshes instead of enervates me. Before me spreads away this beautiful lake. . . ." Headley positively started to gloat. A noble trout leaps. The sun sets. One by one, bright stars appear in the night sky. "If one is not entirely spoiled," Headley

---

[2] Perhaps not surprisingly, Murray ultimately found himself unsuited for the ministry, and wound up running an oyster restaurant in Montreal.

promised his urban readers, "he soon attunes himself to the harmony of nature, and a new life is born within him."

Nor was it only the physical climate of Manhattan before air-conditioning that could be remedied in the Adirondacks. Where the missionary Roubaud encountered his sea of war-painted faces "adorned with every ornament most suited to disfigure them in European eyes," Headley's romantic wilderness was a place where true human features were revealed.

"In the woods, the mask that society compels one to wear is cast aside, and the restraints which the thousand eyes and reckless tongues about him fasten on the heart, are thrown off, and the soul rejoices in its liberty and again becomes a child in action," he told his readers.

"Nature and the Bible are in harmony[3]—they both speak one language to the heart—yet in the wilderness there is no formality in the expression of one's feelings. A man 'laughs when he is merry, and sighs when he is sad,' without thinking or caring how it would appear in the saloon or grave assemblage."

In his essay "Nature," Emerson said simply, "In the wilderness we return to reason and faith." And when in 1858 he, too, went to spend a month in the Adirondacks at Follensby Pond, along with Louis Agassiz and eight other "luminaries," he wrote in his poem-journal of the trip, "Up with the dawn, they fancied the light air / that circled freshly in their forest dress / Made them to boys again. . . ."

The reinvigorating power of the wilderness is also at the heart of Cole's *Course of Empire*. The return of wilderness in the last two paintings isn't driven by plants alone. Hordes of barbarians, presumably still strong from their wild existence, overpower the corrupted civilians. The irony is obvious; it is a grand achievement to conquer wilderness and build a civilization, perhaps the greatest achievement human beings can muster. But those who remain closest to the land are always the stronger. The arc of civilization leads inevitably to corruption and defeat.

Already in the 1840s, Headley worried about the American criminal justice system in the more sophisticated sections of the country. After

---

[3] One guide, Alvah Dunning, might have disagreed. "That's a damn lie," he once said while reading Genesis. "It says here the Lord opened the flood gates of heaven and it rained down forty days and forty nights and drowned the earth to the tops of the highest mountains. Why, I've seen it rain here for forty days and forty nights and it never raised Raquette Lake more than a foot."

observing a trial in the Adirondacks, he said approvingly that the locals were not yet "sufficiently educated to understand that the science of law as reduced to practice now-a-days, is based on two great principles—first, to give the scoundrel a better chance than the honest man—and second, to make technicalities weigh against truth and justice."

Thomas Cole, meanwhile, was concerned about what he called the "meager utilitarianism" of the age, though his Adirondack paintings of Schroon Lake, Schroon Mountain, and Indian Pass are less full of stormy foreboding than some of his more well known paintings of the Catskills and other points south.

Emerson warned, "Things are in the saddle and ride mankind."

Suddenly, the polluted image of civilization created a dissatisfaction with the names assigned by political patronage to the park's most notable features. Romantics always preferred Native American names, even if they were of very dubious lineage, to those of politicians or foreign tyrants. In the style of Cooper, Lake George was almost always referred to as Horicon. After Hoffman, who seemed to have something of a genetic memory for what he claimed were long-lost names, Marcy was reverentially called "Tahawus, or cloud-splitter."[4] Old names kept the New World feeling new.

The notion that hope for the nation resided in its wild roots, which ultimately overpowered the romantic's faith in inevitable progress, had not yet coalesced into an effective preservation movement. But its corollary, the idea that salvation of the individual lay in keeping a foot in both worlds, was self-evident to the (mostly white, wealthy, and male) writers who went to the park in the nineteenth century. Headley, who explained in his introduction that he first went north in the aftermath of "an attack on the brain," concluded after getting there that "without frequent communion with nature every man degenerates."

It wasn't only emotional and spiritual health that could be improved by Adirondack air. By the end of the century, the region drew tuberculosis victims by the thousands. The founder of the movement, Dr. Edward Livingston Trudeau, arrived barely alive—"Why, Doc, you ain't no heavier than a dried lambskin"—at Paul Smiths in 1873. Just as

---

[4] Donaldson points out that if Tahawus was in fact an old Indian name, Cheney probably would have known it and told Emmons. The guide Orson Phelps named Haystack, Skylight, Upper and Lower Wolf jaw, Gothics, Saddleback, Slide, Gray, Flattop, Sable, and Basin Mountains. Nippletop, Phelps said, "was named by its creator; the name suggests itself at sight."

Adirondack Murray had implied he would be in *Adventures in the Wilderness,* Trudeau was all but cured within a few years. He spent the rest of his life fighting the disease, which was the scourge of the age. By the 1890s Trudeau's Adirondack Cottage Sanitarium at Saranac Lake was the world's foremost center for the study of the disease, and consumptives of all ages spent winter nights bundled by the hundreds in bearskins on its porches, "taking the air."

Not every sufferer from consumption was taken with the beauty of the Adirondacks. Robert Louis Stevenson was one who came looking for a cure in 1887 and found it "a bleak blackguard beggarly climate, of which I can say no good except it suits me." While there he wrote most of *The Master of Ballantrae,* which ends with death in a decidedly unromantic Adirondack wilderness.

But for those who were inclined to believe in the salutary power of wilderness living, there was no better proof than the Adirondack guide. The man at the oars, pronounced Murray, was "uncontaminated with the vicious habits of civilized life."

The Adirondack guide was not, however, uncivilized. At least not in any sense meaning "bloodthirsty." Without exception the top tier were said to be modest and unassuming men. Hence the continual

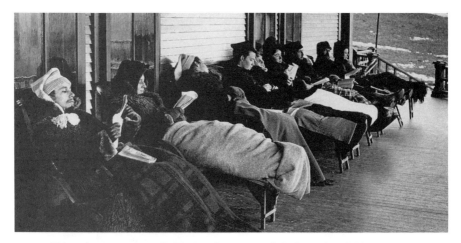

Tuberculosis patients at the Trudeau Sanitarium (which was founded by the great-grandfather of cartoonist Gary Trudeau) in Saranac Lake, circa 1900. COURTESY OF THE ADIRONDACK MUSEUM, BLUE MOUNTAIN LAKE.

comparisons to Natty Bumppo, besides the obvious desire to piggy-back on the unprecedented commercial success of Cooper's novels. Cooper himself thought that what made his Leatherstocking novels so popular was the protagonist's ability to find the middle road between savagery and civilization. Bumppo, the novelist told lecture audiences, possessed "the better qualities of both conditions."

Once again, it was a trait first identified in an Adirondack guide by Charles Fenno Hoffman. "I had heard of some of his feats before coming into this region, and expected of course to see one of those roistering, 'cavorting', rifle-shirted blades that I have seen upon our western frontier," Hoffman said of Cheney, "and was at first not a little disappointed when a slight-looking man of about seven and thirty, dressed like a plain countryman, and of a peculiarly quiet, simple manner, was introduced to me as the doughty slayer of bears and panthers." His disappointment didn't last long.

Even writers who had already read Hoffman's book before they arrived at the McIntyre Iron Works felt constrained to profess surprise at Cheney's mild exterior. Charles Lanman specifically sought out Cheney because of his reputation "as the guide of all travelers in this region." Expecting "to see a huge, powerful and hairy Nimrod," he found Cheney instead to be "small in stature, and bearing more the appearance of a modest and thoughtful student."

Of the guide Mitchell Sabattis, who was an Abnaki Indian, Headley wrote that when they parted he "shook his honest hand with as much regret as I ever did that of a white man. I shall long remember him— he is a man of deed and not of words—kind, gentle, delicate in his feelings, honest and true as steel. . . . I never lay down beside a trustier heart than his, and never slept sounder than I have with one arm thrown across his brawny chest." Brawny *and* delicate.

Orson "Old Mountain" Phelps, arguably the most famous guide of them all, was downright philosophical. "If ever a man was formed to sit on a log, it was Old Phelps," wrote Charles Dudley Warner in a profile that appeared in the *Atlantic Monthly* in May of 1878. Warner wrote that life in the Adirondacks "had highly developed in [Phelps] the love of beauty, the aesthetic sense, delicacy of appreciation, refinement of feeling . . ."

The title of Warner's piece was "The Primitive Man," and its gist was that Orson Phelps was just such a creature. Warner, who was an occasional collaborator of Mark Twain's, said Phelps was the long-

The legendary Adirondack guide Mitchell Sabattis. COURTESY OF THE ADIRON-
DACK MUSEUM, BLUE MOUNTAIN LAKE.

sought missing link who "would satisfy the conditions of the Miocene environment and yet would be good enough for an ancestor."[5]

Among the evidence offered for his status as the former were Phelps's habits of personal hygiene. "His clothes seemed to have been put on him once and for all, like the bark of a tree, a long time ago," Warner noted. And Phelps himself famously added, "Soap is a thing I hain't no kinder use for."

His lingo was famous. Warner said Phelps "used words sometimes like algebraic signs." When asked for the next day's plans, he told Warner, "Waal, I callerate, if they rig up the calleration they callerate on, we'll go to the Boreas." Phelps called a hike on a trail, which he probably cut himself, "a reg'lar walk." Off the trail was always "a random scoot." Unless, of course, it was through a dense enough thicket to be a "reg'lar random scoot of a rigmarole."

Old Mountain's acceptability as an ancestor was obvious from his aforementioned sensitivity. Those who complained that Phelps might be lazy, Warner said, would have said the same thing about Socrates.

Orson Phelps loved the attention. In later years, when crowds of tourists stopped at Keene Flats (now Keene Valley) to see the wizened old primitive with an immense white beard, for a small fee he supplied them with autographed copies of Seneca Ray Stoddard's photo of himself. For a little more of their money they could possess his own line of trail maps and guidebooks. For a while there was even an "Old Mountain Phelps" model fishing rod for sale.

In some respects, though, Phelps's primitive persona was a self-conscious act that he put on for the customer as part of what writer William Chapman White described as a conscious mission to promote the Adirondacks. When he wasn't guiding people to the summits of the High Peaks, dropping pearls of wisdom along the way like "Them Gothics ain't the kinder scenery you want to hog down," Phelps was writing his own regular column for a local newspaper. Locals called him "Greeley," because of his devoted allegiance to the *New York Tribune* and the opinions of its editor. A writer for *Putnam's Magazine*, Kate Hilliard, writing under the pseudonym Lucy Fountain, discussed the finer points of Tennyson's poetry with him.

---

[5] As this sentence shows, Warner had a keen eye for the pretentions of his century, as well as a healthy capacity for wit and humor. His Adirondack short story "How I Killed a Bear" is still hilarious today.

Later in life Phelps began work on a major treatise about, among other things, Adirondack geology. Unfortunately he never completed it, but the twenty-two neatly handwritten ledger book pages he did fill are notably lacking in "algebraic" English.

This isn't to say Phelps's style wasn't both unique and refreshingly free of the breathless descriptions used by the romantics he sometimes guided. "The summit of Dix is an odd thing," he wrote, a "sharp, narrow, curved, uneven ridge covered with balsam brush from two to four feet high, and as thick as hair on a spaniel dog; a look at it reminds one of a look at an old poor cow doubled up to lick her hip, and for a man to travel it with a knapsack on would be like ants taking [a] big egg and traveling the cow's back."

Charles Dudley Warner knew of his subject's writerly leanings, and he disapproved. "When the primitive man comes into literature," he sniffed at the end of his profile of Phelps, "he is no longer primitive."

Warner and the other writers knew full well that the myth of the happy primitive was by no means a new fantasy. In 1530 a German writer named Hans Sachs wrote a book called *Lament of the Wild Men about the Unfaithful World* extolling the wonderful simplicity and peace

"Keene Valley—Noon Mark, Adirondacks," with Orson "Old Mountain" Phelps in foreground. Circa 1880, by Seneca Ray Stoddard. COURTESY OF THE ADIRONDACK MUSEUM, BLUE MOUNTAIN LAKE.

of those who eschewed urban materialism and lived in the woods. By the early 1700s the "noble savage" was a stock character in literary critiques of modern civilization.

In reality, of course, the life of an Adirondack guide could be as normal as anyone else's. John Cheney lived with his wife and two children in a tidy little cabin not far from the ironworks that employed him. The walls were decorated with engravings of the Declaration of Independence, George Washington, and Andrew Jackson. Mitchell Sabattis, meanwhile, was a good Methodist who played the Sunday hymns on his violin. Orson Phelps, for a time, was the postmaster of Keene Flats.

Life had its disappointments, too. When Cheney was seventy-four, one of his sons went insane and fired a gun at him, wounding the old man in the face slightly. The younger Cheney then went on to set fire to the boardinghouse Cheney and his wife were operating and danced around the yard while it burned, brandishing his shotgun at anyone who tried to stop the blaze.

Sabattis, meanwhile, battled mightily with alcohol for much of his life, though he eventually won. And Alvah Dunning, beloved guide of President Grover Cleveland[6] and J. P. Morgan, only came to Raquette Lake in the first place after fleeing his hometown to escape prosecution for wifebeating.

Finally, it was hard work to be a good guide. Charles Lanman, who was always a bit less dewy-eyed than his fellow writers, said, "The life of a guide, notwithstanding the gush that has been written about it, is a hard one, and there are few who would not abandon it to engage in a less arduous mode of earning a livelihood. . . . It makes them old before their time."[7]

---

[6] Dunning was on good enough terms with Cleveland to feel that he could write to the White House, "Some time ago Ike Kenwell asked me to catch you some lake trout. I done so. He offered to pay me but I did not take any pay. Just now I am out of baking powder and if you would send me some I would be very much obliged to you." Though the president had no connection with the Cleveland Baking Powder Company other than a shared name, two cases of the stuff were sent right out to Raquette Lake.

[7] Stories of unhappy endings for guides abound. A guide named Chris Crandall lost a leg in a hunting accident; he worked for a while after that but ultimately shot himself in the head with a rifle, using his remaining foot to pull the trigger. A guide named Sam Dunakin was so drunk so regularly that he lowered the end of his dock below the level of Fourth Lake on the Fulton Chain so that he could row right up onto it and roll out of his boat; drinking apparently affected his walking more than his rowing. A guide named Eula Davis was found shot in his cabin by another guide, Ernest Duane. The bullet that killed him went through Davis's wallet; when a few days later Duane was caught spending ten-dollar bills with holes in them, he was arrested and convicted of murder.

But none of these pesky details mattered to the romantics who visited the park in the middle decades of the last century. In the Adirondacks, any sorry dehumanized denizen of the civilized world who was flush enough to pay a guide two dollars and fifty cents a day could come up for a few weeks and commune with a professional primitive. It was not for nothing that Orson Phelps called those who made the journey to Keene Valley to visit him "pilgrims."

15 *At Play in the Great Longhouse*

Despite his spreading fame as a guide, John Cheney always preferred to describe himself as a hunter. Had he lived only a few decades earlier that is no doubt how he would be remembered. Born in 1800 near Lake Champlain, Cheney, like Nat Foster and Nick Stoner before him, moved deeper into the Adirondacks as the nearby game gave way. He arrived in Newcomb around 1830 with nothing but his gun, his dog, and a knapsack.

In the next thirteen years he killed six hundred deer, forty-eight bears, nineteen moose, four hundred martens, thirty otters, seven wildcats, six wolves, and one panther. He also took a single beaver, which he believed was the last of its species in the entire state of New York. For three years the animal eluded Cheney, but, he explained to a visitor, "I finally fixed a trap under the water, near the entrance to his dam, and it so happened that one day he stepped into it and drowned."

All of the writers who hired him peppered their tales with accounts of some of Cheney's more exciting hunting exploits. The time he broke his rifle over the head of a wolf, after which he always hunted with only an eleven-inch pistol, was usually included. So was the time he was snowshoeing down a mountain and fell into the winter den of a large bear. The bruin had Cheney in a deadly bear hug when the master's loyal dog came and drew the beast off, allowing Cheney to find his pistol in the snow. According to some versions of the story, Cheney was the only one of the three who lived to tell the tale.

There was also the time Cheney turned and saw a great panther crouched and ready to spring upon him. He raised his pistol slowly, and just as the great cat leapt, he shot it through the brain. This story illustrated the powerful presence of mind of the great woodsman.

"Being a little curious to know whether he was not somewhat agitated in finding himself in such close proximity to a panther all ready for the fatal leap, I asked him how he felt when he saw the animal crouching so near," Joel T. Headley wrote.

" 'I felt,' [Cheney] said coolly, 'as if I should kill him.' " Whether Headley saw evidence of comic timing in Cheney's reply, he doesn't say. He does report that it was characteristically succinct.

John Cheney's desire to be remembered more as a hunter than a guide was partly a result of his living during the transition between the two professions. But even before Ebenezer Emmons, then Charles Fenno Hoffman, and then the other writers, painters, lawyers, doctors, and bankers began arriving at Upper Works looking for his services, John Cheney's position in the world was fundamentally different from the trappers of the previous century. To Stoner's generation the wilderness next door was, practically speaking, no-man's-land. Or everyone's land. But Cheney had a real job as company hunter, woodsman, "and factotum" for the McIntyre Iron Works. The company owned a sizable chunk of the neighborhood.

The significance of this was not lost on Hoffman. "The demolition of the pine forests, and the conversion of less valuable wood into charcoal, will rapidly clear the country, and convert the lumber-men and charcoal-burners into farmers," he wrote, "while the old race of hunters already begin to find a new employment in acting as guides to the owners of lands."

Most of all, though, in Cheney's desire to be perceived as a hunter is a recognition that despite all of the romantic talk of free air and regained vigor, most who came to the Adirondacks and hired guides came there to kill animals. The best thing a guide could do for a "sport" was to get him within range of something to shoot or hook.

They were generally very good at their job. Individual guides came down differently on the great debate over deer-hunting methods; still hunting versus dog driving versus jacking. "The only manly way to kill deer is by 'driving' them, as I do, with a couple of hounds," said Cheney. Mitchell Sabattis was more likely to jack. And Alvah Dunning was famous for his ability to call animals to the water by bleating like a fawn. One way or another, though, good guides all got plenty of venison for their clients, even if they had to shoot it themselves. The major exception was Old Mountain Phelps, who preferred to climb mountains.

And if a rare client was a somewhat ambivalent hunter, like Headley—"I sat and shivered, thinking there would be vastly more poetry in staying by the campfire, and eating venison already killed, than waiting for that which was yet running on the mountain"—there were trout galore.

The accounts of the fishing in the region would be almost unbelievable were it not for the consistency of the reports and a few early photographs. "Fifty fine fellows" in two hours of casting flies here, though of course the biggest one of the day got away; "forty pounds of trout in two hours" there; a half bushel in half an hour on the Cold River. And the fish could be big. Headley watched an unnamed woman land a nineteen-pound lake trout at Moose Lake.

This was the bloody flip-side of the romantic image of wilderness, and there are several ways to account for it. It was fun and fashionable, for one; in the northeastern cities, at least, hunting had progressed from something virtually everyone in America did for food to something the wealthy did for sport. Nor was the long-term health of the game population of much concern in a period when the deer herd was in all likelihood exploding because of rapidly increasing forage land in areas of the park where loggers and charcoal makers were at work. Besides, though the earliest calls for some kind of protection began to be sounded in the 1860s, few of the romantic tourists doubted that the Adirondack wilderness would eventually succumb to civilization. So why not enjoy the sport while it lasted?

Mostly, though, the hunt fit right into the notion of wilderness under which the romantics were operating. Both the preference for Native-sounding place-names like Tahawus and the habit of writers of the time to adopt faux Indian pseudonyms like "Piseco," "Wachusett," and "Nessmuck," suggests that a large component of the romantic idea of wilderness was nostalgia for an imagined aboriginal past. Never mind that the country was currently waist deep in the bloody

Unidentified Adirondack fisherwoman. COURTESY OF THE SARANAC LAKE
FREE LIBRARY.

business of Native removal in the West; there hadn't been any serious
threat from the Iroquois for at least three-quarters of a century, and
Americans wanted to play in the Great Longhouse. They wanted to be
Indians, and Indians killed and ate game pretty much all the time,
didn't they? It was the way of the wilderness, and the romantics
wanted to be a part of it all.

Once in a while, writers voiced sympathy for the fate of individual
fish or deer. "I can't help it, my speckled beauty," wrote Headley of a
fish, "it's a world where we prey on each other. Beside, I have had
nothing but fried pork for three days, and I already gloat in imagination over your salmon-colored flesh. I have gone but half a mile [on
the river], and let us see, I have forty. That will do for today, and we

will return home." Similarly, the literary consensus was that the eye of a dying buck was a noble thing.

The guides, too, occasionally displayed a complex attitude toward their prey. Cheney stopped Hoffman from gratuitously shooting unneeded partridges by saying, "It's wrong, it's wrong sir, to use up life in that way." Of deer, the old guide said, "I wish I could get my living without killing this beautiful animal! but I must live, and I suppose they were made to die. The cry of the deer, when in the agonies of death, is the awfullest sound I ever heard."

But even John Cheney's sympathy evaporated when it came to predators. "I'd a good rather hear the scream of a panther," Cheney went on to say, "provided I have a ball in my pistol and the pistol in my hand." Similarly, Mitchell Sabattis stopped Headley from shooting a mother duck only a short time after he himself attempted and failed to kill a nesting eagle. "Only the mountain has lived long enough to listen objectively to the howl of a wolf," wrote the great naturalist Aldo Leopold almost a century later in explanation of his own slowness at perceiving the ecological and aesthetic value of predators.

One of the greatest Adirondack guides, Alvah Dunning, was one of several people credited with shooting the last moose in the region in 1862. Yet he never could understand the disappearance of the animal. "What caused the moose to all leave in one season right after the Civil War, is a mystery I never could solve. They were thick thirty years ago. I killed eight big ones in five days. My father, myself, and two others killed 100 moose one winter."

In old Alvah's defense, the extermination of the moose was no doubt hastened by the opening of the forest by loggers and miners, which created conditions that favored deer. The two animals rarely cohabitate, because the deer carries a parasite that is deadly to the moose. Also, the eradication of beaver, and thus beaver ponds, from the park dramatically decreased the supply of moose food. Still, the demise of the big ungulate was one of several signs, on a variety of fronts, that the sporting bonanza couldn't last.

Already in 1853, when Charles Lanman "awoke from a piscatorial dream, haunted by the idea that I must spend a portion of the approaching summer in the indulgence of my passion for angling," the fishing was in decline all around the perimeter of the park. "The days of trout fishing in Lake Horicon are nearly at an end," he moaned. "A few years ago it abounded in salmon-trout, which were frequently caught weighing twenty pounds, but their average weight at the present is not more than one pound and a half, and they are scarce at that."

Of course, Lanman didn't let the status of the stocks prevent him from setting up a buoy in Lake George and then dumping around it "suckers, perch, and eels, which are cut up and deposited, some half a peck at a time." After a while, he promised, the big trout would show up and "so long as you keep them well fed, a brace of them may be captured at any time during the summer." He did this in good conscience because he was certain, in the time-honored way, that any problems were caused by the despicable methods of other fishermen.

"In the autumn," he reported, "when [the fish] have sought the shores for the purpose of spawning, the neighboring barbarians have been accustomed to spear them by torch-light. . . ."

Buoy fishing notwithstanding, "my advice to those who come here exclusively for the purpose of fishing is to continue their journey to the sources of the Hudson, Schroon Lake, Long Lake, and Lake Pleasant."

This he proceeded to do himself, accompanied for a while by a wandering violinist who entertained him with bawdy songs deep into the night. "Next morning we plunged again into the forest, and as we rode along, I noticed trees at certain intervals, marked 'H,' which after vainly attempting to account for, I finally inquired the reason of," he wrote. " 'Oh, it means highway,' was the reply."

At stops all along the way, dozens of brook and lake trout rose to take flies, chunks of salt pork, mice, and various other things Lanman put on the end of his line. In the heart of the park in the 1850s, he was pleased to report, the fishing was still very good.

That too would change. Beginning in the summer of 1869, the back-to-nature crowds grew exponentially. The immediate cause was the publication of Adirondack Murray's *Adventures in the Wilderness* on April Fool's Day of that year. In a few months it went through eleven printings. As important as book sales, though, were the number of readers who could now afford to actually take Murray's advice to go to the woods—and did. The Civil War was over and the industrial revolution was in full swing. People traveled. By July of 1869, the *Boston Daily Advertiser* was covering the phenomenon that became known as "Murray's Rush" in a series entitled "With the Multitudes in the Wilderness." The term that stuck was "Murray's Fools."

Part of Murray's success was due to the fact that he wrote a very enjoyable book, full of improbable adventures and anecdotes that he advised the reader to believe only if inclined to do so. And whereas earlier writers had generally been quite honest, even macho, about some of the hardships encountered by the traveler in the Adirondacks, Murray made it all sound easy.

Of the spring hordes of insects, for instance, Headley had said, "By the time I had taken ten or fifteen [fish], I was compelled to fling down my rod and run and scream, for the blood was pouring in rivulets from my neck, face, and hands." Murray on the other hand, who admitted he never went before the relatively bug-free month of July and encouraged others to do the same, described the black flies as "one of the most harmless and least vexatious of the insect family." Mosquitoes, meanwhile, were likely to be worse in the majority of New England villages. "There is nothing in the trip," he promised elsewhere in the book, "which the most delicate and fragile need to fear."

Within a few years there was a stern backlash against Murray in the press: it wasn't as easy as he said it would be. The bugs were in fact horrible, if you arrived in June; the hotels were too few and too full; the guides were unavailable or corrupt. Most of all, there was no way the preacher and his guide went over the Phantom (Buttermilk) Falls.

If Murray exaggerated the ease with which one could visit the Adirondacks, he was only off by a few years. Railroads didn't yet cross the heart of the park but they could get you reasonably close. Where they stopped, you could usually get a stage or a steamboat. And everywhere, even before Murray's Rush, hotels sprouted like poplars in an abandoned clearing. In 1850 there were only a handful of places a visitor to the Adirondacks could stay. By 1875 there were more than two hundred hotels in the future park.

The first were almost accidental inns, founded by locals who realized they could make a better living taking in guests than by farming or trapping, which then grew into large establishments. Jesse Corey, a former trapper, opened a place called Corey's at the Indian Carry, between the Raquette River and the Saranac Lakes, in 1850. The first of a succession of hotels called the Raquette Lake House opened in 1856 at the carry between Raquette and Forked Lake. The Rainbow Inn, on the lake of the same name, was founded around 1860 by James

Wardner, who had also been a trapper. There were popular places called Martin's, Moody's, Kellogg's, Bartlett's.

In Keene Flats, as Keene Valley was first known, a farmer named Smith Beede, who for years had been taking in boarders at his home, built a proper hotel called Beede House on what is now the site of the venerable Ausable Club. Business rapidly became so good for Farmer Beede that he gave up agriculture altogether in favor of real estate development.

These early hostels were essentially way stations, where a client might meet up with a guide, lay in a few essentials, and then shove out into the wilderness for a few weeks. One of the more famous among them was located in the former home of the unfortunate aristocrat Charles Frederick Herreshoff. In 1837 Otis Arnold and his family from Boonville moved onto Brown's Tract and simply occupied the Herreshoff Manor, abandoned three years before by Nat Foster. The original plan was to farm. But so many fishermen wandered up asking for lodging that Arnold's, as it was known, was soon a full-fledged hotel serving as many as two thousand visitors a year. The rate was a dollar and a half a day, meals included.

By the time Otis Arnold's life came to its own suicidal end—in 1868 he filled his pockets with rocks and drowned himself in Nick's Lake, after having shot and killed a guide he falsely accused of stealing a dog collar—he had ten thousand dollars squirreled away in his attic.

In happier times, Arnold's six daughters were famous among travelers. They rode wildly through the woods bareback with their long hair streaming behind them, like a sort of Amazon cavalry. They lit smudge fires under the cows they were milking to keep the black flies away. And one of Queen Victoria's ladies-in-waiting, Amelia Murray, believed that they had never seen another woman besides their mother before she visited the place in 1856.

Women writers like Murray and her predecessor Harriet Martineau are evidence that though the profession of guiding was strictly male in the nineteenth century, the clientele was not. Nor did women travel only by the relatively less strenuous method of riding in the front of a boat rowed by a brawny guide. From Keene Valley in particular, women in bulky Victorian skirts regularly took part in multiday hiking trips into the High Peaks.

The participation of women accelerated during the second half of the century, as the scattered homegrown hunter's lodgings were joined by more formal hotels. The first of these were built in the Lake George and Luzerne area in the hope of luring guests away from the swank and popular spas just to the south at Saratoga Springs.

Beginning in the 1790s Saratoga was perhaps the premier destination in America for people with money. De Tocqueville visited it. So did George Washington. But by the middle of the 1800s, the regulars were ready for something new. Developers on the shores of Horicon hoped to cash in. By 1876 there were twenty hotels clustered around the southern end of Lake George.

The grandest of these—as grand as anything Saratoga had to offer—was the Fort William Henry Hotel, which was located exactly where Monro had surrendered to Montcalm. There was a small hotel of that name on the site by the 1850s, but in 1868 construction began on a truly monumental Victorian pleasure palace.

When completed it was more than three hundred feet long, with a mansard roof and piazzas, and thirty-foot-tall Corinthian columns running the length of it. There were six-story towers on either end,

The veranda of the Fort William Henry Hotel, circa 1880, by Seneca Ray Stoddard.
COURTESY OF THE ADIRONDACK MUSEUM, BLUE MOUNTAIN LAKE.

and rooms for nine hundred guests starting at thirty dollars a week. There was a stagecoach office, a telegraph office, a cigar store, a book-store, a billiard hall. Dances were held every Thursday night. Fort William Henry was the place to be in the 1870s.

In the 1880s the tonier option was much farther into the heart of the park, at Blue Mountain Lake. In 1879 Frederick Durant began building Prospect House. His uncle, Dr. Thomas C. Durant, had already built the Union Pacific Railroad and was now planning to lay tracks across the Adirondacks in order to get more logs out and get more tourists in. The tycoon's son William West Durant had begun building the first of his influential Adirondack Great Camps. Frederick expected his great hotel would ensure him a piece of the action.

The hotel that rose in the middle of nowhere was 225 feet long and six stories tall, with great porches on all sides. All of the three hundred rooms had running water, many had baths, and plenty had fireplaces. There was a steam-powered elevator. There were bowling alleys, a wax museum, and a two-story outhouse. There were concerts in the evenings, and water sports in the afternoons. Most exotic of all, Prospect House was the very first hotel in the world to have electric lights. Among the six hundred guests during the 1880s were Tiffanys, Astors, Stuyvesants, and the like.

Sadly for Frederick, his Uncle Thomas ultimately decided not to have the railroad go through Blue Mountain Lake. This took some of the steam out of the growth projections for the hotel. Worse, in the 1890s, Prospect House wasn't really where you wanted to be anyway. Not when you could be at Paul Smiths.

Probably the most famous Adirondack hotel of all time, Paul Smiths, started out as a small informal place. Smith, a giant Vermonter whose real name was Apollos, was an Erie Canal boatman who loved Loon Lake. After guiding independently there for a few years, in 1852 he opened a little men's-only place that he called the Hunter's Home. The first floor had nothing but a living room, kitchen, and a barrel of whiskey with a dipper. Four cents a drink on the honor system. The second floor was a bunk room. It was wildly successful.

In 1858 with some financing from his patrons he opened Paul Smiths on Lower Saint Regis Lake. There were seventeen rooms to start with, but over the next three decades it grew to five hundred rooms stretching along the lakeshore. Mrs. Smith's cooking was famous, his stories were famous, many of the regulars were famous. In the 1890s it held its own with Newport as a summer resting place for the robber barons of the industrial age.

By the turn of the century, though, the hunters and anglers who thought they knew the Adirondacks back in the good old days were complaining mightily in the hook-and-bullet press that the park was ruined. And the problem wasn't just the numbers of people, it was the type. A popular and vaguely xenophobic weekly tabloid called *Forest and Stream* warned its readers, "Between the fish-hog, the Italian railroad hand, the night-hunter, the pseudo-sportsman and the like, this grand region is becoming yearly less and less like its old self and a few more years will witness its entire destruction from a sportsman's and nature-lover's point of view."

Charles Dudley Warner wrote in the *Atlantic* that "those who are most refined and most trained in intellectual fastidiousness" were the best fit for time in the wilderness.

For some, like Warner, the Adirondack guide was only half of the whole. Imbedded in the endless deep thinking about the simplicity and nobility of the guide is the clear implication that for the desired effect the other half, the literate client, is also necessary. Only communion between the properly civilized urbanite and his adequately rustic alter ego conjured up the desired noble savage. When both were worthy, even the woods could be dispensed with; well-loved guides occasionally accepted invitations to visit their clients in the off-season in the city.

The current crowd of visitors to the Adirondacks, Warner complained, left the place "strewn with paper collars and tin cans."

It was as if Thomas Cole's cycle of corruption and degradation had reached into the inner sanctum and produced a horrible caricature of the old ideal. The historian Philip Terrie argues in his *Wildlife and Wilderness* that a large part of the animosity toward the new crowd was fueled by class snobbery among those who could afford to come to the region before the hotels and railroads made it accessible to the more recently gentrified masses. One doesn't have to read many articles in *Forest and Stream* to sense that this might be the case. Paul Smiths, said a writer for the magazine, was a place of "embryo sportsmen in velveteen and corduroys of approved cut, descanting learnedly of backwoods experience . . . anon some millionaire Nimrod or piscator of marked renown drags in from a weary day with a basket of unusual weight, or perchance a fawn cut down before its time."

The biggest complaint in *Forest and Stream* and elsewhere was not the paper collars or velveteen clothing, however, but the scarcity of game. "It appears evident that, for the general public, the Adirondack deer supply cannot hold out much longer, unless more efficient protection is afforded them," reported *Forest and Stream* in 1894. "They would long ago have been exterminated, if it were not for the large areas of private parks, where they do receive protection."

The private parks didn't help the guides, though. "With the end of free hunting, the guides who now make their living from hunters will lose their occupation, and as a class disappear. Those still employed will become appendages to hotels, clubs and permanent camps, and will be much less numerous than they used to be," the magazine pointed out.

The apparent depletion of the deer herd was hastened by the fact that, in the off-season, many guides were engaged in market hunting. Some venison was shipped out of the region on trains; some went to the rapidly growing number of logging camps, full of men who preferred their beans with meat. A guide from Lake Placid was said to have shot in a single day 160 deer that were yarded up in the snow. Another guide, named Elijah Simonds, was believed to have killed more than 2,000 white-tails in his long career, along with 3,000 foxes, 150 bears, 12 wolves, and 7 panthers.[1]

As bad as the nouveaux rusticators were, though, the highest scorn was reserved for the "hotel guides" who led them. For several years during the 1880s photographer and publicist Seneca Ray Stoddard omitted lists of guides from his annual Adirondack guidebooks, saying that the profession had sunk to the point where the word was meaningless. Stoddard's postmortem was a dramatic overstatement, of course. Old-style guiding continued quite strongly until the Great Depression, at least.

---

[1] In a similar fashion, the High Peaks guides sowed the seeds of their own demise by making it too easy to get around in the woods. By the 1860s Phelps had cut not one but two trails to the summit of Marcy. He also blazed paths up Skylight, Hopkins, and Giant. In 1860 a guide named Hickok cut a trail up Whiteface from Wilmington. Lyman Epps Sr., one of the African Americans given land by Gerrit Smith, cut the first trail to the Indian Pass in the 1850s. Orson Phelps's son, Ed, and two other guides cut the Range Trail that passes over the summits of Upper Wolf jaw, Armstrong, and Gothics. When, in the twentieth century, wilderness fashion turned toward self-reliance, it followed routes blazed by the guides of the nineteenth.

"Hotel guides" at the guidehouse at Paul Smith's, by Seneca Ray Stoddard. COURTESY OF THE ADIRONDACK MUSEUM, BLUE MOUNTAIN LAKE.

The Adirondack Guides Association, which was formed in the 1890s in an attempt to professionalize the trade, struggled along until the 1950s. Guiding has never died out.

But the heyday of the mythic Great Adirondack Guide did not extend far into the twentieth century. Of course there were (and still are) exceptional guides here and there, beloved by their clients, but within a generation the Adirondack guide who had once provided access to a nostalgic vision of wilderness was becoming an object of intense nostalgia himself.

In the May 3, 1883, *Forest and Stream,* a writer who went by the name of Piseco contributed a long correspondence "about certain changes which have taken place in the character of the [Adirondack] guides, as a body, through the introduction or intrusion into their ranks of men who, while styling themselves guides, and as such receiving guides' pay and employment, have little, if any, right to claim either."

In an obligatory manner Piseco gently thumbed his nose at the multitudes, who "from their Pullman cars . . . are transferred to huge Concord stages and sent bowling over good roads behind four horses into the very heart of the mountains, and are welcomed to the hotels (whose verandahs are covered with gaily dressed ladies, all flirting, fanning and watching the girls playing croquet or lawn tennis in front) by swallow-tailed-coated waiters, and shown into reading rooms, barrooms, bedrooms, as their wishes dictate, and after shaking off the dust of travel, they can adjourn to the parlor and listen to pianos, or to the dining room, and from a well-arranged menu select their dinner."

Piseco spent most of his considerable effort complaining about the system of territoriality that had developed in the guiding profession, whereby a person was forced to change guides from lake to lake. He griped about the related problem of having to pay the first guide's way back to his home base. He hated paying a full day's rate when all he wanted was a half day.

Piseco carped about a guide who refused to show him the best fishing holes "until through self interest I gave in and fed him liberally." He fulminated about another guide who didn't adequately "bait his buoy." He said he'd seen guides spearing lake trout, or offing too many deer. Worst of all, one guide even broke his fishing rod while getting into the boat.

The good guide, Piseco said, the Great Adirondack Guide of the old variety that was harder and harder to find, was something altogether different. The good guide "selected camping grounds, felled trees and peeled bark for our shanties, fitted up balsam beds, shelves and racks, kept the camp-fires and smudges going night and day, prepared and cooked the meals, washed dishes and, nights or early morning, left me sleeping to slip away and return with venison or fish.

"When through restlessness I wearied of one spot and proposed change to some other," Piseco said, an old-fashioned guide didn't complain. Rather, he carried everything, leaving Piseco "struggling along with perhaps my rod and creel only." Best of all, a good guide was very contented with two and a half dollars a day.

The worst thing about the new hotel guide, everyone agreed, was that he was lazy and greedy. Even Adirondack Murray had said so back in 1869. This was a fatal sin for a guide. For the Great Adirondack Guide of yesteryear had far more important duties even than any of his vague philosophical roles. Namely, he did all of the work.

"Your guide if he knows his business, will do all the cooking, and wash out your undergarments," reported Adrion Ondack, another of *Forest and Stream*'s rugged correspondents.

Before getting around to the laundry, though, the guide rowed you to camp in a boat he probably built himself. The Adirondack guide boat is a thing of great beauty. The first in the classic style was probably built by Mitchell Sabattis around 1849. But many other guides and a few professional boatbuilders took pride in building and maintaining them. The ribs were cut from the roots of spruce, or tamarack, where the curve of the grain closely matched that desired for the shape of the boat. The planking was pine or cedar, cut three-tenths of an inch thick and laid flush. Add five thousand tacks, three thousand screws, and a couple of coats of clear varnish, and the boat was done. A good builder could finish one in a month. A good guide could row one loaded down with a client and gear twenty or thirty miles in a day, portages included.

After which he would build a fire and prepare "a royal dinner—venison broiled, roasted and fried, pork and beans, a course of finer game consisting of frogs' hind legs, capped off with a dessert of pancake and rice pudding, coffee, cigars, whiskey, brandy, and a delicious glass of West India Shrub, the recollection of which still makes the teeth water."

While this was in the making, the clients enjoyed a pipe, or perhaps angled for trout, or began drinking. While it was being cleaned up, again by the guides, the clients might play whist.

Before dark, the guide also built a lean-to if there was not one already on the site. First a frame of saplings was constructed. Siding and roofing was acquired by girdling good-sized spruces and hemlocks at the base and again as high as could be reached, and then peeling the bark away. This killed the trees of course, but guides figured they would make good firewood in a few more years. If it was too late in the season to peel bark, a roof could be made of fir, spruce, or hemlock bows.

This was not low-impact camping. One stormy night that Hoffman spent with Cheney "tree after tree came down." To stay warm they built a fire with twenty-foot logs, managing to ignite a couple of nearby trees in the process. Cheney reassured Hoffman that they would fall the other way when they burned through.

When a gale kicked up, Cheney exclaimed, "Tormented lightning! . . . This is too pesky bad," and cut down yet another tree to block the wind. Hoffman said the guide's last words of the evening were, "Well it's one comfort, since it's taken on to blow so, I've cut down most of the trees around us that would likely crush us during the night." John Cheney found it impossible to understand how people could survive on the Great Plains in the absence of trees.

The Adirondack lean-to is a standard icon in the lore of the park, and travel writers often marveled at their guides' indomitable self-reliance and great skill in building them. But according to Charles Lanman, even the shelters of the most famous guides were not always all they were later cracked up to be.

"The storm did not set in until about midnight, and my first intimation of its approach was the falling of rain-drops directly into my ear as I snugged up to my bed-fellow, for the purpose of keeping warm," he said of a night in a hemlock shanty on the side of Marcy with Cheney. "Desperate indeed were the efforts I made to forget my condition in sleep, as the rain fell more abundantly, and drenched me, as well as my companion, to the very skin." But the storm got worse.

"Finally Cheney rose from his pillow (which was a log of wood), and proposed that we should quaff a little brandy, to keep us from catching cold, which we did, and then made another attempt to reach the land of Nod." Lanman complained no more.

There were no doubt countless wet and cold nights such as Lanman's in the century of the Great Adirondack Guide. Cheney, especially, was famous for setting off into the woods with the barest minimum of equipment. "Got your pork? Got your matches?" he'd ask his clients just before setting off. "All right! Let's go!" But the image of a shivering fisherman snuggled up next to his guide in a leaky lean-to is not the image of the period that endures.

In the Adirondack Museum is a painting by Arthur Fitzwilliam Tait called *A Good Time Coming*. It is one of the best-known paintings of the Adirondacks that is not by Thomas Cole or Winslow Homer. It has a little bit of the feel of George Caleb Bingham's *Fur Traders on the Missouri,* at least in the bearded visage of the man seated at the far right of the picture. In the background, a rustic is approaching from the lake with a string of trout and a rifle. There are dogs, and a guide cooks over the open campfire. But the giveaway that these are not fur traders is the figure at the center of the painting. He is wearing a necktie and filling his tin cup with champagne.

And in the Concord Free Library in Concord, Massachusetts, is another painting, this one by William James Stillman. It is less famous than *A Good Time Coming* but is still quite well known among Adirondack buffs because it is the only image of Emerson's famous Philosophers' Camp done by someone who was there. In one corner, Louis Agassiz and three others earnestly dissect a fish. James Russell Lowell, Stillman himself, and several comrades practice shooting in another corner. Emerson stands alone, self-reliant in the center, absorbing it all.

Here is a memory of the Adirondacks that resonates. Guides and scientists and philosophers and jurists and painters gathered among the tall trees at the shore of Follensby Pond. The Philosophers' Camp! "Ten scholars," Emerson wrote in his memorial poem, "made free men of the forest laws. . . ." Ten famous white intellectuals, playing Indian.

One final image. This one of Thoreau, back in Concord, writing in his journal. The hermit of Walden Pond probably wasn't invited; at any rate he didn't go to the Philosophers' Camp.

"Emerson says that he and Agassiz and Company broke some dozens of ale-bottles one after another, with their bullets, in Adirondack country, using them for marks!" he wrote on August 23, 1858. "It sounds rather Cockneyish."

16   *Nowhere Like This*

At the end of an immense and rotting log that lay sticking out into Nellie Pond trout were rising, but not to assorted dry flies. This was in June. Brian McDonnell and fellow guide Jack Drury had steered the canoes across four deserted wilderness lakes. They carried the boats on their shoulders over the intervening portages, one a mile long and partly flooded. They pitched the tents, a floorless one for themselves and a modern hiker's model for the two city clients. They found a suitable tree and hoisted the food bag twenty feet up into the air; "Bears, sure, but more likely raccoons." They collected wood.

Meanwhile out on the log, the brook trout remained uncooperative. So once camp was made, McDonnell suggested a return to the canoes.

"I once ran into Lee Wulff on the Saranac River," he said as he silently paddled the umber-colored Kevlar craft around the shoreline of Bessie Pond. Bessie lies about a hundred yards from Nellie in a section of the park called the Saint Regis Canoe Area. About thirty feet behind the canoe and ten feet down, a big silver spoon McDonnell was trolling fluttered around in the water. It was supposed to attract monster trout to the barbed Mickey Finn fly that trailed a few feet farther back. Lee

Wulff, who died in 1991, was perhaps America's greatest and most famous fly fisherman; he was a man of legendary patience who became particularly well known for taking Atlantic salmon on dry flies with extremely light tackle.

"I was out with some clients and he was out fishing with his wife," McDonnell continued. Joan Wulff is herself a legendary angler, who for many years held the world record for distance casting.

"We talked a bit about the fishing, and then separated," McDonnell said. "And when I got off the river and signed out at the register, I noticed they had signed out just ahead of me. So, of course, I looked to see what they said. They had written 'Lee and Joan Wulff: fishing slow, biting worms best.' " He laughed.

Not long after, McDonnell reeled in a very nice, foot-long brookie. The bright red spots surrounded by orange halos that ran the length of its body shimmered. And on its dorsal fin was the tell-tale splotch of white that marked it as a member of the native Adirondack strain of brook trout. It was a beautiful fish, and it made the angler happy to have caught it.

Back at camp, though, it was discovered that, in the same amount of time, the two companions in the other canoe had caught and kept a string of six fish. They released as many more. Worms.

After the fire became a comfortable blaze, and the trout were eaten, whiskey was poured into Sierra Club cups. Talk turned to other trips. Some were in the Adirondacks, like the backside of the Seward Range, or the ninety-mile canoe race from Old Forge to Paul Smiths. But McDonnell was just back from a twelve-day sea kayaking adventure in Fiji with his wife, Grace, who is also a well-known Adirondack guide. So there was talk of bonefish, and a guy with a corrugated steel canoe. Then Jack Drury told of a trip up Mount McKinley many years ago during which a climber fell into a crevasse and died. Personal encounters around the globe with bears and insects were compared.

Talk turned as well to the profession of guiding. Drury runs a wilderness leadership training program at North Country Community College in Saranac Lake. McDonnell, in addition to running All Seasons Outfitters out of Saranac Lake, occasionally serves as president of the revived Adirondacks Guides Association. "One of the reasons the profession has been rejuvenated up here in the past few years is that as society has become more and more urbanized there are fewer and fewer people who have the necessary skills and the outdoor knowledge to go into the wilderness," said McDonnell at one point.

"Also," he went on, "with the growth in rock climbing and ice climbing and even hunting and fishing, the guide is becoming more and more of an instructor. It's not just a 'conquer the mountain' mentality that's making more people look for that kind of trip. I don't know if it's television, or computers, or just the age of quick response, but people want little bites of wilderness. They want to be quickly immersed for a very short period of time and then get back to their real life. So you have rock climbing and ice climbing—the idea of challenging oneself to the edge of one's limits. In some ways I think it's an attempt to have adrenaline replace actual time in the woods.

"Which is fine," he said a moment later. "But in my opinion it's no substitute. The reason for wilderness is to escape, is to get out and completely immerse yourself in the wildness of it all. I can see it in people I guide; it takes two days to get unwound and get out of their normal routine. And then they're in tune with what's around them for a few days. But the last two days of the trip, people are already starting to get geared up for going home. If you're only out there for three days, you're really just on hold."

The fire burned low. The talk died down. The bottle was put away. Tents seemed a good idea.

Happily, the next day and night were much the same. There were more lakes to explore, more fish to catch and not to catch. Not another party of human beings was seen. Rather, there were beaver, mink, muskrat, a mother merganser with a half dozen chicks, and trees too big around to hug. There was time to swim. To walk the tops of eskers. To return to camp at dusk as Venus rose, and sit on a log and trade a few more tales. And that evening the pines did, in fact, whisper.

The last day out, for a change of pace and a chance to teach some map and compass skills, McDonnell led by following his clients on a random scoot of a rigmarole up the side of the trailless Long Pond Mountain. It's not a particularly big mountain, but from the top the view is of almost nothing but forests and lakes and distant peaks. There are, here and there, a few roofs disturbing the illusion of seamless wilderness. To the south the ski slopes on Big Tupper are easy to spot as are a few buildings in the town of Tupper Lake. The airport at Saranac Lake is discernible with a little looking.

"Guide and client at Upper Ausable Inlet, with Mount Haystack in the background,"
by Seneca Ray Stoddard. COURTESY OF THE ADIRONDACK MUSEUM, BLUE
MOUNTAIN LAKE.

These intrusions are only the anomalies, really, in what is one of
the more remarkable views in the park. From the top of Long Pond
Mountain, even more than the summits of some of the High Peaks to
the east of it, the improbability of space like this in the crowded northeast corner of America is evident. The land below is not dominated by
awesome and lonely peaks, or terrifyingly sublime precipices. The
country stretching away in the three directions that offer views is gentle and well-watered, seemingly livable and inviting.

"You know what I said the other night by the fire about feeling
sometimes like I need to find some other place to live, that this place
is becoming too filled in, too crazy with people and politics?" McDonnell asked over a hiker's lunch of crackers, cheese, dry summer
sausage, and water. "Well, then I come to someplace like this and the
feeling goes away. And I think, where else would I go?"

17 *Feller-Buncher*

John Courtney III stood on the shiny steel tank treads of his purring machine and lit another cigarette. "A good operator, one who knows what he's doing with a feller-buncher, can cut and stack, oh, probably a hundred trees or more an hour," he said. "But the problem is, you can't find anyone that's any good. No one wants to learn. No one wants to work. So I end up doing it because we just can't trust anyone else."

By "we," he meant himself and his father, John Courtney Jr. Together, they ran what was one of the largest independent logging operations in the park, one of the largest in the state for that matter. In addition to this feller-buncher, they owned another one, a half dozen skidders, a giant chipper, a few semis, and assorted loaders, pickup trucks, bulldozers, and the like. In the winter of 1995, the Courtneys employed about twenty-five men, give or take a few.

A feller-buncher is like a bulldozer equipped with an enormous set of hydraulic claws on the front. The claws are capable of holding a mature tree in place while powerful pincers, like a gigantic pair of loppers, shear it off just above the ground. Then, like a rumbling beetle maneuvering the carcass of a praying mantis, the machine carries the tree upright for a distance and then lays it down—"bunches" it—neatly in a stack with about a dozen other logs. There it stays until another logger driving a skidder comes to drag the logs out of the woods.

For larger trees, John explained, the loppers can be replaced with a saw head. With that, the feller-buncher can fell and bunch trees up to two or three feet in diameter. But here, on Champion International's land just inside the park's northern border, there aren't many trees that big to cut. As his father would say, the Courtneys were just cutting junk out of the junk.

"I just know how to tell which ones to leave," Courtney explained when asked about the park regulations on how heavily one can cut private timberland without a special permit. "It's either thirty or thirty-five square feet of basal area per acre. Which isn't really a whole lot to leave behind, to tell you the truth. Basal area is the amount of growing stock of timber with tree diameter above six or eight inches. You just look at 'em and you know. It's not every single acre that has to be that way. You can cut one a little thicker and another a little lighter. When you've cut long enough, you just know what that many trees looks like."

The younger John Courtney is a good-looking guy, in his thirties, with blond hair and a ready smile. He works hard, and it's easy to imagine he knows how to have fun as well. "Hey," he said at one point, "I bet you've never seen this before," and he jumped off the treads of the feller-buncher and tramped a few dozen yards through the snow to a good-sized white birch.

The tree was one that he had chosen to leave standing. All the way up it, papery bark was peeling off in sheets about the size of phone bills. They flapped lightly in the February breeze. Courtney took out his cigarette lighter.

"This is cool," he said, and lit the tree on fire.

It took a while for the flames to take hold, longer than Courtney expected. "Usually they just go up like a torch," he said and moved back in front of the radiator of the idling feller-buncher to keep warm. His jacket was up in the heated cab and all he had on was a T-shirt. He shook his arms occasionally as he watched the tree. A moment later he said, "There it goes, now, that's more like it."

Crackling, sputtering flames licked their way up the birch, then split outward where the trunk branched. Flames worked along the dividing lines of the tree like cartoon fuses for a complicated series of bombs. Occasionally, burning bits of bark fell down to the snow, like embers from a Roman candle. Then, in less than a minute or two, all the loose bark was consumed and the fire was out.

"The best thing is," Courtney said, "it doesn't hurt the tree at all. Come back here next year and you won't be able to tell." He stood a moment watching the smoking tree.

"But you wouldn't want to try that in the summer," Courtney said and then said it again a few seconds later. "No, it wouldn't be too good an idea in the summer."

He climbed back up into the cab of the feller-buncher and pushed forward on the two levers that control the machine's movement. The feller-buncher moved through the woods on its shiny steel tank treads, and wiggled back and forth a little to position its hydraulic pincers around the base of a tree.

From a safe distance away the tree appeared to shiver only a little before being lifted straight up and carried, wobbling slightly, over to the pile. Only when Courtney allowed the tree to tip down onto the bunch did a sound resembling a tree falling ring through the woods. Then, off the great machine shambled, over the frozen ground, felling and bunching its way through the forest.

18   *Logs!*

In his unfinished book on the Adirondacks, Orson Phelps devoted several pages to a description of the view from the summit of a peak called Giant of the Valley, or simply Giant. First he looked north, to "an ocean of mountain summits." Then northwest, "down the beautiful Ausable, naturally walled by its everlasting walls of mountains." To the south was Slide Mountain, "looming up among countless numbers that are lower." West was "Tahawus, a mountain on top of mountains, and high ones at that." Southeast lay "the broad blue surface of Schroon Lake . . . and a chipped sea of broken hills that an India-rubber imagination would not think of counting."

Finally, Old Mountain Phelps looked toward New England, the wellspring of American industry. "Our next and last look is to the east, which takes in the Green Mountains of Vermont. . . . and a clearer view of Lake Champlain than [from] any other mountain," he wrote. "It has all been lumbered over and mostly burned, which gives it a desolate look."

Logs! Two and a half centuries before Phelps, Samuel de Champlain looked in the reverse direction, from lake to mountains, and reported, "The country is all covered with great and high forests." And it was. But almost as soon as people of his race moved into the woods they began cutting down trees. Perhaps a million acres cleared to make room for farms. Another quarter million for charcoal for the iron mines. Miles of "corduroy" roads, paved with logs. Miles of railroads with wooden ties. Thousands of cords for potash, for cooking, for steam, and for heat. Wood was the primary fuel of the pre-coal economy; in Manhattan in the middle of the nineteenth century the average family spent a tenth of their income on firewood.

Logs! In 1850 New York surpassed Maine and became the biggest lumber state in the union. New England by then was almost exhausted. The century of summers that belonged to quiet guides like Mitchell Sabattis and sensitive sportsmen like Joel T. Headley was also a century of winters that rang with the sound of axes. It was a time of springs when logs by the million floated out of the mountains to a place on the Hudson called "the Big Boom." It was a century during which the Adirondacks spawned a hundred timber companies that eventually failed and one called International Paper that still owns more land in the park than anyone besides the state itself.

The harvest began slowly enough. In the earliest days, every town or village worth the designation had a sawmill. There were seven thousand mills in the state of New York by 1850, two thousand of them in the Adirondacks. But these were mostly primitive operations, some nothing more than a long saw and a pit deep enough for one person to go below and help the one above hew. They weren't really in the lumber industry any more than the local gristmill was an agribusiness. And even when the sawyers were replaced by a waterwheel, the work was so slow you could "roll on a hardwood log—go in to breakfast and come out about the time the board was ready to drop from the saw."

Then, as now, the Adirondack forest was dominated by hardwoods—maples, beeches, and birches. But hardwoods don't float very well, and water was the only economical way to move a log in the days before roads and railroads. So the earliest loggers took only pine, which was easy to saw, grew near navigable water, and floated well enough to support a man.

White pine probably made up no more than 3 percent of the forest that Champlain saw stretching endlessly westward from the shore of his lake. But with millions of acres of virgin forest in the Adirondacks, the earliest loggers could afford to be selective. Young trees were left standing, not out of conservation, but merely because there were plenty of giants around for the taking—trees two hundred feet tall, with diameters of greater than six feet. Trees that were seedlings around the time Columbus was born.

By the 1820s the easy pines were already gone from the shores of Lake Champlain and along the Hudson. By 1830, the timber boom was already over in Ticonderoga. The center of operations moved to Glens Falls, on the Hudson, and the tree of choice became spruce.

Spruce probably made up about 15 percent of the original Adirondack forest. It's not a towering giant of the forest like the pine, but it floats. And that's all that mattered to the timber speculator and lumberjack alike. Once the pines were gone, to the logger spruce was the only tree in the forest.[1]

For the rest of the century, the term "merchantable timber" meant spruce alone. Land was valued and sold according to how much spruce it had on it. When the spruce was gone, a tract was considered worthless. Worse than worthless, even. Seventy-five percent of the trees were still on the ground—the giant maples and birches—but without spruce the forest was a liability that was best allowed to revert to the state for nonpayment of taxes.

It is tempting to say that there was no philosophical concept of wilderness at the heart of the logging enterprise as it developed in the Adirondacks in the second half of the 1800s. This isn't to suggest that the men who ran logging companies were somehow greedier or more driven by economic forces from outside the region than were the builders of mines or hotels. They weren't. And the early farmers possessed no greater degree of "respect," in any modern sense of the word, for the original ecosystem of the Adirondacks than the timber cutters. The environmental impact of logging on the forest, at least in the decades before railroads allowed the harvesting of hardwoods,

---

[1] The only other tree that was taken in any significant amount during the first half of the century was the hemlock. More than a hundred tanneries were located around the periphery of the park by 1840, and beside most of these were barn-sized piles of hemlock bark, which provided tannin for the leather curing process. Crews of men delved into the backcountry every spring and early summer, when the bark was loose enough to peel. The chopper would fell the tree, then the fixer would notch it at four-foot intervals and slice the bark up the length of the log, then the spudder would go to work with a two-foot wedge called a spud and remove the bark. Probably two-thirds of the hemlocks in the Adirondacks were stripped of bark and left to rot before the tanning industry moved to the Midwest.

was actually far less severe than that of charcoal making or field clearing.

Because of the nature of their chosen endeavors, however, farmers and miners took a longer view of the region. They attempted to transform the wilderness into something else, be it a pastoral idyll or a manufacturing center. They imagined towns growing, maybe even cities. They built houses that in a few cases are still standing. They built churches. If only by default, as the reflected opposite of these imagined futures, as everything the Adirondacks were not but could yet be, they possessed an idea of wilderness.

Logging camps, by contrast, were usually built to fall down within a few years. With the exception of a handful of experiments in sustainable silvaculture on large private estates, the logger's wilderness strategy was to cut out and get out. The timber industry had done pretty much that in New England before it got to the Adirondacks, and there was still a continent of forest to go between New York and Alaska. From the company offices where land was bought or sold or abandoned, the land and waters of the Adirondacks were merely variables in a series of calculations regarding merchantable timber and distance to market. There was no forest, really, only trees. And only spruce trees, to be specific. The schism between human and wild was, in a sense, total.

To stretch the model of the three earliest European responses to wilderness to something approaching an extreme, the logging industry's strategy was closer to the Dutch traders' in Albany than to that of the Jesuit missionaries or the English colony builders. Individual lumberjacks had to physically go into the forest, to be sure, and they developed an intimate knowledge of the natural world from their life there. Many were guides in the off-season. But if there had still been enough Iroquois in the Adirondacks, and if they could be convinced to cut the spruce for cheaper than the French Canadian immigrants and others who populated the typical logging camp, one imagines the lumber barons perfectly happy to sit in a fortress in Glens Falls and wait for the logs to come floating down.

Cutting was usually done during late fall and early winter. This was in part because timber left lying through the summer attracted woodworms, and even more because most loggers preferred to spend the warmer months farming or guiding. Smaller crews were employed through the summer and early fall building logging roads and constructing camps where the seasonal men would stay.

The first time through a piece of forest, the loggers took nothing smaller than twelve inches in diameter. Using single-bit axes they chopped a notch halfway through the trunk about two or three feet off the ground. Careful loggers would lay their ax in the notch with its back at the inside. If the notch was true, the handle would point toward the intended direction, and a final chopping opposite and slightly above the notch could begin. If, on the other hand, the ax pointed toward another tree, a few more swings of the ax corrected the cut. This was worth the little bit of extra effort; trees that got hung up on other trees were called "widowmakers."

Generally, though, the loggers were very good. At Indian Lake, Headley observed some men across the lake "driving trees." For three hours he watched "five as good choppers as ever swung an ax" notch trees almost to the point of falling. But instead of felling the trees one at a time, they moved up the hill in a line. And after about twenty trees were notched, the top tree was felled directly onto the one below it. Like dominos, Headley said, the whole row fell.

After a tree was felled it was cut, or "bucked," into salable logs, which were sometimes called "markets." The standard Adirondack log was thirteen feet four inches long, and its value was calculated on the basis of how much larger or smaller than nineteen inches it was in diameter at the thin end. Five markets contained around a thousand board feet of sawed lumber.

The number of markets in a given tree, of course, depended on the size of the trunk. Surprisingly, this had little to do with the tree's age. A spruce can live for four hundred years, but it does not grow nearly as consistently as pine, hemlock, maple, and birch.

Spruce seedlings typically take root in the shade of their elders, or perhaps beneath a stand of balsam fir that have recolonized a silted-in beaver pond. For the first hundred years the young trees stretch for the light, gaining significantly in girth only if a blowdown or logging opens the canopy above. A hundred-year-old spruce tree can be eighty feet tall and only a few inches in diameter at the base. Or, if the soil and light are right, the same aged tree could be seventy-five feet tall and almost two feet at the base. On the other hand, a tree with the latter dimensions could be over three hundred years old.

During its second century of life the tree fills out, usually reaching its average height of between eighty and ninety feet and average girth of around nineteen inches. After two hundred years in the forest, spruce begin to grow much more slowly, concentrating on producing cones. According to a study done in 1901, the average length of a spruce crown for all situations and soils was forty feet, and the clear trunk was around thirty feet. From such a tree, "the average length of merchantable log was found to be about 46 feet." Which is to say, an Adirondack spruce usually contained about three and a half market logs.

In midwinter, work started long before dawn, by the light of lanterns stuck on poles in the snow, and ended when it became dark again. A good lumberjack with a sharp ax could cut seventy logs a day for a month. The more he chopped the more he made, and a hundred logs a day was not an unheard-of output. But generally, such a pace couldn't be maintained day in and day out for the whole season of fifteen-hour days. Not without ruining arms and shoulders, anyway.

For this a lumberjack received, at midcentury, about seventy-five cents a day. Unless it was raining too hard, in which case there was no

Unidentified Adirondack logging camp. COURTESY OF THE ADIRONDACK MUSEUM, BLUE MOUNTAIN LAKE.

work and no pay. Pay was often in company scrip that was good only at selected local stores and bars, or at the camp commissary. When the men came into town with their wages—well, loggers were not known as savers.

A logger also got room and board. "Room" generally meant a bunk next to anywhere from fifteen to forty-five other bunks in the attic of a rough log building. It was a decidedly rustic existence. Bunkhouses were thrown together rapidly by advance crews during the fall, along with a blacksmith's shack and maybe an office and commissary. Since the buildings were built to last at most three or four years, freezing drafts were not uncommon; bread dough wouldn't rise unless the cooks kept it warm with lanterns.

If the camp wasn't large enough to justify a freestanding cook-house, the ground floor of the bunkhouse was usually divided into two rooms. One was the kitchen and dining area, where by tradition the men were absolutely forbidden from going except during mealtimes. The other was the "men's room," where the cooks, who were usually women, were not allowed to go at any time.

Interestingly, given the usual pay differential between men and women both then and now, cooks were often the highest-paid employ-ees at the camp. This may have been simply because no woman in her right mind would choose to spend the winter in a barn with forty-five ax-bearing men for less than top dollar. But it is also true that there was plenty of work involved in the job. Loggers and log drivers kept warm mainly by eating prodigiously.

Flapjacks were consumed in almost inconceivable numbers, as were eggs. Breakfasts of a dozen of each were commonplace. Forty men in Jones Ordway's camps along the Rock Creek polished off four hundred boiled eggs at a single dinner. And boiled eggs weren't the main course. Beans were. Beans always were. Beans with salt pork and bread, or once in a while, some venison or bear. After dinner the log-gers retired to the men's room to sharpen their axes, to smoke a pipe. And then upstairs to the hard bunks to sleep, perchance to belch.

If the job of logging ended with the chopping, the money to be made by speculators in the lumber business would have been great indeed. Surveys in the 1880s estimated that there was an average of sixteen large spruces to an acre in the park, or about a day's worth of chopping for a good ax-man. And there were plenty of acres with a great deal more spruce than that. As late as 1870, virgin timberland in the Adirondacks sold for seventy cents an acre. For around a dollar-seventy, then, the boss could expect to have sixty or seventy market logs.

But a log lying on the forest floor fifty, sixty, or even a hundred miles from the nearest sawmill isn't good for much more than sitting on and pondering the hidden meaning of nature. At least half of the labor and expense in the lumber business was spent getting the market logs from where they grew to the market. It was all part of the ongoing calculation.

After felling, limbing, and bucking, the thirteen-foot logs were drawn or skidded by horses or oxen to the nearest skidway. A skidway was usually not much more than a couple of sturdy logs laid side by side, across which the market logs would be piled. The skids were often built up at a lesser angle than the slope of the land, so that a sled could later be drawn up beneath the downhill end to be loaded.

According to Harold Hochschild's history of logging in the Blue Mountain Lake area, a pair of lumberjacks would typically wait at the skidway in order to "jack" the logs up onto it as they were dragged out of the woods by the teamsters. For most of the century, they used what they called a "barefoot lever." This was a six-foot pole of ash or hickory, about three inches thick, with a flattened end. In later decades, these were replaced with pikes and peaveys, which had iron tips, and a hook that went around the log to allow the lumberjack to grab on.

Once up on the skids, a log could be rolled down to its resting place. As the pile grew, the lumberjacks might lay smaller logs perpendicular to the others so that they could roll the heavier logs on up to the top. When, finally, it was as high as they dared pile it, or when all the logs in the vicinity were cut and stacked, the lumberjacks moved on to another skidway. Sometimes, as a crew worked its way up a slope, skidways were built end to end like steps all the way up the mountain.

As soon as enough snow fell to use the rough sled roads that had been built in the fall, the loggers were called off of cutting and skidding. It was time to get the logs from the skidways to the river's edge, or the "banking ground." This was called "bobbing," which was derived from "bobsled," which in turn probably came from the Algonquin word "toboggan." It was an apt usage; at times, a trip down an icy and steep road on top of a pile of logs ten or twelve feet high could be one hell of a sled ride. It could, in fact, be deadly.

Loggers were understandably quite inventive when it came to methods of slowing their own progress down the hill. One common type of sled used in the highest elevations allowed the back end of the logs to drag on the ground. If this wasn't sufficient, or if the logs were on a sled that didn't allow them to drag, various cramponlike devices could be clamped onto the runners. Chains and ropes could be wrapped around the critical areas. Occasionally, a rope might be attached to the back end of a load and then wrapped a few times around a sturdy hardwood at the top of a particularly steep stretch. A couple of loggers could then provide a belay.

As a final resort, hay or dirt could be thrown on the sled tracks. But this was generally avoided. The last thing you needed on your way down the side of a slippery mountain was to smell smoke and look down to see that your runners were on fire.

On flatter ground, the problem was sometimes reversed. It was the job of the company "road monkey," often a teenager, to run along with a snow shovel and a tank of water to even out and ice over the tracks. The road monkey was also responsible for making certain the tracks didn't become so uneven that the load of logs would topple the sled. In the 1890s, special sprinkler wagons came into use on the flats. When finally the logs were at the nearest river's edge, they were once again piled onto enormous skidways, this time to wait for the breakup of the ice in the spring.

In the earlier decades of the industry, when there were still great white pines growing near the water, logs were skidded individually and then lashed together into rafts at the water's edge. It took five days to guide a raft of logs down Lake Champlain to the Saint Lawrence. The timber rafts that went down the Hudson in 1758, and probably earlier, were usually made of already sawed wood. Thirty or more layers of inch-thick boards, sixteen feet long, were crisscrossed over each other. These were held together by "grub stakes," or poles cut from saplings, and then chained together into what was called a "five-platform piece."

As the river widened, larger rafts were made by securing three or more five-platform pieces side by side. A hundred and eighty thousand board feet of green lumber rode pretty low, barely breaking the surface of the water. All the boatmen had were poles and oars to keep the mass in the current. And away from lumber pirates; in 1804 the state Legislature passed a law making it illegal to steal a raft of timber.

But the new law was already almost moot; rafts didn't survive into the spruce era. In 1813 a couple of innovative brothers named Fox, who were cutting spruce in the Brant Lake area, simply chucked their logs into the Schroon River without bothering to make them up into rafts. They set up a boom across the stream farther down to collect them again. Other operators quickly started doing the same, and in 1825 the Legislature again visited the issue of timber thieves, this time requiring that all logs sent down the Hudson be branded. From then on, as logs arrived at the river's edge from the woods, they were stamped with special hammers bearing the mark of the company that owned them.

The loose-log drive was an Adirondack invention that ultimately spread to lumber camps across the country, wherever softwoods were cut. Driving became infused with a lore and tradition that were equal to, or even greater than, those of the logging camp. For as dangerous as felling and sledding trees could be, nothing required more skill and daring than driving loose logs down an icy river to the Hudson and then down that river to the Big Boom at Glens Falls.

The excitement and danger began with the very first stage, at the "rolling banks," or "banking grounds." All winter long the logs accumulated by the riverside on immense skidways. When the logging in the Blue Mountain Lake area was at its peak the pile of logs along the side of Balsam Lodge Stream, the banking ground of Jones Ordway's operation, stretched for three solid miles. As soon as the ice broke up in the spring, it was some unfortunate logger's job to go below the huge skids and loosen the wedge that held the logs in place. It was a task, one romantic travel writer noted, that produced at least as much anxiety as the most dehumanizing urban job.

There was a friendly competition among the hundred or so logging outfits in the Adirondacks to be first on the river. This was only partly a matter of pride; the earlier one's logs were on their way the more water there would be in the river, and the faster they were likely to get to Glens Falls. To boost the flow, loggers often constructed dams both on the rivers they were using and on tiny feeder streams. Where such dams existed—and they were everywhere in the Adirondacks—they were opened a half hour or so before the log drive was to begin. When the resulting surge had reached about two miles downstream, the logs were added to the maelstrom.

More water was also marginally safer for the men. Though too much water could cause large logjams to be even more treacherous than they might otherwise be, insufficient water made jams more frequent. And logjams were even more voracious widowmakers than hung-up trees.

A jam started when one log hung up on a boulder in the river. Then the others would get caught on that key log until the whole thing stopped. If the current was strong enough, and fast enough, logs would pile up on top of each other until some were out of the water entirely. Such jams generally grew up the length of the river as opposed to across it, though if there was a bend in the river they might extend from shore to shore.

Generally speaking, the job of every log driver was to keep those logs moving, thus hopefully preventing jams from forming in the first place. Drivers were positioned permanently at strategic corners, or out in the river on rocks where jams were known to occur. They stood there for hours on some slippery rock, deflecting the oncoming logs with a ten-foot pike, or a peavey. On their wet feet they wore a pair of Croghans—stiff leather boots made by one of three shoemakers in the town of Croghan, New York—over thick wool socks. In their mouths, by tradition, was a pipe.

The guys who always managed to end up tending an easy patch of river were derisively called "high bankers," and a road monkey got more respect. A much more honorable title was that of "rider." Riders floated down the river's edge on a particularly fat log, poking and prodding the shore-bound stragglers, moving them along as a cowboy might encourage uncooperative dogies. Their favorite sport was birling, in which one person tries to run another off a log.

But jams were an inevitable part of the profession, and experienced drivers on any given river knew the bad spots. Among the worst on the upper Hudson were between the village of Blue Ledge and the sharp turn called Deer Den, just below the river's confluence with the Boreas. Also bad was the Hudson River Gorge below Newcomb, where several companies now do a good business taking tourists down the rapids in rubber rafts. It was bad at the Moulton Bars at Warrensburg, and the Boreas River was bad for thirteen-foot logs all the way down its length.

Experienced river drivers also knew the easy stretches, an old logger named "Yankee John" Galusha told a writer named Peter Fosburgh

Driving loose logs, as opposed to rafts, was an Adirondack invention. COURTESY ADIRONDACK MUSEUM, BLUE MOUNTAIN LAKE.

in 1905. Here the riders picked out good logs and rode them for miles, he said, smoking their pipes and watching the scenery go by. Galusha drove logs on the North and the Boreas Rivers for two decades starting in 1876. But when a log rider heard the roar of rapids up ahead, where the Indian River joined the Hudson for instance, pipes and tobacco were put away. "The jam stretch," Galusha said it was called, and the log drivers hated it.

As soon as a jam formed, the foreman asked for volunteers, and whoever felt like a hero that day took his pike, picked up his ax and maybe a stick of dynamite, and went and got in the jam boat. Jam boats followed behind most log drives and were carried around to the front only as needed. They were usually about fourteen feet long and four feet wide, with a relatively flat bottom and no keel for maneuverability. They held three men, with the oarsman in the middle.

The trick to breaking a jam was finding the key log, the single piece of wood that held the whole mass back. When the jam boat approached, from downstream, the bow man hooked onto a stuck log and the oarsman jumped out and secured the boat. Then the men with pikes and axes went to work, slowly and carefully trying to unlock the mess. When the key log was located, they chopped at it very slowly. A few swings, and then a break to listen to the shifting logs. "Did you hear that?" This way, the key log could be coaxed to break slowly, leaving enough time to get back in the boat and get away.

Hopefully. When big jams finally broke loose, they could do so with terrifying speed and noise. So at the first shifting of the mass, the first sound of creaking and groaning logs, the first hint of a bend in the key log, the men got themselves back to the waiting oarsman and the relative safety of the boat. The oarsman's job, in fact, was considered by some to be the most important of the three, and the man who did it was usually paid twice as much as the others. As the logs began to loosen, he had to keep the boat from getting tangled among them and lost, and then once the men were back on board he had to row with all his might to keep from getting crushed in the oncoming mass.

Sometimes, though, the boat would be pulling away from the jam and the logs would stop moving again. This was an occasion for expletives. And, occasionally, explosives. Going back the second time was even more hair-raising than the first. Ultimately, though, every jam was broken. But sometimes men died. Yankee John Galusha remembered the names of seven friends of his who were killed breaking logjams: Dillon, Houghton, Lewis, Frenchie, McGar, Bruno, Culver, and Repetoi.

Repetoi may have perished trying to save another man, whose name was Russ Carpenter. According to one version of the story, the two men had been showing off by racing their jam boats down through a run of logs. At Deer Den, Carpenter's luck failed. His boat was smashed to splinters and he went under the churning mass of logs. Then Repetoi, too, was lost.

Repetoi's body was apparently found soon after, but Carpenter's corpse was nowhere to be found. A few months later, though, some schoolchildren found a red handkerchief sticking up out of a gravel bed near Stony Creek. Stony Creek is more than twenty miles downstream from Deer Den. When the children dug the handkerchief out, they found it was still tied around Carpenter's neck.

Partly because of the dangers involved, the pay was generally better for log driving than it was for cutting and skidding. At turn of century on the Hudson, rivermen, as the ones who worked the shore were called, made about a dollar and a half a day. And the boatmen who worked the jams got more. On the upper drive of the Hudson, from the mouth of the Indian River to the mouth of the Boreas River—"the jam stretch"—the rate was occasionally four dollars a day.

Higher wages may also have been necessary to offset the living conditions during the drive, which were even less hospitable than those in the lumber camps. The men slept side by side in open dirt-floored lean-tos that were anywhere from twenty to forty-five feet long. Each was allotted a strip of floor about a foot wide and slept with either his head or his feet toward the roaring fire that ran the length of the structure.

The workday was marginally shorter than it was during the cutting season, because it was impossible to drive logs by lantern light, but the men were still out by around three in the morning. They stood around, eating beans and eggs, stamping their Croghans in the snow, waiting for first light.

They came back to camp at dark, usually soaking wet. But no one changed. The cook and cookie, no longer women, would have already built the fire up to a roar and the drivers steamed themselves dry while eating ham and beans ladled from an enormous kettle. Then maybe they smoked a pipe, stood around some more, and went back to sleep. It was hard on a body; log drivers over the age of thirty-five were rare. Pretty much anyone who stuck with the business that long, and managed to avoid being killed in a logjam, retired with rheumatism.

The efficiency of loose-log driving allowed spruce logging to work its way up the rivers into the very heart of the park. The same expanding economy that produced romantic travel writers with the time and inclination to craft a literature of wilderness escape had at last discovered where the money could reliably be made in the north woods. Namely, by removing whatever would float.

Logs! Year after year, the timber companies came to the State Assembly requesting that rivers and streams, some of them barely navigable by canoe, be declared public highways. The list is indicative of the loggers' progress. In 1846 the lawmakers opened the Saranac River and all its branches and lakes, followed by the Raquette in 1850; the Moose, Chateaugay, and Schroon in 1851; the Black and Beaver in 1853; the Salmon, the lower West Branch of the Saint Regis, parts of the Oswegatchie and Grass Rivers, and West Canada Creek in 1854; more of the Grass and the Great Chazy River in 1857; more of the Saint Regis in 1860; the West Branch of the Schroon in 1865; the Deer River, Mill Brook, and Trout Brook in 1867; all of the branches of the Sacandaga in 1869; Platt Brook in 1870; Cold Brook and Otter Creek in 1872; and the rest of the Oswegatchie in 1878.

Other laws facilitated the blasting of channels where the streams were too shallow, and the building of dams where the flow was deemed insufficient. During the same winters that Adirondack Murray and his fellow romantic travelers were polishing up their manuscripts and planning their next adventures, loggers were building dams on the tiniest of tributaries, sometimes stepping streams high up the sides of mountains in order to build up a big enough surge for driving the logs.

The dams were like a thousand valves in the great, gravity-fed, hydraulic wood-delivery machine that the Adirondack wilderness was becoming. With enough ice and water, and the judicious tweaking of the controls, a spruce could be cut at three thousand feet up the side of the Seward Range and sent on its way all the way out of the park to the saws at the end of the line.

In truly fast water, logs might go thirty miles in half a day, but normally on the Hudson an unimpeded log traveled only about two miles an hour. From Newcomb, the trip might only take a couple of days. From Durant Lake it might take a month. On the other hand, a log might get stuck somewhere for a few years, waiting for another flood like the one that left it high and dry. In order to round up the stragglers, there was always a second, "fly drive," after the main drive. Timber companies assumed that three years were necessary for all the logs cut in any given year to finally make it through. But eventually, the logs found their way to the Big Boom.

The Big Boom was located below the park at a place the river men called the Big Bend of the Hudson, about four miles above the town of Glens Falls. Built between the years 1849 and 1851, it was quite a feat of engineering and organization. Below the main boom, which stretched from shore to shore and stopped all the logs coming down, the river was divided by smaller booms into several channels leading to various mills and docks. At the head of each fork in the current was anchored a floating platform, and log drivers stood with pikes and peaveys ready to direct the oncoming logs to their left or right. With a poke and a prod, the hundreds of thousands of Adirondack logs that collected above the main boom were sorted and sent to the waiting mills.

By 1862 there were so many logs coming out of the park, and so many companies going after them, that a partnership was formed to sort out the costs of the Hudson River portion of the drive. This was probably an inevitable outcome, given that if two drives met on the river somewhere above the Big Boom, there was no way to keep the logs of one company from mixing with those of the other.

The agreement began with the words "Whereas, the undersigned are engaged more or less in floating logs down the Hudson River and its tributaries." But with the price of driving a log on the Hudson usually working out to around two cents, "more" turned out to be a better description of the logging business in those decades than "less." In 1850 there were 132,000 logs collected at Glens Falls. In 1859, when the Big Boom broke, half a million logs went surging downstream as far as Troy. And in the early 1870s, precisely when Murray's Fools were rushing to the Adirondack wilderness to restore their souls, upwards of a million logs a year were floating down out of the mountains to the Big Boom.

The decline in spruce began soon thereafter. By 1885 some two-thirds of the forest in the Adirondacks had been cut over for spruce at least once. Much of it had already produced a second cut about fifteen years after the first. Whereas the first loggers generally took only those trees greater than a foot in diameter, the second round harvested down to ten inches.

Guide and client crossing a logjam on the upper Hudson River, circa 1900, by Norman S. Foote. COURTESY OF THE ADIRONDACK MUSEUM, BLUE MOUNTAIN LAKE.

After 1868, the development of a wood-pulp-based paper industry changed the calculations of profitability significantly. By the 1880s loggers were being sent back into many places for a third time. Trees five inches in diameter were cut and sent down the river. Spruce was getting hard to find; by the end of the century, some loggers were reduced to peeling hemlock logs, which made them float.

Surprisingly, perhaps, the impact on the forest of all this cutting and skidding and floating was less than catastrophic. Here and there spruce might have accounted for 40 percent of the forest, and once in a while lucky loggers found nearly pure "spruce swamps." But generally spruce was found mixed in with hardwoods on lower slopes; the richer the soil the fewer the spruce. Since spruce probably represented only about 15 percent of the original forest, in all likelihood the ecology of the smaller rivers took more of a beating than that of the forest itself.

According to Barbara McMartin's analysis, "as late as 1885 no more than fifteen to thirty percent of the forest cover had been taken from little more than a third of the original park." McMartin also found that most of the logging done during the period was within a mile of a stream, and six miles at most. In 1885 the state's Forest Commission reported that the "great northern forest contained nearly two million acres of virgin timber and 1.3 million acres from which only softwoods had been removed." The impact of logging on the forest before 1890, McMartin concludes, was "minor."

The loggers, however, were by no means finished. And more importantly for the future of the park, in the last decades of the 1800s the public's opinion of logging in the Adirondacks bore no resemblance to McMartin's modern statistical findings.

19   *Forever Wild*

In the January 24, 1885, issue of *Harper's* magazine two engravings of Adirondack scenes appeared. In the first, cool water flowed merrily down a series of low, moss-covered ledges, shaded by towering trees. "A Feeder of the Hudson, as it was," read the caption.

In the image on the facing page moss, soil, trees, and water are all gone. In their place is a wide vista of dry boulders and parched slopes, rising up to a barren peak. A single smoldering stump dominates the foreground. It was, the caption announced, "A feeder of the Hudson, as it is."

This was the popular image of the Adirondack timber industry at the end of the nineteenth century. To pilgrims visiting Old Phelps, consumptives seeking balsamic breezes, and sportsmen and women after deer and trout, it didn't really matter who had actually cut down the trees. Some of the clearing was done by farmers already gone west. Much was the work of charcoal makers in the employ of iron mines. There were the hemlock peelers who supplied the tanning industry with bark, and there were massive fires ignited by sparks and embers falling from the smokestacks of passing steam engines. Nor did it matter that the cutting was concentrated along the roads and rivers the tourists frequented. As far as the public was concerned, rapacious loggers were destroying the wilderness.

But it wasn't a concern for tourism, or any nascent ideas about the intrinsic value of wild places, that drove the Legislature in 1885 to take the first concrete step toward preserving the Adirondacks. As the second engraving in *Harper's* shows, the predicted aftermath of human civilization was no longer the moist, leafy place that Thomas Cole depicted in the final painting of *The Course of Empire*. The end of civilization was now a barren and dry desert. And a desert at the source of water for the Hudson River and the Erie Canal did not bode well for the future prosperity of the Empire State.

At worst, New York would be deprived of access to the West, the asset that had allowed it to surpass Boston and Philadelphia to become the commercial center of the country. At best, New Yorkers would be held hostage by the railroad interests that had constructed lines paralleling the water route. The creation of the Adirondack Forest Preserve in 1885, and of the Adirondack Park seven years later, was justified in these purely utilitarian terms.

Not even the sporting press, which surely saw the benefit for its readers of habitat preservation, was yet willing to argue in favor of wilderness for its own sake. "If the Adirondacks are cleared, the Hudson River will dry up," *Forest and Stream* warned in 1883.

The popular idea that desertification followed deforestation had its roots in the 1864 publication of George Perkins Marsh's *Man and Nature*. The book contained its share of fine prose about the relationship of the individual to the surrounding world but it was not, essentially, a piece of philosophical nature writing. Nor was it the woodsy proselytizing of Adirondack Murray or Joel T. Headley. *Man and Nature* was perhaps the first truly ecological book; more Louis Agassiz than Ralph Waldo Emerson, more *Silent Spring* than *Walden*.

Marsh argued that when forests are indiscriminately removed, the capacity of the land to hold water is diminished. Wetlands dry up. Runoff accelerates, as does erosion. Marsh was a Vermonter familiar with the Adirondacks, but his primary example of the consequences of clearing were the once lush lands surrounding the Mediterranean. There were places in the Old World, he warned, where "the operation of causes set in action by man has brought the face of the earth to a desolation almost as complete as that of the moon."

Just as Agassiz came to very different conclusions about the past than his contemporaries, Marsh, by "prolonging the harmless and undestructive rate of geological change" forward through time made prognostications very different from those of Thomas Cole and the Romantics. The invading hordes of barbarians in *The Course of Empire* were unnecessary when creeping desertification would do the job of bringing down human society. Even more critically for future images of wilderness, Cole's small solace that in the aftermath of human corruption the world returns to something close to its prehuman condition is absent from Marsh's analysis.

Though Marsh believed a healthy wilderness was self-regulating and self-sustaining, its particular attributes were far from inevitable. By his way of thinking, which is remarkably close to the majority of scientific opinion today, nature will find a new equilibrium after the forests are removed. It might even be a new "wilderness," but there was no reason to assume it would be one of cool waters, moist soils, and reinvigorating balsamic breezes.

Thus the Adirondack wilderness that was once a part of the impenetrable seat of Satan himself; that defeated thousands of farmers and drove Charles Frederick Herreshoff to end his life; that was the antidote to all the ills of urban existence, turned out to be, in fact, a fragile place. If "another era of equal human crime and human improvidence" were to take place, Marsh warned, total extinction of the human species was quite possible.

As contemporary as Marsh's ecological jeremiad sounds, he wasn't a wilderness advocate in the modern sense. He believed sustainable harvest of wild resources was probably possible. Through the application of scientific management, America, with so much forest still intact, could avoid the disasters that befell the Middle East. But only if it discarded the Separatist habit of viewing human endeavor as something apart from the larger workings of the world.

Throughout the 1870s and '80s, Marsh's logic became the basis for a movement to save what remained of the Adirondack forest. The loudest voice of the period was that of an odd crusader from Albany named Verplanck Colvin. As early as the late 1860s Colvin began arguing for a park of some sort in the Adirondacks. And in 1870, he began what would become a multi-decade effort to pressure the Assembly in Albany into acting. That year Colvin submitted a report on his ascent of Mount Seward to the New York State Museum of Natural History that was included in its report to the legislature.

"I desire to call your attention to a subject of much importance," he wrote. "The Adirondack Wilderness contains the springs which are the sources of our principal rivers, and the feeders of our canals. Each summer the water supply for these rivers and canals is lessened, and commerce has suffered. The United States government has been called upon, and has expended vast sums in the improvement of the navigation of the Hudson: yet the secret origin of the difficulty seems not to have been reached.

"The immediate cause has been the chopping and burning off of vast tracts of forest in the wilderness, which have hitherto sheltered from the sun's heat and evaporation the deep and lingering snows, the brooks and rivulets, and the thick, soaking, sphagnous moss which, at times knee-deep, half water and half plant, forms hanging lakes upon the mountain sides."[1]

Colvin's wasn't the most alarmist voice, either. There were worries that the flooding caused by log drivers was dislodging boulders and sediment that would ultimately make its way all the way down to the harbor of New York City and fill it in. There was fear that dessicated wetlands of the Adirondacks would send malarial vapors wafting south. Flash floods threatened.

"In any event," summarized Frank Graham Jr. in his fine political history of the park, "the lumbermen and railroad magnates came to be seen as twin threats to the city's economic well-being, and the Adirondacks a key to its survival."

In 1872, the year that Yellowstone National Park was established, Verplanck Colvin was appointed by the Legislature to survey the Adirondack region. He became a man obsessed. He repeatedly drove his crews to near rebellion with midnight descents down trailless peaks, on which he had lingered too long with his compass and sextant. That first year he and his assistants traced the Hudson to its highest source, a tiny pond on the side of Mount Marcy that Colvin described as a "tear of the clouds," and the name stuck.

[1] Colvin's notion of "hanging lakes" is largely discredited, but studies done across Lake Champlain in the Green Mountains of Vermont during the 1970s by University of Vermont scientists found that pine trees do indeed "comb" between five and thirty additional inches of precipitation a year from the fog.

Over and over again in his semiannual reports, Colvin urged the Legislature to create a park in the Adirondacks: "I shall hereafter show that the practical continuance of the canals, or their enlargement for shipping purposes, whether it be the Erie, the Champlain, or the Black River, depends in the future, as it does almost entirely at present on the numerous rivers of the wilderness," he wrote at the beginning of his 1873–74 report. "There is not a builder, or a farmer throughout the state but is interested in preserving from fire and destruction the vast forest which covers from three to five thousand square miles of northern New York."

The Legislature, being a legislature, responded with more study commissions, which they then usually ignored. One headed by Colvin recommended that a park of about 1.75 million acres be created, and Colvin worked the hallways of the state capitol tirelessly pushing it. During the same period the *New York Times* began a long tradition of editorializing in favor of state action to preserve the forests. But nothing came of Colvin's original park proposal.

The state did, however, begin to accumulate land. As mentioned earlier, throughout the century it was a standard practice among lumber companies to default on their property taxes once the merchantable spruce had been removed from any piece of land. For the state's part, when tax auctions occurred it had long been the policy to accept almost anything rather than hold the land. Land sales occurred at a pace that outdid even the great speculators of the Revolutionary War era. According to McMartin's calculations, by 1900 all of the land in the park with the exception of two townships had been auctioned off at some time for taxes.

It was a thoroughly corrupt system; loggers often defaulted and then rebought land for less than they originally owed. Others were able to buy land that was in default, log on it, then default themselves before ever paying a cent. The system is redeemed in hindsight only by the fact that it allowed the state to collect a sizable nucleus of generally spruceless, but still mostly wooded, lands for the future park.

In 1872, when Colvin began pushing his idea for a park, the state owned only 40,000 acres in the Adirondacks. In 1883 the state quietly discontinued selling land back to loggers, accelerating the buildup that was already in progress. By 1884, when another study commission, under the chairmanship of Harvard professor Charles Sargent, warned

Water conservation was the primary impetus for the state's first actions to protect the Adirondacks. "Bog River Falls, Adirondacks," circa 1885, by Seneca Ray Stoddard.
COURTESY OF THE ADIRONDACK MUSEUM, BLUE MOUNTAIN LAKE.

the Legislature that the region was being reduced to "an unproductive and dangerous desert," the state owned over 700,000 acres.

Or a lot more, or a lot less; one measure of the convoluted nature of the state's holdings is that no two sources report the same number of original acres in the Forest Preserve.

Like Colvin's commission a dozen years earlier, Sargent's recommended that state land in the Adirondacks be kept as a Forest Preserve. Unlike its predecessor, this commission was heeded. On May 15, 1885, Governor David Hill signed a law creating the first half of the two-part legal structure that today regulates development in the Adirondacks. The law stated that all state lands in the various Adirondack counties, plus some land in the Catskills, "shall constitute and be known as the Forest Preserve."

The law further stated, "The lands now or hereafter constituting the Forest Preserve shall be forever kept as wild forest lands. They shall not be sold, nor shall they be leased or taken by any person or corporation, public or private."

Seven years later, it was apparent that unless the scattershot holdings that made up the Forest Preserve were combined into a larger, contiguous reserve, there was no real hope of protecting the watershed. In 1892, therefore, the Legislature and Governor Roswell P.

Flower created the Adirondack Park. A blue line encircling some 2.8 million acres was drawn on an official map, with the hope that the state would concentrate its efforts to acquire Forest Preserve land within "the Blue Line," as the park's boundary thereafter became known. The legislation boldly stated that the new park would "be forever reserved, maintained and cared for as ground open for the free use of all the people for their health and pleasure, and as forest lands necessary to the preservation of the headwaters of the chief rivers of the State, and a future timber supply."

The language was uplifting, but in practical terms it wasn't much of a park, if protection of the land within its borders is the measure. The general hope of the Legislature was that one day the state would own all of the land within the Blue Line, but in 1892 New York owned less than a fifth of it. On the other four-fifths of the Adirondacks there were no restrictions whatsoever.

For that matter, it wasn't much of a Forest Preserve either. Despite the "forever wild" tone of the enabling legislation, there were hardly any restrictions on Forest Preserve land. Fire starters were to be punished, and railroads were required to cut the brush near their tracks. There was to be a warden and some inspectors to enforce the rules. But, significantly, the legislative acts creating both the Forest Preserve and the Adirondack Park contained no specific protection for the trees.

This was not an oversight. As the reference to "future timber supply" in the park's enabling legislation makes clear, neither the Forest Preserve nor the Adirondack Park was created out of a desire to preserve wilderness in any prehumanized sense. The leading early lights of American forestry, Gifford Pinchot, Bernhard Fernow, and Charles Sargent, were all familiar with the Adirondacks and were unanimous in their absolute confidence that "modern," "scientific" forestry techniques could protect both the forest *and* the state treasury. The big woods and the bottom line would, they said, both improve with a little lumbering. Just as it has always been the assumption of the U.S. Forest Service, which these same experts went on to establish, it was believed in Albany that the state could simultaneously save the trees of the Adirondacks and make money off of cutting them down.

Unlike the larger body politic, however, who have yet to stop the U.S. Forest Service from letting large sections of the national forests be clear-cut at a taxpayer loss for the so-called common good, the voters of New York rapidly concluded that the state and its scientific managers weren't up to the job. Pinchot and Fernow and the other experts howled that the problem was unenlightened, corrupt officials rather than the idea of scientific forest management per se. But, as Frank Graham wrote, by the 1890s it was clear that "taking the forester out of the forest" was a necessary prerequisite to protecting the Adirondacks.

The scientific forester's case wasn't helped by the fact that the first person appointed to chair the Forest Preserve commission was an Adirondack lumber baron named Theodore Basselin. Under his watch unscrupulous piano makers stole prime spruce. Corrupt forest wardens helped bilk the state out of revenue by canceling contracts after the lumber had been cut and hauled away. Honest forest wardens were subjected to death threats from bands of lumber thugs. "Despoiling the Forests—Shameful Work Going on in Adirondacks—Everything Being Ruined by the Rapacious Lumberman—State Employees Engaged in the Business," headlined the *New York Times* a few years into Basselin's tenure.

In January of 1894, for reasons unrelated to the Adirondacks, a state constitutional convention was held in Albany. The year before had been one of great drought in the eastern United States. Water levels in the Erie Canal and in the Hudson reached historic lows; forest fires in the Adirondacks reached new highs. To the New York Board of Trade and Transportation, an industry association which had not previously opposed logging on state land, it appeared that Marsh's long-predicted environmental catastrophe was finally at hand. So, at the convention, the board enlisted a Democratic delegate to propose a rather startlingly simple amendment to the constitution: ban logging on the Forest Preserve.

A five-member committee was appointed to look into the amendment and take testimony from concerned citizens. They heard from sportsmen. They heard from doctors impressed with the work on tuberculosis at the Trudeau Sanitarium in Saranac Lake. They even heard from a handful of early preservationists. In the end, though, members were more influenced by the testimony of fire insurers worried about water supplies, of shippers worried about hitting the bottom of dried-out rivers, and of mill owners worried about their hydropower. The legal structure that has resulted in the largest remnant of forest wilderness east of the Mississippi River was largely created as a cushion for future industrial prosperity.

On Thursday, September 13, 1894, despite several attempts by timber lobbyists to have it scuttled, article 7, section 7 was voted on by the Constitutional Convention. It read, "The lands of the State, now owned or hereafter acquired, constituting the Forest Preserve as now fixed by law, shall be forever kept as wild forest lands. They shall not be leased, sold or exchanged, or be taken by any corporation, public or private, nor shall the timber thereon be sold, removed or destroyed."

The amendment was approved by a unanimous vote of all 112 delegates, and the new constitution was approved by the voters in the fall of 1894. From then on, in order for Forest Preserve lands to be altered in any significant way an amendment to the state constitution would first need to be approved by two consecutive sessions of the legislature and then be voted on by the general public. No other land in the nation is so well enshrined by law.

Many at the time believed the "forever wild" clause of the constitution would last only until the arts of forestry and government advanced to a level where they could be trusted to "manage" the Forest Preserve. Nevertheless, logging companies became noticeably less cavalier about letting timberland revert to the state in lieu of taxes, since they might now never get it back. A few firms, like the one that became International Paper, accumulated substantial holdings to feed their mills. It was a wise strategy; despite numerous opportunities, the citizens of New York never substantially loosened the protection given their Forest Preserve by the constitution.

Ten years after passage of the constitutional amendment banning the destruction of any trees on Forest Preserve land, 3.5 million trees were felled on private land in the park. The 1905 timber harvest was the biggest of all time in the Adirondacks, culminating a period during which the forests of the Adirondacks were under increasing pressure from new logging technologies. It couldn't last. After 1905, logging in the park began a steady, though not yet precipitous, decline.

Two factors conspired above all others to accelerate the rate of cutting in the decades on either side of the turn of the century. First, the growth of the modern paper industry meant loggers could make money cutting softwood saplings. Second, the arrival of railroads in the heart of the park meant they could finally go to work in earnest on the hardwoods that dominated the Adirondack forest.

There was a pulpwood mill at Luzerne as early as 1869, but it took a few decades before demand from the paper industry achieved a critical level. In 1890 the state Fisheries, Game, and Forest Commission reported that the practice of taking only those trees greater than one foot in diameter had completely broken down. "The wood pulp men cut all the trees of certain species, large and small," they wrote. "This close cutting of the spruce and other kinds left no provision for future growth. . . ."

Not that the pulp mills accepted only small wood. The largest spruce tree on record in the state of New York, a giant of the species with a forty-one-inch girth, was turned into paper. But in the 1890s trees like that were rarer than twenty-pound trout. By century's end, mills without their own supplies of timber were often forced to accept small hemlock, pine, and balsam. Spruce wasn't entirely gone—Finch, Pruyn and Company floated spruce logs to its paper mills until 1950— but it was scarce.

The rise of the paper industry also hastened the end of the great log drives, and not only because it consumed all the floatable timber. Pulp mills preferred their wood cut short, and as the four-foot "pulp stick" gradually replaced the thirteen-foot "saw log" it made life difficult for the river log riders. Even if a company found a decent supply of big timber, it was not a good feeling to ride a log down the river smoking a nice bowl of tobacco and find yourself surrounded by pulp sticks. There was no way off; a stick four feet long and five inches around won't hold a man up.

The last drive of thirteen-foot logs on the Hudson was in 1924. Long logs went down the Moose River until 1948. The Big Boom closed forever in 1952.

Log drivers were being replaced by railroad teamsters anyway. In 1863 Thomas Durant took over the long effort to build a railroad to the iron mine at Tahawus. Though he never completed the line, by 1871 he had gotten as far as North Creek, opening much of the upper Hudson River area to hardwood logging.

Also in the 1870s, there were lines running north-south outside the western border of the park, and up the Champlain Valley in the east. Off of these, loggers and miners built dozens of spur lines into the park. In 1892, William Seward Webb, a son-in-law of Cornelius Van-derbilt, completed the first railroad to cross the heart of the park, run-ning from just north of Utica to Malone. Off of this line in particular, hundreds of short spurs led up into the forest for the purpose of removing the trees.

One other development: In the 1890s two Swedes (or Germans depending on who's telling the story) arrived at Kunjamuk Mountain in the Adirondacks. They came from one of the legendary logging camps of Michigan or Wisconsin—from Paul Bunyan country. They brought with them a two-handed saw, with which they could easily cut 160 logs a day between them and averaged more than that.

It's not that 160 logs a day for two men with a saw was exponen-tially more than two good men with axes could cut. It was, however, a substantial technological improvement. There is a direct line from the two-handed saw to the chainsaw, to the motorized skidder that replaced the teams of oxen, to the eighteen-wheel semi that replaced the log train. And, of course, to the feller-buncher, with which a good operator in a good stand of timber can cut 160 trees in an hour.

20 *Death and Taxes*

At the modern logging operation run by the two John Courtneys virtually nothing is wasted. Nothing is left behind to clutter the forest floor, or to catch fire. They may be "cutting junk from junk," but industry has found a profitable use for every piece of the tree. Logs cut by the younger John Courtney on the feller-buncher are skidded whole out of the woods to a clearing where his father waits at the controls of an enormous sawyer-sorter that can pick up a log, run it through a machine that removes the limbs, and then swing it 360 degrees to any of a number of piles.

Into the smallest stack go the veneer logs, the best and straightest pieces of hardwood, which might ultimately end up at the skateboard factory in Ogdensburg, or at a furniture maker in Germany. Into another pile go lesser saw logs. Around behind is a stack of firewood.

Everything else—limbs, broken trunks, rotten pieces— goes through the whole-tree chipper. The chipper slurps the trees in, one or two or even three at time, like a six-hundred-horsepower kid sucking in great pieces of spaghetti. At the controls, the elder Courtney keeps the hungry machine well fed. Out the other end, the chips fly into the back of an eighteen-wheel tractor trailer rig to be hauled to a chip-burning power plant. If too many chips slip over the top of the trailer, he adjusts the blower with another set of controls.

"Forty years ago I got into logging," the elder Courtney said one night over supper at a diner in Tupper Lake. "I got a chainsaw and a contract for hardwood pulp for Diamond Match down in Ogdensburg. Eighteen dollars a cord, delivered. When we came to Tupper Lake in 1958 there were eight sawmills—Jamestown, Lake and Lake, Edgar, Draper, Elliott Hardwood. But they all closed in the seventies. There's one mill now in Tupper, it just opened a year ago and I don't know how long it will last.

"But I've seen it all come and go. When we first started we had the first privately owned rubber-tired skidder in this area. I also was the first one to haul the tractor trailer in this area, privately owned. I was the first to start chipping whole trees in this area. In fact, I'm still the only one in town who has a whole-tree chipper.

"It's like a plant or an assembly line. You got to have a constant flow of logs to keep the bills paid. We got about sixteen guys on our payroll, at around ten bucks an hour plus health care, and a dozen independent truckers. That feller-buncher machine my son's using costs around two hundred twenty-five thousand dollars, and the skidders to haul the logs out are around a hundred fifty thousand apiece. And we haven't even talked about a loader—for a halfway decent loader you're talking anywhere from fifty to a hundred twenty-five thousand. So if you get yourself a new skidder, loader, and a chainsaw you got to make sure some company is going to buy your wood. Then you got to make sure you got wood to cut, because you can't sell it if you can't buy it."

The calculations are endless, and even when you've done them right everything can go wrong. "You know it's . . . it's tough," he said. "Never was easy, though. You got the weather, you got the market, there's so many unknowns. We had ten days of rain and warm weather last January and that cost us sixty thousand dollars. You can't skid, you can't haul, and it's too much money to build a road."

A waitress arrived and said, "Hi John, you need a menu this evening?" He took one and studied it. "And hell, I can tell you injury stories. We once carried two men out of the woods dead in the space of twelve days.

"One guy went in to steal some gas and motor oil from the job site on a Saturday night. It was raining. He was drunk and he drove his car into a ditch. He and his wife were together, and he got into the loader that we had at the site in order to pull his car out. But somehow, attaching a chain or something, he got his head in between the loader and the back of his car and the loader just came ahead a bit and wedged his head between it and the rear taillight of the car. Then it pushed the car ahead enough that the pressure came off and he dropped down to the ground. Then the loader ran over him."

After a moment of silent thought Courtney said, "And the thing is, if he wanted gas he only lived two blocks from me. He knew he could have come and I would have just given it to him. But he wanted to steal it."

The man who had died twelve days earlier was a more traditional logging accident. "He'd been drunk all weekend," Courtney said, "then he came to work on Monday morning and cut himself a whole bunch of trees leaning into another one. So he went underneath to cut the one out holding them all up and it came down and hit him on the head. Killed him deader than dead. It was bad."

Loggers, apparently, still party like loggers. "I learned long ago not to hire all my guys from one town," Courtney said at one point. "That way they don't get in the barroom together, get to drinking, then on Monday morning you got all kinds of trouble. Sometimes, a little knowledge and a lot of mouth mixed well, you get yourself a state of war.

"They discuss the job. This is done wrong, that's done wrong. They get in trouble with each other too. This one doesn't like that one's wife enough. That one likes her too much. They're human, you know. So I try not to hire more than one or two from an area. Right now we have only one guy from Tupper."

Dinner arrived and Courtney ate in silence for a few minutes.

"The real problem now is that these machines are smarter than the help," he said. "We just can't get anybody to run the things right. We've been through about eight guys since November and we haven't got anybody yet. This is what's happening with society today. We got machines with circuit breakers and hydraulic systems, electric over hydraulic, hydraulic over electric. You gotta know how to look at a schematic, you gotta know hydraulics. Almost no one even touches a chainsaw anymore.

"It's not the equipment. Or the wood. Or the markets, or the financing that bothers us. It's the personnel. We can't get the people who want to take the responsibility."

He sighed and then said, "People don't give a shit. They don't care. We've lost something in this country. TV has taken and given everyone an illusion. They never show anyone who's struggling to make a living or what they have to do, they always show the multimillionaires. *Days of Our Lives*! You never see them doing anything unless they're shooting one another or spending a million dollars. We live in an illusion here.

"If you got a warm place to live, the roof doesn't leak, you got food on your table and love in your home, that's about all you need. And your health, that's all you need. We don't need all these other things that we're driving to get, as far as I'm concerned.

"I'm sorry if I talk in circles sometimes," he said at one point. "I sit on the Town Board. I'm president of the New York State Timber Producers Association. I'm president of the Tupper Lake Woodsman's Association. And I sit on the Empire State Forest Products Association. And I run my own business. So my mind just goes.

"Every day I'm out there, six days a week. I get out there around five in the morning and I get home around six at night and then, depending on the night, anywhere from zero to ten phone calls a night. Scheduling trucks, scheduling wood. And I do my paperwork on Sunday. For forty years. I've been traveling sixty, seventy miles a day for twenty years. What I spent on gas I could have 'bout the best place in the Adirondacks.

"But I don't have time to hunt and fish. Never did that stuff. My wife and I go to Myrtle Beach every year. After you been fighting the black fly six days a week you don't really care to go out and get bit for three more hours on Sunday in order to catch a couple, three little trout when you can go to the store and three dollars will buy all you want. Fighting the fly is part of the Adirondacks heritage I'd just as soon weren't there." Courtney laughed his big friendly laugh.

"My son works hard, too," he went on. "Last Sunday he rebuilt the transmission on a skidder. He's been working with me since he was four years old. He'd stand there between my legs for hours while I was sorting logs with a crane, all afternoon. I used to carry him on my shoulder when I'd walk wood." It's always a good idea to walk a piece of land and see for yourself what kind of trees are on it before you bid on the opportunity to cut them.

The waitress came and cleared the plates. Courtney asked about pie. "I skipped the gravy," he said coyly to her, "so I can have the pie, right?" She laughed and said, "Sure, John, you can have the pie."

"This is something I would like to bring out," he said when she had gone. "You listen to all the environmentalists talk about the pristine Adirondacks and all this, and at the turn of the twentieth century they *raped the wilderness* here. I mean, they cut everything standing. And yet here it is all 'pristine' again today. We loggers are doing things ten times better than they did in the old days, but we're still not good enough in the eyes of the environmentalists. I mean, if I spill five gallons of hydraulic, or even twenty gallons of hydraulic, up here in the woods, and nobody goes there for thirty years, between the sun and the evolution of the soil that dissipates naturally. But if I go in New York City and throw a hundred gallons down the manhole, and every other contractor does the same thing, you got a very different type of problem. But there's no leniency."

The pie arrived, and Courtney took a bite and chewed it thoughtfully. "So while the environmental groups are worrying so much about the environment, the business is going overseas where there's no environmental regulations at all. And if this continues to happen we're going to be a second- or third-grade country just because the greenies have put us there. They used to be the brownies in pre-German days. Pre–World War Two German days, I'm talking about. That's what they were. That's what helped knock out the German economy. It was the environmentalists."

Courtney quickly pointed out that he didn't mean to suggest that he was entirely against the existence of the Adirondack Park. "There's a lot of regulations I'm not opposed to," he said, but allowed a little later that he'd like to see some logging in the "forever wild" Forest Preserve. "All that timber in there is overmature. It's overripe. What they can't understand is that timberland should be cultivated, harvested so that it could be just as good for the environment and also just as good for mankind." Gifford Pinchot would have agreed.

Courtney shrugged resignedly and then added, "Hey, but maybe my theory isn't right. We all have a right to our thoughts. That's one thing they haven't taxed yet." He took another bite of pie. "They're trying to restrict our thoughts, though. Not the Adirondack Park Agency, but a certain group out there that wants to control everything you do.

There's talk now about planting a microchip in you when you're born and then put that in the computer and then they'll know everything about you as long as you're on the face of the earth. They'll know when you're married, where you move to, where you go out at night.

"Oh yeah, it's true," he said a little louder, apparently sensing some disbelief. "I've read about that. New World Order! If people don't wake up and get ugly, boy . . ."

As worrisome as they are, though, the lamentable quality of today's workforce and the possibility of environmental brownshirts and World Order microchips are not what concern Courtney the most. His primary fear when he ponders the future of his industry in the Adirondacks is much more mundane. What will make or break the logging business is the same as it ever was: the calculation.

"The biggest threat of all to logging here is taxes," he said several times during dinner and then again the next day on the way to the job site near Malone. "In Maine, taxes on timberland are around a dollar an acre, whereas here it runs six, seven. So if you're sitting on the board of directors or are the CEO of a major company like Champion, and you got a hundred thousand acres that's worth, say, three hundred an acre, that's a thirty-million-dollar asset. And you're harvesting it only every forty or fifty years, so if you put that thirty million in the bank at just six percent you're doing a lot better than logging it, given the taxes you're going to pay over that time. This is the real problem.

"International Paper just went and gave a bunch of land to the state so they wouldn't have to pay taxes on it. Champion's land is all for sale, Domtar's land is all for sale. Some of Finch and Pruyn's is for sale . . . well, no, I guess they say right now it isn't. But there's always talk of Finch and Pruyn selling. This is what will happen with the large landowners, and then there won't be any land left to log."

In his fear of taxes the elder John Courtney, who died suddenly of a massive heart attack while out walking a piece of timberland with his son in May of 1996, had what would probably have seemed to him to be some strange bedfellows. Harold Jerry, for instance, who is currently Governor George Pataki's head of the Public Service Commission. The commission has nothing to do with the park per se, but Jerry's top-floor corner office at the state government's Empire State Plaza in Albany probably qualifies him in Courtney's mind as a "high-priced bureaucrat." If North Korean architects trained in the former

East Germany were asked to design a monument to faceless bureaucracy, it would probably look much like the Empire State Plaza.

But Chairman Jerry is an unusual bureaucrat. His day job is to regulate the electric and telephone industries, but he spends his weekends deep in the Adirondack woods in a cabin with neither power nor phone. He is a very trim and handsome man, who eats his lunch out of a reusable nylon bag. An entire wall of his office is taken up with a huge collection of topographical maps of the park.

Jerry is more than just an interested part-time resident of the park. Twenty-eight years ago, when then-Governor Nelson Rockefeller appointed a commission to study the future of the Adirondacks, Harold Jerry was its staff director. That commission ultimately resulted in the creation of the Adirondack Park Agency (APA) in 1971, part of whose mission was to undertake the first effort at regional zoning on the park's private lands.

"I have always felt that the most important mistake that we on the study commission made was we assumed that ownership of the paper company lands was immutable," he said while nibbling at some raisins from his lunch bag. "We figured subconsciously that the paper companies would always maintain their holdings because they needed them as a resource base for their mills.

"However, this assumption has turned out to be shaky at best and probably erroneous, because what has happened is that they have found that in many instances it is more economical to import the raw materials from elsewhere, Canada or abroad.

"Now, some of the companies, for example International Paper, the largest private landowner in the park with somewhere around 330,000 acres, have actually increased their holdings slightly in the last twenty-five years. On the other hand, others have been quite willing to sell all or most of their holdings. As far as I know today, Champion International and Domtar—and we're talking a couple hundred thousand acres of open space—are both interested in selling, at a minimum, a conservation easement on their land, and possibly selling them outright. So we have as of this moment a couple hundred thousand acres of timberland in the northern portions of the park the fate of which is uncertain.

"The point I'm trying to make is that even today the preservation of the open space in the park is threatened. About a thousand houses a year are being built up there. That sounds like chicken feed if you come from New York City, but the fact of the matter is if you build a thousand houses for a thousand years you've got a lot of houses. And if you build them for just a hundred years you've got a lot of houses. And so in the last twenty years there have been twenty thousand new houses built in the park.

"I'm not trying to say they were all built in the backcountry. But, theoretically, even on resource management land [the Park Agency's strictest zoning classification, and the one that applies to most large holdings of timbered land] you can still put a house on every forty-three acres. So my wife and my children and I, who own sixteen hundred acres where we've done some logging, could build forty houses on our property. And of course it isn't just the forty houses that causes the destruction of the open spaces so much as it is the roads that connect them. The minute you build a house you've got a road, and there goes the backcountry.

"This brings us back to the paper companies. Since the park's most essential element is open space, the fact that these paper companies have historically acquired, managed, and maintained open space has been very fortuitous. But then, as I said, the paper companies realized they could get along without some of their land, and that some of it had infinitely more value for real estate development then it did for growing trees. Trees grow very slowly, particularly in the Adirondacks. You can't even get syrup out of a maple tree for forty years."

Chairman Jerry put a single raisin in his mouth and looked up at the big map on the wall.

"Let's talk about real estate taxes. This is a big player. First of all the park is six million acres, about 3.5 of which are private and 2.5 million are public. The state pays local taxes on its land in the park. This is not known to most of the rest of the taxpayers in the state. If they realized it they might rise up and rant because in the rest of the state, with the exception of the Forest Preserve lands in the Catskills, the state does not pay local taxes.

"A couple of years ago the average tax on the average forested Adirondack acre was about four dollars, compared to about a dollar and a quarter in Vermont, New Hampshire, or Maine. So you had a heavy tax on the open space here. However, ninety-nine percent of the paper company land is leased for exclusive hunting and fishing use to hunting clubs, and those leases pay at least the four dollars they need for taxes plus probably some more.

"Therefore, as a political matter, when you start talking about providing a subsidy for keeping forest land open the guy downstate says, What are you talking about?—they're covering that real estate tax with the leases. And there may be nothing wrong with that argument except that land in the Adirondacks continues to get subdivided.

"So, if we want a park and the open space that's necessary to it, we've got to decide if we are willing to subsidize the forest land owners to keep that land open. But it seems politically unlikely," Chairman Jerry reiterated matter-of-factly.

If there is an irony in the Adirondacks today it is this respect-bordering-on-nostalgia for the logging industry among the majority of the park's most informed supporters. The Forest Preserve and the Adirondack Park were created a century ago to protect the land from the perceived depredations of lumber barons and crooked politicians, but the tens of thousands of mailers sent out annually by various conservation organizations interested in protecting the park don't usually mention feller-bunchers and skidders. They don't send out photos of clear-cuts because there are no large clear-cuts in the park. Fear of loggers is one more Adirondack phenomenon that has found more fertile ground in the Far West.

What the fliers do mention fairly regularly are the thousand new homes that are built on private land within the park every year. What the conservationists do fear are the calculations of the construction industry. They worry that the new "camps," thousands and thousands of them, great and otherwise, will permanently change the wild character of the park.

21 *Birth of a Great Camp*

One summer afternoon in 1883 a steam train pulled out of New York City and headed north, up the Hudson. On board one of the cars were three horses, two dogs (Muggins and Sport), one carriage, three cases of wine, two packages of stovepipe, two stoves, one iron pot, four washstands, one barrel of hardwood, seventeen cots, seventeen mattresses, four canvas packages, one buckboard, five large barrels and one half-barrel, two tubs of butter, one bag of coffee, one chest of tea, a crate of china, a dozen rugs, four milk cans, two drawing boards, twenty-five trunks, thirteen small boxes, a boat, and a hamper. The Stokes family—mom and dad, seven children, one niece, ten servants, a woman named Miss Rondell, and a coachman—was going camping in the Adirondacks.

Camp Chronicles, the short memoir in which the above list appears, was written by one of the children on that trip, Mildred Phelps Stokes Hooker. She wrote it as a Christmas card to her neighbors on Upper Saint Regis Lake in 1952, by which point she had been coming to the lake for seventy of her seventy-two years. *Camp Chronicles* is at times bittersweet about an era already slipping away; toward the end Hooker laments seeing only strangers in church. But mostly it describes with a good deal of style and humor the progression of Upper Saint Regis from wild lake to elite summer community.

The Stokeses' destination that summer of 1883 was Birch Island. Anson Phelps Stokes, Mildred's father, had visited Paul Smith's Hotel in 1876 and "was so charmed by the beauty and peace of the Upper Lake—there were no camps at all on it then—that he bought the island from a Mr. Norton for $200." He paid another five hundred dollars to the Mutual Life Insurance Company to buy off a claim they had on the property. He explained to his daughter that "it was cheaper to pay them than to hire a lawyer to prove that he didn't have to."

As the inventory of equipment suggests, the Stokes family weren't exactly engaged in what modern hikers would consider "low-impact camping." But neither was it yet the sprawling collection of permanent buildings that would later become known as a Great Camp. Along with everything else on the train car were five large boxes of tents, and four bundles of heavy wooden poles. There were about a half dozen tents for sleeping in, another one for dining, and one fourteen-by-fourteen-foot canvas "parlor."

It was a stylish form of roughing it. A picture of one tent included in *Camp Chronicles* shows walls decorated already with the Japanese fans that would become standard in later camps. There were needle-point chairs and thick carpets covering the wooden floor. Dark curtains that hung over the doorway contrasted quite elegantly with the clean white of the tent walls.

Over the years, though, the tents were gradually replaced with permanent log cabins. A dock and a handsome boathouse with a second-story veranda were built. A central lodge, also of logs, was added. The dining room was expanded. Nearby Chicken Coop Island, so named because it housed the flock brought each year "to kill as needed," became "known as Hog Island when the pigs moved in, and as Pearl Island when it achieved the distinction of housing humans."

When the family first came to Upper Saint Regis Lake, according to Stokes's Christmas card, they had trouble deciding on which end of their little island to stay. In the end, though, it didn't matter since the compound spread to include the entire island.

It was still a "camp," of course, for as A. L. Donaldson famously put it: "If ever an exact little word gradually went to seed and ran wild, not only in a wilderness of mountains, but in a wilderness of mean-

The boathouse at Levi Morton's camp on Upper Saranac Lake. COURTESY OF THE
SARANAC LAKE FREE LIBRARY.

ings, it is this one. If you have spent the night in a guide's tent, or a
lean-to built of slabs and bark, you have lodged in a 'camp.' If you
chance to know a millionaire, you may be housed in a cobblestone castle, tread on Persian rugs, bathe in a marble tub, and retire by electric
light—and still your host may call his mountain home a 'camp.' "

Or as Seneca Ray Stoddard said in the 1888 edition of his guidebook: "These camps are never really completed, for one of the fascinating features of the camp is that it is bound by no rules of time and
architecture. It expands and blossoms with the passing seasons."

Organic metaphors do nicely for both the progress of individual
camps from picnic spot to sprawling architectural folly, and for the
changing meaning of the word "camp" itself. But they are not as useful at explaining the larger phenomenon of camp building in the
Adirondacks, which on most lakes was spearheaded by an entrepre-
neur of one sort or another. It was not by mistake that the hotelier

Paul Smith spent most of his earnings in the early years buying up as much land around his hotel as possible, until he ultimately owned some forty thousand acres.

Smith knew how to work an opportunity when he saw it; he once remarked, after a train leaving his hotel was robbed, that the thieves should have known that he had already relieved his guests of all of their money. The price of admission on the Saint Regis Lakes by the middle of the Gay Nineties was better than $4,000 an acre. In 1896 Smith sold four acres for $20,000, exactly the amount he'd paid for thirteen thousand acres not too many years earlier.

"I never saw anything like it," he said to a reporter from *Forest and Stream* in 1890. "There's not a foot of land on that lake for sale this minute, and there's not a man in it but what's a millionaire, and some of them ten times over. . . . I tell you if there's a spot on the face of the earth where millionaires go play at house keeping in log cabins and tents as they do here I have it yet to hear about."

Smith's tone of wide-eyed innocence belied the fact that he had sold most of the millionaires their land. And that he knew his clients' preference for not socializing outside of their own crowd well enough to limit sales to "the right sort," whatever that meant.

What it meant twenty miles away in Lake Placid was always made perfectly clear. There the primary developer was Melvil Dewey, who also invented the library cataloguing system that bears his name. It was the policy of Dewey's powerful Lake Placid Club that "no one will be received as member or guest against whom there is physical, moral, social, or race objection, or who would be unwelcome to even a small minority. This excludes absolutely all consumptives, or rather invalids, whose presence might injure health or modify others' freedom or enjoyment. This invariable rule is rigidly enforced: it is found impracticable to make exceptions to Jews or others excluded, even when of unusual personal qualifications."

Sadly, Dewey was by no means the only racist in the park. To the most influential of all developers of the period, however, money was money. Whether because he was possessed of a more enlightened mind, a more desperate pocket, or just more land to unload, William West Durant was perfectly happy to sell land to anyone with the money to spend. It didn't matter if you were a Vanderbilt or a Guggenheim, a Morgan or a Morton, if you had the cash, Durant had the land and a camp to go with it. And it was Durant and his wealthy clients, more than anyone else, who developed the notion of Adirondack camps as more than simply wooden tents.

William West Durant was the son and heir of Dr. Thomas C. Durant, who was forced out of the Union Pacific Railroad Company by some of his associates not long after the golden spike was driven in 1869. This probably spared Dr. Durant from being implicated a few years later when the company's financing arm, the Crédit Mobilier, became the center of a major scandal involving influence peddling in Congress. By then he was safely concentrating on a little side-project he had purchased in 1862, the Adirondack Railroad.

The Adirondack Railroad was originally organized in 1848 as the Sackets Harbor and Saratoga Railroad. This was one of the several phantom lines that were expected to save the McIntyre iron mine at Tahawus. It was to be financed in the usual way for railroads, through government largesse. The organizers had an initial grant from the state allowing them to buy up to a quarter of a million acres of state land in the vicinity of the proposed route for a nickel an acre, well under the going price.

The payoff for the company would supposedly come when the railroad raised the value of their holdings astronomically. When that, and other similar land grants, failed to produce enough railroads, the State Legislature passed another law allowing would-be tycoons to condemn other people's land lying in their way. But still, at least in the case of the Sackets Harbor and Saratoga line, not a mile of track was laid.

By the time Dr. Durant got involved in the railroad in 1862, the Legislature had given the builders the right to mine iron and sell logs off of the surrounding land. Still the deal wasn't sweet enough; the elder Durant convinced the Legislature to pass yet another law giving most of his land an exemption from all state land taxes for twenty years. In return, he promised to lay 185 miles of track across the middle of the Adirondacks, from Saratoga Springs to Ogdensburg.

Given Durant's railroad-building experience and the terms of his grants from Albany, in 1864 the *New York Times* confidently and favorably predicted that the Adirondack region would shortly "become a suburb of New York." As it turned out, though, the man who put rails across the continent was unable to get more than sixty miles built in the Adirondacks. In 1870 he ran out of investors, and efforts to get a direct subsidy from the state failed. The railroad got only as far as North Creek, 125 miles short of its intended destination.

Quite conveniently for Durant, though, sixty miles of track was precisely the minimum he needed to take full advantage of his land options from the state. By 1870, when construction halted, Dr. Durant owned in the neighborhood of 700,000 acres of land in the central Adirondacks, most of it tax exempt. He controlled a good deal more land than the state of New York, which in 1872 owned only 40,000 acres in the region.

During most of the fifteen years that Dr. Durant was busy with the Union Pacific, his son William had roamed around Europe with his mother, Heloise, and his sister, Ella. But when the national recession known as the panic of 1873 arrived, coinciding with a downturn in Dr. Durant's own health, the father sent word to his scattered flock to come home and help him revive the family fortunes.

When the call to come home caught up with him, young William West Durant and some friends were hunting big game and dabbling in archeology in Egypt. In his years abroad, William West had attended prep school in England and university in Germany. Fluent in French and Italian and proficient in German, by all accounts W.W. was enjoying his life as the playboy son of an American railroad magnate. According to Craig Gilborn's biography of the family, *Durant,* the young heir was not, at twenty-three, overly excited about the prospect of a career as a real estate developer in the north woods. He didn't even really like his father. So after returning to New York, he traded mortgage-backed securities on Wall Street for a few years instead.

When William West Durant finally did make a trip north to Raquette Lake in 1876, he had a broken leg. He took the train to Albany, where he changed to another one bound for Saratoga, and then another on the family line up to North Creek. Then, along with his father and sister, he climbed into a carriage for the nearly eight-hour ride to the small settlement at Blue Mountain Lake. There they met guides who could row them up through Eagle Lake, Blue Mountain Lake, and Utowana Lake—what used to be called the Eckford Chain Lakes. At the outlet of Utowana, William's guide, David Helms, carried him and his crutches over the three-quarter-mile carry to the Marion River, which flows down into Raquette Lake.

Raquette Lake is the heart of the central Adirondack lake country. Leading from it to the west, the Fulton Chain of lakes runs to Old

Forge. To the east lie the Marion River Carry and the Eckford Chain. Finally, Raquette Lake itself flows northeast into the river of the same name and then into the fourteen-mile-long Long Lake and on into Tupper Lake. At Coreys it is possible to portage over to the Saranac Lakes and beyond.

Thus, despite the fact that the Durants owned little of its shoreline, Gilborn makes the case that Raquette Lake's location made it strategically important to the family's development plans. Their vast holdings lay in all directions from the lake, and it was one of the few great frustrations of the senior Durant's life that he was never able to purchase more of the lakefront from the state of New York.

And Raquette Lake was beautiful. When William West and his father and sister arrived there in 1872, there were not more than a handful of rough camps and lean-tos on its ninety-nine-mile shoreline. One of these camps had been started by Dr. Durant a few years earlier on a half-mile-wide peninsula called Long Point that the Durants did own. Sometime during this trip William West, who had not particularly excelled on Wall Street, apparently changed his mind about the real estate business.

But the one-story main lodge, open dining room, and handful of log cabins and tent platforms that constituted his father's camp on Long Point was not stylistically what William West had in mind for a family residence. In 1879, in a grove of white pines on the southwest tip of the point, on the opposite side from where his father had built, W.W. began construction of what is generally considered to be the first "artistic camp" in the Adirondacks.

The main building, called the Swiss Cottage, was two stories tall with a large living room and four bedrooms. Logs were selected carefully for size and quality, and notched only on the bottom side rather than the more common "Lincoln log" corner. Instead of the usual stovepipe, W.W. had grand stone chimneys built. Instead of minimal and rough furnishings, interiors leaned toward the luxurious.

The tradition of separate buildings for separate functions was maintained, so that there were twenty-six structures by the time he sold the camp in 1895. In all but the most utilitarian of woodsheds, however, artistic touches were added. Under eaves and along porch fences the craftsmen, who were primarily moonlighting guides and lumberjacks, created intricate rustic details using naturally curved, unpeeled limbs and branches. On one porch railing, they spelled out

Laurence, Heloise, and Basil Durant at play in the nursery at Pine Knot, circa 1885, by Seneca Ray Stoddard. COURTESY OF THE ADIRONDACK MUSEUM, BLUE MOUNTAIN LAKE.

"W.W.D." Some interior ceilings were papered with birch bark, while some exteriors were sheathed in hemlock bark. Here and there, red-painted window trim leavened the woodsy effect.

Durant didn't stop with the buildings. He had his crew create lawns and footpaths. Rustic planters and window boxes were constructed. Occasional hollowed-out tree stumps were planted with annuals. There were fern glens, and vines planted along the porches of the cottages. Kerosene lanterns were hung for light and effect. And, of course, it was all furnished with rustic pieces made from twigs and found wood.

A houseboat with four rooms, running water, a kitchen, and bath was built. It was sheathed in cedar bark, and Durant christened it the *Barque of Pine Knot.* He used it first to escape the black flies, and then later, when he was being sued for divorce, to escape his wife. He called the camp itself Pine Knot, in honor of an enormous, three-foot knot of wood found during the construction.

Much has been written over the years about the possible sources of Durant's architectural inspirations, most notably by Craig Gilborn and by Harvey Kaiser in his *Great Camps of the Adirondacks.* Durant may have been familiar with rustic gazebos and the like built in the 1850s and '60s in Manhattan's Central Park and Brooklyn's Prospect Park. At his prep school, Twickenham, Alexander Pope had built one of England's first picturesque gardens. Also, there is much that is Swiss, Scandinavian, Russian, and Bavarian about the style of Pine Knot. Durant would have seen buildings in those places during his travels. He was also familiar with the Swiss-style Wayside Hotel in the Swiss-named town of Lake Luzerne, in the southeastern corner of the park.

Equally important inspirations for the main architectural features Durant used at Pine Knot and his later camps were the circumstances of building in the middle of the woods. Large overhangs kept snow and rain away from foundations, and stone foundations kept logs from rotting. A gently sloped roof supported by heavy timbers could hold the ten or more feet of insulating snow that would pile up in the winter. Tall chimneys with caps to trap sparks reduced the chance of fire, and multiple buildings meant that any fires that did start could be contained before they destroyed the whole place. Bark was far more readily available than plaster or wallpaper. Rustic was fashionable, but it was also practical.

This doesn't mean that Durant's architectural achievements were accidental or the inevitable result of cost cutting. The log exterior on the second floor, and on many later camps, was in reality a facade covering a more traditional balloon frame construction. Durant took pains to develop special stains and preservatives that were applied to the unpeeled logs to slow the progress of wood borers. Peeled and sawed pieces were rubbed with beeswax to give them the proper degree of refined rusticity. He used milled lumber in the interiors both at Pine Knot and at his later camps. And when local logs were inadequate, wood was occasionally imported from Canada or the American south.

Pine Knot rapidly became a minor tourist attraction. It was "unquestionably the most picturesque and recherché affair of its kind in the wilderness," Seneca Ray Stoddard wrote in his 1881 edition of *The Adirondacks, Illustrated*. Stoddard, it might be noted, was occasionally employed by the Durants in a public relations capacity. But Donaldson concurred. "It became the show place of the woods," he wrote in his history of the region. "Men took a circuitous route in order to gain a glimpse of it, and to have been a guest within its timbered walls and among its woodland fancies was to wear the hall-mark of the envied."

This, of course, was exactly the result that Durant desired. Pine Knot inspired a slew of building, both on Raquette and on the lakes connected to it. The Stott family began Camp Stott on Bluff Point in 1877, which was later sold to the publisher Robert Collier. After paying off a grumpy Alvah Dunning, who was living in a truly rustic shanty with a bark roof held down by rocks, a Durant cousin built Camp Fairview on Osprey Island in 1880. Another cousin built a camp called Cedars up on Forked Lake in the same year. A former governor of Connecticut, Phineas Lounsbury, began a camp at Echo Point in 1883.

Around this time it was decided that a brochure was in order, and Edward Bierstadt, the brother of the painter Albert, was hired to take pictures. The resulting book of photos, *The Adirondacks, Artotype Views among the Mountains and Lakes of the North Woods,* prominently featured Durant properties.

In 1885 Dr. Durant died, leaving William West in charge of, though not the sole heir to, the family business. William immediately set about selling the railroad and several large parcels of land, which together netted him nearly a million dollars by the end of the decade. A few months after depositing over $600,000 in his account he visited

"Duryea's Cottage, Blue Mountain Lake," circa 1886, artotype by Edward Bierstadt.
COURTESY OF THE ADIRONDACK MUSEUM, BLUE MOUNTAIN LAKE.

his sister in London and presented her with a check for $25,000. That, he told her, was her half of the estate. It was a bit of avarice that would return to haunt him.

He himself, meanwhile, commenced living like the superrich he hoped to entice to the Adirondacks. In 1890, he commissioned the building of the *Utowana*, a 190-foot oceangoing yacht of the sort that once inspired J. P. Morgan to tell a curious visitor, "If you have to ask, you can't afford it." When it was finished he sailed it to Europe where he entertained assorted royals and old school chums.

Also in the 1890s, Durant built Uncas and Sagamore. These two camps, along with another one built on land sold by Durant (Kamp Kill Kare),[1] were pronounced in 1903 to be "the finest trio on the North American Continent" by Henry Wellington Wack, the founding editor of *Field and Stream*. "I doubt if there is any forest villa in Europe to compare with either [*sic*] of them in any respect," he swooned.

In 1890 a crew of two hundred began building Uncas, which was named for the character in *Last of the Mohicans*. The site was a 1,500-acre parcel that included all of Mohegan Lake, not far from Raquette Lake. Though its later owners, the J. P. Morgans, added to it significantly, originally Uncas was less sprawling than Pine Knot. It was self-sufficient, with a farm and blacksmith shop on the premises to supply it. And whereas Pine Knot developed over the course of thirteen years, gaining a structure here and there whenever the spirit moved Durant, Uncas was planned and completed in two years.

There were stylistic differences as well. Instead of notching the logs, which produced the overlapping corners reminiscent of frontier cabins, here they were mitered. Moving even further along the scale from primitive to haute rustic, on the main lodge Durant used "peeled poles" rather than leaving the bark on the logs. Bark wasn't eliminated entirely, however. Some of the cabins were completely sheathed in it. Instead of hewn-stone chimneys, at Uncas he insisted that only uncut faces of fieldstone be visible. As at Pine Knot, it was furnished

---

[1] In 1896 the Forest Preserve Board bought 24,000 acres from Durant. In the middle of the parcel was a thousand-acre tract around Sumner Lake that was mysteriously not included in the sale. Two years later it came out that Teddy Roosevelt's lieutenant governor, Timothy Woodruff, who was also the chairman of the Forest Preserve Board at the time, had bought the parcel for himself from Durant. He built Kill Kare there, and renamed the lake Kora, after his wife. The press was not impressed, but an official inquiry a decade later proved inconclusive as to the ethics of the transaction.

in a rustic manner. In general, though, Uncas was less twiggy than its predecessor.

At his last major camp, Durant moved even further away from the primitive roots of his style. It was begun in 1896 on a peninsula sticking into Shedd Lake. "Shedd," however, had inappropriate connotations, so Durant borrowed again from James Fenimore Cooper's lexicon of Indian words. Both lake and camp became Sagamore.

Though, as at Uncas, numerous buildings were added by later owners—this time the Alfred Vanderbilts—Durant's original conception of Sagamore continued the process of simplification and consolidation.[2] The main lodge was, and is, an immense three-and-a-half story Swiss chalet. Logs were no longer structural but became details, sawed in half and attached as siding to a modern frame structure. There are still projecting roof rafters and peeled-log beams between the floors, but they too are nonstructural. The interior of Sagamore was finished with plank floors, wainscoting and burlap-covered walls, and a stone fireplace in every room. Had things gone the way Durant hoped, Sagamore would have been his year-round home.

Despite the architectural differences among the three camps, Uncas and Sagamore clearly developed the aesthetic framework Durant created at Pine Knot in the 1880s. The same can be said, in fact, about a majority of the other large camps constructed in the Adirondacks. "Before [Pine Knot] was built there was nothing like it," Donaldson wrote in 1921. "Since then, despite infinite variations, there has been nothing essentially different from it." In part because architecture reminiscent of Pine Knot can be found not only all over the populated parts of the park, but at National Park Service headquarters all over the country, it is as the creator of the "Adirondack style" that Durant is most often remembered.

There is more to his story, however. For though Durant's first love was clearly style and architecture, his business was land development.

"I firmly believe," he told the *New York Daily Tribune* in 1886, "that the Adirondacks are the resort of the future."

Durant's vision of an empire of vacation homes represented a marriage of sorts between the pastoral dreams of previous speculators like

---

[2] Even after Alfred's widow, Margaret Emerson, finished adding on to Sagamore and it could easily house a hundred guests, it was rather small compared to their 137-room mansion on Fifth Avenue or The Breakers, their "cottage" in Newport, Rhode Island.

John Brown of Providence, and the romantic travel prescriptions of writers like Adirondack Murray and Joel T. Headley. But whereas Brown hoped to cull buyers from the surplus farmers of New England, and expected these yeomen to come and transform the wilderness into the small farms and towns they were leaving behind, Durant looked elsewhere for customers. He trolled among creators and owners of surplus wealth that the industrial revolution was producing up and down the East Coast.

By almost any definition a lake surrounded by pleasure homes is no longer properly described as a wilderness. And few would describe the vast pleasure palaces Durant designed as wilderness living. But it was precisely the proximity of the health-giving wilds of the romantics that made Durant's land valuable. It was not only an affectation that Durant's customer base referred to their Adirondack spreads as "camps." Wilderness was the commodity they thought they were paying for.

The main impediment to the kind of development the Durants hoped to foster in their central Adirondack holdings was transportation. They established a stagecoach line, the 4&6 Overland Company, that took passengers over the thirty miles of bad road from North Creek, where their railroad ran out of rails, to Indian Lake and Blue Mountain Lake. There, the senior Durant had established a line of rowboats to take people on over to Raquette Lake.

As rustic and traditional as they may have been, rowboats didn't quite jibe with the image William West was trying to create with his camps. This was, after all, the age of steam. In 1878 he built a dam across the Marion River to raise the level of the water in the channels between the lakes of the Eckford Chain and inaugurated his Blue Mountain and Raquette Lake Steamboat Line. Later Durant dredged the channels, which eliminated the need for all the passengers to crowd in the bow to raise the stern over the shallowest parts of the route. Durant ships ultimately plied Long Lake, the Raquette River, and Tupper Lake.

Not everyone was happy with Durant's brand of progress. This may have been because the convenience of arriving at camp by steamship was somewhat offset by the fact that Durant's dams flooded and killed thousands of trees along the shoreline. Around 1895 someone, possibly a nascent environmentalist but more likely a displaced guideboat

W. W. Durant's ferryboat "Killoquah," on Raquette Lake, by Seneca Ray Stoddard.
COURTESY OF THE SARANAC LAKE FREE LIBRARY.

rower, stole the Durant craft *Buttercup* from its mooring in the middle of the night and sent it to the bottom of Long Lake.

Durant, though, was undaunted by his Luddite neighbor. He strung telegraph wires in from North Creek. And to further ease the passage from there, in 1900, he built the shortest standard-gauge railroad in the world. The Marion River Carry Railroad took passengers over the three-quarter-mile distance between Utowana and Raquette Lakes. Also in that year he oversaw the completion of the Raquette Lake Railroad. This ran alongside the Fulton Chain from Raquette Lake west to Thendara, where it connected with William Seward Webb's line. Passengers could finally travel all the way from Manhattan or Philadelphia to Durant country by rail.

Durant's board of directors on the Raquette Lake Railroad, which included railroad magnate Collis Huntington, J. P. Morgan, William Seward Webb, and a pair of Whitneys, gave him confidence. So certain were these men that they could ultimately get permission from the Legislature for their plans that they simply started laying track before they had the necessary enabling legislation in hand. There is also some evidence in their plans that, as critics of the Raquette Lake Railroad at the time contended, Durant and his associates were hoping to facilitate logging on Forest Preserve land. After all, the forever-wild clause of the constitution was only a dozen years old, and it was still widely assumed to be temporary.

In some ways, Durant's courtship of the elite of American industry also harked back to the earlier speculator John Brown's practice of offering free land to the first few pioneers if they would promise to stay put long enough to attract others. By virtue of his father's achievements, William West Durant had very real expectation and hope of being included in a league with the super-wealthy. He moved in their world. But beyond whatever personal social aspirations he harbored lay the realtor's certainty that wherever the robber barons went to play, others would surely follow. And they did.

But while it served William West Durant's larger purposes to sell Pine Knot to the builder of the Southern Pacific, Uncas to J. P. Morgan, and Sagamore to the grandson and principal heir of Commodore Vanderbilt, it curiously didn't make him rich. In fact, for all his apparent success, Durant was rapidly losing money.

When he sold Pine Knot in 1895 he told the buyer, Collis Huntington, that he needed the money to pay for the building of Uncas. A costly divorce at the time from his first wife, Janet Stott, doubtless added to his cash-flow problems. Huntington paid him $35,000.

According to some sources, Durant didn't so much sell his second camp to J. P. Morgan as lose it when Morgan called in a loan secured by the property. Morgan, who was introduced to Durant by Huntington, offered to buy Uncas outright, but Durant refused and took a loan instead. After Morgan foreclosed on Uncas, tradition has it, he almost never went there.

By the time Durant sold Sagamore in 1901, his empire was crumbling around him. The sources of Durant's troubles were many. But the biggest, at least at the end, was a lawsuit against him by his sister, Ella. She charged that he had mismanaged their father's estate and had deprived her of her share of the proceeds. The suit was actually launched as early as 1895, but it had been thrown out on a technicality. Within a few years, though, it was reinstated and the trial proper began on January 5, 1899.

Ella was altogether of a stronger will than her father or her brother or her mother ever expected a woman to be. By all accounts, her immediate family wanted her quietly and profitably married, not publishing poems and plays in Europe. And certainly not launching lawsuits over business deals she couldn't possibly understand. But that wasn't Ella; when an employee of William's told her that her brother was about to flee to England, she promptly had W.W. arrested. Collis Huntington bailed him out for ten thousand dollars.

It was a long and tortuous trial, and not surprisingly the press loved it. It came out that after Dr. Durant's death Ella had never wanted to sign over her power of attorney to William West in the first place. She had said then that she had "no confidence in her brother, that she knew he would cheat and rob her if he got the chance." It also became clear that William West had indeed been systematically funneling land and other assets out of the original Adirondack Company, which he was supposed to be managing in the interests of the whole family, into another entity called the Forest Park and Land Company, which he alone owned.

In the years leading up to the trial, Durant did what comes naturally to any flashy real estate developer with cash-flow problems. He sold his big yacht and began subdividing. Selling big camps on small lakes to the very rich had always been only the first half of his plan. The second half of the scheme was to divide up the shores of the larger lakes and sell more modest camps to less prominent but still wealthy businessmen, doctors, and politicians.

In 1898 and 1899, he divided the north shore of Rich Lake in Newcomb into forty-two lots of three to seven acres apiece. He furiously built and sold a few smaller camps elsewhere in the Newcomb area. But his main effort was at Blue Mountain and Eagle Lakes, where he carved out two hundred shorefront lots.

A map of the proposed project in the Adirondack Museum in Blue Mountain Lake looks eerily like something that might be brought before the Adirondack Park Agency by a cash-hungry large-landowner today. The legend across the top reads "The Eagle's Nest Country Club." There is a golf course, tennis courts, a clubhouse. Along the western shore of Blue Mountain Lake are a series of two- and three-acre lots bearing numbers in the hundreds. Each site is drawn long and thin to maximize the number of waterfront lots.

The golf course and country club opened in 1899, but by then events were moving too fast for Durant. On August 13 of the following year his main backer, Huntington, died of a heart attack at Pine Knot. Though Durant insisted the deceased had promised to continue financing the development of Eagle's Nest and the other projects, there was nothing in writing. The executors of the estate decided instead to call in their outstanding loans to Durant. Nor were Webb, Morgan, or Whitney, to whom he turned next, inclined to help him out.

In December of 1900, Durant went to J. P. Morgan and offered to sell 60 percent of the company to him for $400,000. All but forty thousand of this was to go to his creditors, principally the Huntington estate, and the rest was to finish the steamboat line and the golf course at Eagle's Nest. But Morgan, after asking the executors of the Huntington estate exactly how dire Durant's situation was, offered him only $350,000 in exchange for virtual control of the company. Durant refused on the grounds that he was being asked "to shut my eyes and open my mouth without knowing what will be thrown into it."

He decided instead to sell Sagamore. It "cost me a great deal more than any of the other camps I have built," he said of the camp, "and is much more elaborate in the way of gas and water works, heating by furnace as well as by fireplaces, system of draining, roads and stocking the lake with fish, than anything I before attempted."

He estimated construction costs to have been around $250,000, but he offered to sell for fifty thousand less than that. Alfred Vanderbilt, who had inherited more than $46 million on his twenty-second birthday, talked Durant down to $162,500 for the camp and the fifteen hundred acres that went with it.

With a few more land sales, Durant might have managed to stay afloat for a while longer. But at the end of 1901, the court ordered him to pay his sister $753,000. When he appealed the decision he lost again. The judge was quoted in the *New York Times* as saying, "This property came into the hands of the defendant as the trustee for the mother and sister. . . . He succeeded in vesting the title of the whole of this very large estate in himself. His mother became dependent, his sister languished in want, and he reveled in luxury."

After that, the end came fast. In 1904, the last of his Adirondack assets were sold off at auction. William West Durant moved out of the park.

In Utica, where he went first, he met and married his second wife, Annie Cotton. He tried for a while to get into the optical business in Washington, D.C., but failed. He tried raising mushrooms in Maine, but failed to make a living at it. He worked for a while for a land development company on Long Island that went bust. In between, he went back to the Adirondacks and managed hotels, sometimes working for people who had once worked for him. During the First World War he was in the Adirondacks making a living doing deed searches for wealthy clients. Like William Gilliland a century and a half before him, he was reduced to helping others secure title to land he himself once owned.

But though Durant's real estate aspirations were reminiscent of earlier generations of Adirondack speculators, his response to failure was significantly healthier than Charles Frederick Herreshoff's. By all accounts Durant remained a happy man through it all. In 1931, three years before his death at the age of eighty-three, he was invited to Eagle's Nest by Harold Hochschild. Eagle's Nest was once to have been the country club and golf course at the heart of Durant's big subdivision on Eagle and Blue Mountain Lakes. Hochschild's father, who made a great fortune in international mining, got the site during the final breakup of Durant's holdings in 1904. Now the younger Hochschild, himself a mining magnate, wanted to interview the old developer. Hochschild, who later founded the Adirondack Museum, was doing research for *Township 34,* a history he was writing of the area around Blue Mountain Lake.

"I was handicapped," Durant explained when he got up to his former country club turned great camp, "by having been brought up in wealth without being taught the value of money."

22 *Haute Rustic*

Camp life went on in the Adirondacks without William West Durant. By the first decades of the twentieth century, just as Durant predicted it would be, the park had become a major summer destination. At the Raquette Lake railroad station a special shed was constructed to house the private sleeper cars of the wealthiest regulars. Alfred Vanderbilt's car, the *Wayfarer*, was often there, as was Collis Huntington's *Genesta*, William C. Whitney's *Wanderer*, and Robert Collier's *Vagabondia*. J. P. Morgan Sr., the richest of them all, just rented an ordinary Pullman car.

On the Adirondack and Saint Lawrence line, William Seward Webb had not one but two private railroad stations to serve his camp, Nehasane. He had, after all, built the railroad. Webb's instructions were that under no circumstances should the trains stop at either station unless a passenger could produce a signed invitation to the camp, and Webb's orders were generally followed to the letter by railroad staff. In 1892, when he wired his chief engineer that a spur to Loon Lake Hotel was required so that President Benjamin Harrison could take his invalid wife there for a visit, the men graded and laid the required mile of track overnight.

Interior of living room in the main lodge at William Seward Webb's camp, Nehasane, circa 1890, by T. E. Marr. COURTESY OF THE ADIRONDACK MUSEUM, BLUE MOUNTAIN LAKE.

People who owned their own railroad cars and stations, who for that matter owned their own railroads, were unlikely to be content continuing their journey with the hoi polloi on Durant's public steamships. In the early years of the twentieth century private steamboats like the *Stella,* which was owned by Durant's cousin Charles, or A. T. Strange's *Lorna Doone* met owners and guests at the Raquette Lake station. Lucy Carnegie had a steamer named *Raquette* that ferried guests over to the camp she had purchased from the Ten Eyck family. A New York wine merchant named Frederick Hasbrouck had a steamer named the *Mohawk 2* to take him and his guests to the family camp up in Raquette Lake's North Bay.

Motorboats—gloriously polished wooden boats with newfangled gas engines—gradually replaced the steamers. The publisher Robert Collier always made a point of having the fastest boat on Raquette Lake and the Eckford Chain. First it was a boat called the *Skeeter,* which could go twenty-five miles an hour with its sixty-horsepower engine until 1913, when he crashed it into a steamer. It was no great loss because he had already replaced it with the *Stop Thief,* in which his passengers could enjoy the serenity of the Adirondack lake country at forty-five miles an hour. The following year he bought a raftlike rig with an airplane engine. It was purported to be a hydroplane, and when it worked it could even beat the *Stop Thief.*

Collier was also the first to bring an airplane to the Adirondacks. The Curtiss-Wright biplane arrived in a boxcar on a summer day in 1912 and crashed into the lake a month later. Nonetheless, by the mid-1920s floatplanes were becoming standard accoutrements of the super-wealthy in the Adirondacks.

August was by far the most popular month to be in the park, and not only because the black flies and mosquitoes were fewer then. Suntans were not yet fashionable, and after spending July on the shore in Rhode Island, society women, in particular, wanted to regain their white skin before returning to their respective cities in the fall. They came for the shade.

Perhaps because the Adirondacks became a station on the annual migrations of the very rich, in most places camp life gradually became more formal and stylized. "Some of us took a firm stand against evening clothes," wrote Hooker [in *Camp Chronicles*] of life on the Saint Regis Lakes. "We always told our guests not to bring them and I believe Dr. James, after due notice, even went so far as to throw a guest in the lake because he came all dressed up." Her mother, she said, preferred flannel suits and "coarse stockings" to tuxedos.

But the battle to keep the place relaxed was apparently a lost cause. "I once saw one of our neighbors in full evening dress and bedecked with diamonds paddling in a canoe with a man in a 'boiled' shirt en route to a dinner at the Vanderbilts!" [This was not Alfred Vanderbilt, of Sagamore, but his relative Frederick Vanderbilt.] Even Mr. Hooker himself eventually blinked, though his daughter implies that it wouldn't have happened if he hadn't been acting in his official capacity as commodore of the Saint Regis Yacht Club.

"The time came when he felt that in politeness to his guests, who most of them dressed in the evenings, he should wear a dinner coat too," she wrote. "We protested but father was firm and sent for his coat to Lenox. When the night of the party arrived Father sat at the head of the table in all his glory, but there wasn't another tuxedo to be seen. All the guests, in deference to what they knew was Father's preference in camp, had come in camp clothes. . . . It was soon after this that our nice green yacht club coats were introduced so that everyone would know what the well-dressed man should wear."

The evolution toward haute camp life could have been due to the influence of Durant's introduction of artistic camps, a logical result of packaging and selling of wilderness as a salable commodity complete with its own design aesthetic. Or it could have been that champagne and caviar were the inevitable outcome of events when the elite of the Gilded Age got involved in a place. It could also be that, after years of bringing more belongings up to camp than one brought home, a critical mass of material objects was reached that simply demanded a more formal style of living. But whether architecture and interior decoration drove the lifestyle, or the lifestyle drove the design, Adirondack wilderness retreats became increasingly baroque.

At the Adirondack Museum are two photographs of the mantel in the central cottage of Camp Fairview, which belonged to William West Durant's cousin Charles W. Durant. Craig Gilborn, former director of the museum, included them in his book *Durant* because they show the process of accumulation that almost inevitably filled the Great Camps to overflowing with what one critic of the Victorian age in the Adirondacks called artistic clutter.

Adolph Lewisohn at the boathouse of his camp on Upper Saranac Lake, circa 1904, photographer unknown. COURTESY OF THE ADIRONDACK MUSEUM, BLUE MOUNTAIN LAKE.

In the first photo, taken in 1885 by Albert Bierstadt, the handsome fieldstone mantel is decorated with a single white plaster figurine, a large Japanese fan, and two framed engravings. Twenty-one years later, when the second photograph was made, the figurine has been joined by another and both are raised nearly to the ceiling on rustic birch-wood pedestals. These pedestals were apparently constructed to make room on the mantel for the mirrors, photos, plates, vases, bundles of feathers or arrows, and miscellaneous unidentifiable objects that crowd the shelf to overflowing. The Japanese fan is still there, but only a corner of it is visible.

"It was the Vanderbilts, by the way, who put the Japanese touch to the Pratt Camp," wrote Hooker. There had been something of a Japan craze in the country ever since Commodore Perry's "opening" of that country in 1853, and Japanese paraphernalia was almost as popular in the camps as dead animals and twig furniture. But the Vanderbilts had actually traveled to the Far East, and they came back more enthusiastic than most.

"They sent for an army of little Japs," Hooker recalled, "who had just completed the Japanese Village for the Buffalo World's Fair, to come and make their camp over. They not only had the cabins Japanized, they dressed all their maids in kimonos! They had taken over a stout English maid of Mother's, and she nearly died of embarrassment when she had to appear before us in this odd new uniform."

Viewed from a canoe portaged over from the wilds of the Saint Regis Canoe Area, or from the front of Bob Inslerman's trapping boat, the pagoda-like buildings of Pine Tree Point make it one of the more easily identifiable camps on Upper Saint Regis today. But it is by no means the only summer home in the neighborhood that departs from the familiar log style.

The boathouse of nearby Katia is a rounded, medieval-looking building constructed entirely out of boulders. With its three arched doorways facing the lake, and conical roof, it is particularly graceful and lovely in the autumn mist. The owner of Katia, George Earle of Philadelphia, liked his boathouse so much that on the other side of the ridge from Katia, on Spitfire Lake, he built a camp for his daughters called Camp Cobblestone. Here everything is made of smaller stones, and the effect is not as good as at Katia. This camp, in the mist, looks like something built by trolls.

As the camp phenomenon progressed, architectural follies became more common. At Marjorie Merriweather Post's sprawling Topridge, one of the forty-odd buildings is a replica of a Russian dacha. At Kill Kare, in addition to the gondola that was imported from Venice, there is a reproduction of a Norman chapel. Robert Collier's camp on Raquette Lake had a gazebo on a tiny islet a hundred feet into the lake, accessible by a small footbridge. And his neighbors at the Inman family camp had a dance floor built out over the water, which went nicely with their floating vegetable garden. The open-air bowling lanes at Sagamore were built on six-foot-deep solid concrete foundations to prevent frost heave.

Finally, there is Litchfield Park. Edward Litchfield was a lawyer from Brooklyn who, in 1893, bought 8,600 acres southeast of Tupper Lake. He put a fence around it and tried unsuccessfully for a while to keep it stocked with game, some of it exotic to the region. In the middle of it all, a workforce of six hundred built him a French baronial manor out of reinforced concrete sheathed in granite.

The argument has been made by architectural historians that much of the essential appeal of the Great Camps to their owners was the

Two views of the master bedroom at Kamp Kill Kare, circa 1900, photographer unknown. COURTESY OF THE ADIRONDACK MUSEUM, BLUE MOUNTAIN LAKE.

improbability of such grandeur in the middle of the woods. And, it might be added, the power that such improbability implied. The architect of several camps, William G. Distin, had a client who approved initial sketches and promptly left for Europe. The client said, "I want it finished the day I get back," and Distin received a cable sometime later that said, "Will arrive Thursday. Please buy dishes and fittings and have roast lamb for dinner." Distin, the story goes, came through and was rewarded handsomely.

The pursuit of the novel and the improbable wasn't limited to the architecture. The headboard of a famous bed at Kill Kare is constructed of an entire peeled tree, complete with a stuffed owl sitting on one branch. At the same camp, in addition to the more usual bowling alley and squash court, there was a gun house with over two thousand pikes, guns, swords, powder horns, and related paraphernalia. And all of the trash cans at Adolph Lewisohn's camp on Upper Saranac—some forty in all—were made of hollow logs, each embraced by a stuffed bear cub. A *real*, formerly live stuffed bear cub.

Stuffed game, big and small, was an almost universal design motif in the camps. One of the first buildings Vanderbilt added to Sagamore was a fifty-by-sixty-foot trophy room with an office at the back for the full-time staff taxidermist. The Litchfield Chateau is decorated with the skins of lions, tigers, zebras, elephants, hippos, giraffes, water buffalo, grizzlies.

It wasn't just trophies, either. Virtually anything seen moving outside could be shot, cleaned, stuffed, and brought inside. In many camps, small animals like squirrels and raccoons were set in lifelike poses under eaves, over doors, or incorporated into articles of furniture. Bear cubs peered around corners. Hats and coats were hung on hooves and antlers. Branches filled with stuffed songbirds hung over mantels.

The pelts and trophies indicated the odd relationship of the grandest camps to the woods and waters of the park. Along with the intricate and beautiful rustic furniture built by guides and caretakers in the off-season, the taxidermica served to connect the camps stylistically to the wilderness that the dead animals had once inhabited. More than that, though, the wilderness as expressed in the decor of the Great Camps was a fashion motif, a complete aesthetic that included everything from clothing to furniture to behavior. In 1922, Emily Post's book of eti-

Stuffed game, not always from the Adirondacks, was a nearly universal design motif at the grander camps. COURTESY OF THE ADIRONDACK MUSEUM, BLUE MOUNTAIN LAKE.

quette devoted a chapter to the special requirements of an Adirondack house party.

Ultimately, the moose heads and bear rugs were totems not so much of connection to the world God made, but of success back home in the human sphere. They were a sign of ample free time. And the camps, at least those that were big enough to have their own bowling alleys, billiard halls, putting greens, tennis and squash courts, and dance floors, were more like private theme parks than merely comfortable hunting outposts. They were, in their most extreme cases, almost a parody of the observation by the philosopher Hans Peter Duerr that "we should turn wild so as not to surrender to our own wildness, but rather to acquire in that way a consciousness of ourselves as tamed, as cultural beings."

The materialism explicit in the grandest camps shouldn't be emphasized to the point of overshadowing all else, however. Most of the camps in the Adirondacks were, after all, much more modest in scale. There were, and are, small camps up and down the Fulton Chain, around the back of Schroon Lake, and in a thousand other

Camp Cedars, on Forked Lake, circa 1930, by Margaret Bourke-White. COURTESY OF
THE ADIRONDACK MUSEUM, BLUE MOUNTAIN LAKE.

places. A hundred camps, most of them relatively compact compared
to those in the Saint Regis and Raquette Lake areas, rose on the
shores of Lake Placid between 1880 and 1900. They are often delight-
fully rustic in design, but they are simply summer places on the lake,
like summer places anywhere, enjoyed immensely by their owners and
resented occasionally by those who would prefer to see the land unin-
habited. Or at least, inhabited by themselves.

Furthermore, from the beginning there was an element of preservation in the urge to have a piece of wilderness to call one's own. As
early as 1864 the *New York Times*, in an editorial often quoted because
it described the region as "a tract of country fitted to make a Central
Park for the world," recommended private action to slow the progress
of logging.

"And here we venture a suggestion to those of our citizens who
desire to advance civilization by combining taste with luxury in their
expenditures," the editorial read. "Let them form combinations, and
seizing upon the choicest of the Adirondack Mountains, before they
are despoiled of their forests, make of them grand parks, owned in
common and thinly dotted with hunting seats."

The idea did not fall on deaf ears. By the 1890s there were some
sixty associations and hunting clubs that together controlled hun-

dreds of thousands of woodland acres. The largest of them all was the Adirondack League Club, which in 1893 owned or held hunting rights to some 200,000 acres in the southwest corner of the park. In the middle of the park, the Tahawus Club leased 96,000 acres from the now moribund Adirondack Iron and Steel Company (formerly the McIntyre Iron Works). In Keene Valley, the Adirondack Mountain Reserve, which is associated with, but not the same thing as, the Ausable Club, collected around 40,000 acres including the headwaters to the Ausable River and many of the state's tallest mountains.

The usual arrangement included a large central clubhouse and individual parcels out in the wild somewhere for members' personal camps. They were, in essence, immense cooperative Great Camps, and in virtually all of the many battles to come over the future of the Adirondacks, the power and prestige of the wealthy club members was wielded in favor of conservation and protection for the region. In 1902 some of the principals of the Adirondack League Club founded the Association for the Protection of the Adirondacks. With headquarters in New York City, the association became the leading defender of the forever-wild clause of the constitution during the twentieth century. In an era before mass environmental mailings and phone banks, the influence of the elite who populated the membership lists of the various clubs was even more critical than it is today.

It wasn't only business leaders, either. At various times Presidents Benjamin Harrison, Calvin Coolidge, Herbert Hoover, and Teddy Roosevelt visited the Adirondacks, along with scores of lesser politicians. The then Vice President Teddy Roosevelt, who was a member of the Tahawus Club, was lunching near the summit of Mount Marcy on September 13, 1901, when a guide rushed out of the woods with a telegram: President McKinley, who had been shot by an anarchist the week before, had taken an unexpected turn for the worse. After a breakneck descent back to the club and a hellish midnight buckboard ride that took five hours and exhausted three teams of horses and guides, Roosevelt arrived at the North Creek station and was administered the oath of office on a special train that was there waiting for him. His driver on the last leg of the trip, a guide named Mike Cronin, became a national hero.

Keene Valley and Saint Huberts, meanwhile, developed as favorite summer nesting grounds for prominent intellectuals. When the biggest

A happy moment at the Lake Placid Yacht Club, circa 1890 (photographer unknown).
COURTESY OF THE ADIRONDACK MUSEUM, BLUE MOUNTAIN LAKE.

farm holder in the valley, Smith Beede, decided to build a hotel on his land in 1876, he sold his old farmhouse and a few acres to the philosopher William James and three friends from Boston, Doctors Putnam, Putnam, and Bowditch. Putnam Camp, as they renamed their retreat, was often filled with faculty members from Harvard and elsewhere, and still is today.

It was James who invited Sigmund Freud and Carl Jung to the Adirondacks in 1909. "Of all the things that I have experienced in America, this is by far the most amazing," Freud wrote in a letter home. "Imagine a camp in a forest wilderness situated somewhat like the mountain pasture on the Loser, where the inn is. Stones, moss, groups of trees, uneven ground . . ."

Beginning in 1889 another group of philosophically inclined nature lovers gathered across the valley at a place called Glenmore. The leading light this time was Dr. Thomas Davidson, who was joined by Professors John Dewey of the University of Chicago, Josiah Royce of

Harvard, Max Margolis of Columbia, Harry Gardner of Smith, President James Angell of Yale, and others. The company was so rarefied and scintillating that William James was persuaded to leave his beloved Putnam and come join in the woodland conclave.

Literary types and social reformers, meanwhile, were more likely to be found nearby at a cooperative camp called Summerbrook. There the guest list over the decades on either side of the turn of the twentieth century included Maxim Gorky, Lillian Walds, Clarence Darrow, Upton Sinclair, and Jane Addams.

Last to officially arrive in the valley, but certainly not least among the associations, was the village of Saint Huberts and the hotel that would become the Ausable Club. Even before Smith Beede opened his hotel he began selling lots in the area to regular visitors. The first to buy, in 1870, was probably William Neilson, a mining executive from Pennsylvania who had come to the Adirondacks in connection with some local iron mines and had fallen in love with the territory. Felix Adler, the founder of the Ethical Culture Society in New York City, was another early homeowner on the heights, as were a number of his fellow ethical culturalists, including S. Burns Weston, whose son, Harold Weston, became a well-known Adirondack artist. Adler and the senior Weston founded, in 1897, the Adirondack Trail Improvement Society, which built and continues to maintain ninety miles of trails in the area around Keene Valley. Yet another neighbor was Robert W. DeForest, president of the Metropolitan Museum of Art.

In 1886, Neilson learned that a lumber company was poised to buy most of the land in the surrounding High Peaks. He quickly convinced a group of friends from Philadelphia and New York to purchase the 25,000 acres in question and form the Adirondack Mountain Reserve in 1887. Three years later the AMR bought out Beede's hotel, although the original building burned to the ground the same year. In 1903 its replacement, the St. Hubert's Inn, closed after losing money for a decade and a half; it was purchased by the AMR and opened as the Ausable Club in 1906.

The club and the AMR have their own long list of wealthy members and worthy guests: Mark Twain, John Burroughs, Henry Sloane Coffin, Woodrow Wilson, Charles Lindbergh. In the 1920s the executive committee held important discussions on how to cope with the new influx of chauffeurs. At some point it was determined that the

"Ladies Writing Room" was underutilized while the less spacious bar was overcrowded and so the two were switched.

But the headiest times at the Ausable Club were probably during the Second World War, when Secretary of War Henry L. Stimson and Assistant Secretary of War John McCloy, both club members, would arrive periodically for brief respites from the grim work in Washington. While most other members were forced by gas rationing to make use of the club shuttle bus, Stimson and his entourage arrived in camouflaged government automobiles.

The secretary of war was at the club, in fact, on the day the *Enola Gay* dropped the atomic bomb on Hiroshima. He rushed back to Washington where he convinced Truman to change the target of the second bomb from Kyoto, the religious and cultural capital of Japan, to Nagasaki. When the long war finally ended on V-J day, he and McCloy returned to the club and Stimson was given a standing ovation when he entered the dining room. "Let's have dinner," he said promptly and sat down.

The AMR and the other private associations not only used their considerable political and economic clout to influence the State Legislature in the direction of further protection of the Adirondacks, they tended to have more stringent controls on hunting and fishing than the state regulations required. The Adirondack League Club was a pioneer in game management; no deer were taken there before the first of September, two weeks later than the state season, which prevented the death by starvation of many fawns. The AMR, meanwhile, took more of a preservationist approach by banning hunting altogether. Fishing was and is restricted to members and guests; today there's a strict catch-and-release policy—with barbless hooks—for the four species of trout stocked in AMR lakes and streams.

Private land was also where the earliest attempts were made to restore, reintroduce, and in some cases introduce species of game missing from the park. At Nehasane, for instance, William Seward Webb put a ten-foot-high fence around 10,000 acres of what at one point was an almost 200,000-acre estate. He stocked the place with moose, elk, and black-tailed deer. But, as was usually the case, none of the animals survived for very long.

Webb also hired Gifford Pinchot in 1896 to come up with a management plan for the timber resources. As mentioned above, Pinchot, who later became the first head of the U.S. Forest Service, had bitterly opposed the forever-wild provision of the constitution as a needless waste of state assets. He viewed any forest "strictly as a factory of wood." But he was equally opposed to the wanton destruction by the prevailing practices of the logging industry in the Adirondacks and elsewhere. His science wasn't nearly up to the job, but Pinchot's insistence that sustainable yield be the long-term goal of logging was a step in the right direction.

Finally, it's worth noting that many large tracts of private land eventually came to be part of the Forest Preserve. Webb and his heirs eventually sold virtually all of his lands to the Forest Preserve. The Pruyn family, owners of Santanoni, sold their ten-thousand-acre tract to the Nature Conservancy for future inclusion in the Forest Preserve. The AMR, in a series of transactions ending in 1978, sold all of their High Peaks holdings to the state, retaining only a thin strip of land surrounding the Ausable Lakes.

There were also, over the years, countless gifts and sales of land that were not as large in acreage as the great tracts already mentioned, but were nonetheless of great strategic importance to the protection of the park. The Loines family, for instance, collected much of the land on the western shore of Lake George's Northwest Bay, and then gave the critical river frontage along Northwest Bay Brook to the Nature Conservancy, effectively preventing any future bridge being built to the exquisite and still wild promontory known as Tongue Mountain.

Quite understandably, though, there were many already in the Adirondacks who resented bitterly the locking up of the woods, for whatever reason. In the 1890s William Rockefeller bought a tract of land north of Paul Smiths that included the entire town of Brandon. The entire town, that is, except the homestead of one Oliver Lamora and a few of his neighbors. Lamora refused to sell out, even though traveling very far off his yard generally meant getting arrested for trespassing.

Lamora was found guilty of that offense often enough that he gradually became a national hero of sorts for standing up to the robber baron. He even had the gall to argue in court that he should be allowed to fish in Rockefeller's lakes since they were, after all, being stocked with trout by the state of New York.

In the middle of all this, in 1903, one of Rockefeller's colleagues in the private-park fraternity, Orlando Dexter, was shot dead in front of the post office in the town of Santa Clara, just south of Brandon. Dexter had a seven-thousand-acre spread that he had fenced in, which was presumably the source of local anger toward him. Everyone in Santa Clara supposedly knew the killer, but no one ever revealed his or her identity. From then on, Rockefeller kept armed guards posted on towers around the perimeter of his camp. He also used his clout in Washington to have the Brandon post office moved to his Great Camp at Bay Pond.

Lamora eventually died, alone in his defiance, and his son accepted a thousand dollars for the old homestead. William Rockefeller's heirs still own their camp at Bay Pond, though they are currently selling a handful of house sites and shares in the property in order to offset the costs of maintaining a 21,000-acre estate.

Making too much of the excesses and implied inequities of the Great Camps overshadows the reality that it was (and no doubt is) just plain good fun to own or know someone who owns a fabulous Great Camp. Guests at Sagamore were met at the dock by a pair of matching carriages with matching horses ready to whisk them up to the lodge. Once there, after connecting with their appointed local leader in the "guides room," they could fish for trout spawned at the camp's own hatchery. They might go out in boats with guides on nearby larger lakes, or hunting in the fall. In the winter, Vanderbilt and his pals piled onto strings of toboggans to be pulled around the frozen lake by fast horses, with a silver trophy for whoever could stay on the longest.

Whatever they did during the day, though, Sagamore guests got back in time to change for cocktails and dinner. Afterwards, if they were male, cigars were in order in the building over the waterfall called the Wigwam, which was decorated with paintings by Renoir and Remington.

At Santanoni, the Pruyn family treated guests like Teddy Roosevelt to hunting and fishing trips out on Moose Pond, which they owned. There was no need to carry much gear since a building at the pond was fully equipped with guide boats and fishing tackle. The Whitneys and Rockefellers also had (and have) cabins and lean-tos on different ponds around their property for picnics or overnights. Guides, and often more elaborate staff, invariably went along to bait hooks, build fires, cook meals, and clean up.

The main lodge at Kamp Kill Kare, circa 1900 (photographer unknown). COURTESY OF THE ADIRONDACK MUSEUM, BLUE MOUNTAIN LAKE.

For the entertainment of their visitors at Kill Kare, each August the Garvan family, who bought the camp from the Woodruffs a few years after it was built, invited the entire baseball teams of Yale and Harvard up to the camp to play a series of games. They also brought a chef up from Delmonico's to prepare meals. At Adolph Lewisohn's, meanwhile, among the staff of forty or so who accompanied the family each summer was a professional chess player. And at Eagle's Nest, according to the bittersweet memoir *Half the Way Home* by the founding editor of *Mother Jones* magazine, Adam Hochschild, one rarely had lunch without first taking a trip around the lake on water skis.

Lavish entertaining required good help and plenty of it, and the relationship between staff and owner was often quite close. In particular the job of camp superintendent, or chief caretaker, is an honored profession in the Adirondacks. At Sagamore, where the job was occasionally handed down from generation to generation, there was a school for the children of the twenty or so year-round employees. These employees would be augmented by the fifteen or so miscellaneous maids, butlers, cooks, secretaries, and others who usually arrived with the Vanderbilts at camp.

Not surprisingly, outfitting and running the biggest camps required prodigious amounts of money. Immediately after buying the

Ten Eyck camp, on Raquette Lake, Lucy Carnegie reputedly spent $200,000 to remodel and enlarge. This was in 1902, when a copy of the *New York Times* cost a penny. Even at camps with their own farms, dairy herds, and blacksmith shops, all of which had to be staffed throughout the year, many supplies had to be carried in by boat or over the ice in winter.

But servants and caviar weren't required elements of camp life. At a thousand more modest lodges and clubs all over the Adirondacks people grew up and grew old happily jumping off of docks, sailing over to church, racing canoes, building new cabins, fishing, bowling, dancing, playing Ping-Pong, wandering beneath pines. Climbing mountains. Falling in love. Talking about trees. Wondering how it was that Labor Day came so awfully fast this year.

"All felt as lazy as possible, realizing it was one last Sunday in camp," someone wrote in the communal diary of the Stott camp on the first day of September in 1895. "The moonlight and open camp were more than enjoyed in the evening. Then the maidens gathered around the fireside and talked until after midnight, ensconced in easy chairs and loose flowing garments."

23   *The Collector*

The current owner of J. P. Morgan's old place in the Adirondacks drives a vaguely beat-up compact car with New York license plates that read UNCAS. When Howard Kirschenbaum and some friends bought Durant's second masterpiece in 1975, it was a bit run-down. Long gone were the days when a private train waited over at Raquette Lake, kept fully stoked "up to steam" at all times in case the proprietor of Uncas desired a quick return to Manhattan. But the price was right: "It was basically being given away," said Kirschenbaum recently.

Uncas's progress to the bargain basement was not altogether unique among the greatest of Adirondack camps. As the twentieth century wore on, the money that built and maintained many of the largest camps dissipated. Vacation tastes changed, favoring the coast. Hunting and fishing declined in popularity, as well as in local quality. Maintenance costs increased. Progressive federal taxes were introduced. The children and grandchildren of moguls who were uninterested or unable to afford their sprawling camps looked for buyers. Sometimes camps were simply given away to worthy institutions, or to the Forest Preserve.

Pine Knot, Eagle's Nest, Sagamore, and Topridge have all done time or are currently serving as conference and training centers for various not-for-profit enterprises. Nehasane went into the Forest Preserve, as did Santanoni. More than a few Great Camps succumbed to fires, mysterious and otherwise.

When Kirschenbaum bought Uncas it had been a Boy Scout camp for almost a decade. Judging by reports from the early seventies, earning a historic preservation badge was not a priority at the camp. Craig Gilborn, who visited Uncas in 1973, wrote that "the Manor House had become a nearly-empty shell." Kirschenbaum himself is a little more generous about the condition of the place when he acquired it in 1975. "It was structurally sound," he said, "but frayed."

Kirschenbaum already owned Durant's other masterpiece, Sagamore, which he had purchased a few months earlier. Alfred Vanderbilt's widow, Margaret Emerson, had donated the estate to Syracuse University in 1950, but by the seventies the maintenance proved to be more than the institution wanted to bear. Sagamore and fifteen hundred acres were all set to be sold to the state for inclusion in the Forest Preserve when architectural preservationists around New York, and to a lesser extent the rest of the country, became alarmed.

Under the forever-wild provision of the constitution, Durant's most famous camp—where Hoagy Carmichael supposedly wrote "Stardust" while riding a beat-up Model-A Ford up the driveway—was to be torn down to make room for trees. In an unusual last-minute deal, however, the state carved eight acres that included the camp out of the purchase. A frantic search for a buyer willing to accept a long list of restrictions ended with Howard Kirschenbaum's business, an outfit that ran teacher training seminars. The price for Sagamore was $100,000.

"So within the course of a year I suddenly became the owner and manager of not one but two Great Camps, and I began to find out what that meant," Kirschenbaum recalled twenty years later. "And pretty soon my interest in historic preservation began to equal my interest in education. Since then I've been pursuing two careers simultaneously."

In other words, Kirschenbaum became one of the leading crusaders for the preservation of the remaining architecturally interesting camps of the Adirondacks. In this quest, he is not one to give up, even when the odds of success seem remote. Soon after the purchase of Sagamore, it became apparent that the sale had not included some service buildings that were located a quarter mile from the main complex. The collection of sheds went into the Forest Preserve, apparently doomed to destruction. Kirschenbaum went to work lining up allies for an unlikely effort to amend the constitution of the state of New York.

"These were the eleven caretaking buildings, the men's camp, the barns, the blacksmith shop. . . . At first glance you might have agreed [with the state] that they had no architectural significance. But at second glance you find that part of the value of a Great Camp is being able to see how it functioned almost as a little village; a place where people lived throughout the year. Where they had their blacksmith shops and whatever else they needed to create the crafts that ultimately became synonymous with the Adirondacks. To have half a camp is to not have a camp at all.

"With a Great Camp itself, it's mostly an hour of work here patching this, a day there replacing that, a thousand-dollar investment there, five hundred here. So to actually wake up one morning [in 1983] and find that the voters of New York had overwhelmingly passed our constitutional amendment to save the Sagamore outbuildings was something very tangible," he said. "It was enormously satisfying."

Kirschenbaum is a slender man with sandy hair that is beginning to show signs of gray, and he wears wire-rim glasses. He talked over lunch at a picnic table outside the main dining hall of a Great Camp. It was not at Sagamore Lodge, however, with which he is no longer involved. Nor was it at Uncas, where, he said at one point, "I go on the weekends to do a little reroofing strictly for my own pleasure." Kirschenbaum was seated at a picnic table outside the main dining hall of yet another falling-down masterpiece he has taken under his wing—White Pine Camp.

White Pine Camp is on Osgood Pond, not far from Paul Smiths. It originally belonged to a family named White, but is better known for having been, in 1926, Calvin Coolidge's "summer White House." The camp is not in the Durant style; it has instead a sort of proto-modern feel with funky roof lines more evocative of sixties beach bungalows than of artistic log cabins. But as Kirschenbaum is quick to point out, there are unpeeled logs supporting porch roofs, and the boathouse has many rustic details.

"May I help you? Are you waiting for your lunch?" he said at one point to an elderly couple who wandered up to the picnic table. Kirschenbaum and some associates have a twelve-year plan to restore

White Pine and turn it into a sort of museum of the Great Camps. There is much still to be done, but tourists already tour it.

"No?" he said when the two visitors shook their heads in unison. "Well, be sure to walk down to the lake and across the footbridge to the bowling alley. I'm sure you'll enjoy that. The bowling alley is really something special."

As they picked their way down the path Kirschenbaum continued on a thought that had been interrupted, "I think what brought the wealthy families to the Adirondacks and got them involved with building and living in these camps was not unlike what brought the average person who wanted to live in a little log cabin or even camp out in the open.

"It was consistent with a long American back-to-nature movement that had been revived after the Civil War. A belief that leaving the city with its unhealthy air, claustrophobic living conditions, crime and poverty, and coming to the natural area brought them closer to . . . people would say God. Nature. Closer to themselves. Closer to basic values that they held.

"And to relax and to recreate, of course, to put it in less romantic terms."

Perhaps because of his many years of working in education, Kirschenbaum often begins a thought by restating the question he is interested in answering. "There's the issue of continuity," he said at one point. "If there's one specific place in the Adirondacks that you keep coming back to, what does that do to your sense of attachment and value that you give to the wilderness? How is that different from persons who hike through and camp all over?

"I think those families who returned summer after summer, whether it was to the North Woods Club or the Ausable Club or to a nice camp or lodge on Osgood Pond, became fiercely attached to what they grew up with. And they still are attached. They don't even improve their buildings. A lot of times the walls have studs showing, and people who could well afford to insulate and cover them keep it the way it is. Because, they say, 'That's what camp always was.'

"I'm thinking specifically of the Brandreth family in Brandreth Park, or the Rockefeller family at Bay Pond Park, or members of the Adirondack League Club over by Old Forge. They really invest a lot of resources in keeping things the way they remember them. . . . And families with small individual camps on two-acre lots, they join the

Adirondack Council or some other environmental group. They write letters to preserve the park and to resist development, often with a great deal of passion.

"So the Great Camps are alive and well, depending on how you number them. If you number them at around forty—those of the largest scale and the most interesting decorative features—about half are still in private ownership. If you add the grand camps—fine lodges with a few auxiliary buildings that go with them, quality structures architecturally—you could number those in the hundreds, and they are predominately in private hands. . . .

"Should they all be preserved? Well, you know, how many fine examples of Victorian architecture are enough? How many great Art Deco buildings are enough? I don't think that you can put it terms of a 'should.' But I grieve every time a lovely structure that contributes to our heritage, whether it's a Great Camp or something else, is lost. It's a little piece of our tradition that's gone. So once in a while we fight like hell when something really valuable like Santanoni is at stake."

Boat landing at Echo Camp, Raquette Lake, circa 1886, artotype by Edward Bierstadt. COURTESY OF THE ADIRONDACK MUSEUM, BLUE MOUNTAIN LAKE.

Santanoni is a haunting collection of structures on Newcomb Lake just south of the High Peaks. It was designed by the New York architect Robert Robertson, who was a member of the nearby Tahawus Club, and built for the Pruyn family beginning in 1888. There are five thousand square feet of porches around and between the five main cottages of the camp. Fifteen hundred trees were used in its construction.

In the 1970s Santanoni's owners decided the best use for their ten thousand Adirondack acres was as forever-wild parkland; they sold it to the Nature Conservancy with the understanding that the state would eventually buy the land when it could. No provisions were made for saving the camp itself, and Santanoni now lies five miles into the Forest Preserve.

There are many in the park who believe the sanctity of the Forest Preserve requires that the camp be razed or at least allowed to decay into the forest that surrounds it. "Look, maybe if I spent more time studying the houses of the robber barons I'd be more interested in saving them," a senior official at the Adirondack Park Agency has said. "Given the choice, though, I'd prefer more wilderness." He then went on to quote the Adirondacker and early wilderness advocate Robert Marshall, whose logic Kirschenbaum himself had perhaps unconsciously borrowed when asked how many Great Camps are worth saving. Marshall, who was one of the founders of the Wilderness Society, famously answered the question of how many wilderness areas the country should have with the reply, "How many Brahms symphonies do we need?"

But of course Kirschenbaum and his fellow architectural preservationists, who once got the state constitution amended to save a men's dormitory, were not going to let Santanoni go without a fight. Nor, for that matter, was the town of Newcomb, which has struggled financially ever since the National Lead operation at the old McIntyre mine closed.

"I'm on the citizens' advisory committee for Santanoni," Kirschenbaum explained, "and a number of us pushed for a more active use there. A classroom for schoolchildren, perhaps, where they could stay overnight in simple accommodation. No motorized traffic, something small scale and in harmony with the Forest Preserve, but using it in some fashion.

"I don't know if you've ever skied down there in the winter but it would be nice to be able to get there and have a fire in the fireplace and be able to get a bowl of soup and a sandwich. Some of us have been saying that there could be this more active use of the camp and not be in conflict with the Forest Preserve.

"And the environmental members of the advisory committee, those that represent various environmental groups, are generally saying 'You're right. That's the right thing to do with Santanoni. That's the best use of Santanoni.'

"But they've got trouble with the precedent of watering down [the forever-wild provision of] the constitution. The environmental groups just don't trust the Department of Environmental Conservation. They worry the state might open soup kitchens all over the preserve. The metaphor you always hear is 'Don't let the camel get its nose under the tent.' I'm not sure what it means, I don't know what a camel does when it gets its nose there, but I've heard the line five times in reference to the DEC in this process."

After years of debate, a compromise has apparently been reached between those who love fine buildings and those who love the forever-wild clause of the constitution precisely because it has no room for buildings. "It basically says Santanoni's buildings can stay if they're not really used, but just kind of preserved passively as kind of an archeological site," is how Kirschenbaum described it with a strong hint of displeasure in his voice.

But nothing is really over. Nothing, it seems, is ever over when it comes to the politics of the Adirondack Park and how many roads and buildings a place can have and still be "forever wild."

"It may require a constitutional amendment to do it, but some of us are seriously working to see some soup down there," Kirschenbaum said in all seriousness. Then he smiled, and a few minutes later excused himself to return to his office in what used to be White Pine Camp's caretaker cottage.

Down the hill from the picnic table, across the rebuilt footbridge from which Calvin Coolidge used to cast flies at rising trout and then along the shoreline past the bowling alley, is one of White Pine's two boathouses. The dock is in disrepair, and the building itself is listing a little, though not precariously. It does not feel unsafe to venture in.

Lying diagonally across the rough wooden floor is an enormous wood-and-canvas canoe, almost thirty feet long. There are several holes in its hull, and patches of rot, but it is cheerfully colored. Someone long ago painted bright blue and yellow stripes diagonally along both bow and stern.

In foot-high rustic letters just beneath the gunnels amidships they painted the boat's name; *Poetry in Motion.* And in slightly smaller letters, running along the entire length of the boat, are the hand-painted names of children long grown up who presumably once paddled the great canoe around Osgood Pond or some other Adirondack lake. *Don, John, Tom, Brian, Loren, Brian, Bumper, Eldred.*

There's a curious forlorn quality to the *Poetry in Motion* that will most likely survive the growth of a tourist destination around it. It is not an eerie thing, though, like the black log buildings of Santanoni. There, if you peer into the main lodge, the only surviving bits of the old days are a ghostly white stuffed beaver keeping company on the mantel with a nearly featherless stuffed egret.

The *Poetry in Motion* is just somebody's old friend, left behind to decompose while far across Osgood Pond, in front of another camp barely discernible through the trees, paddles still flash on certain summer afternoons.

24 *A Home in the Woods*

Noah John Rondeau, one of the most famous in the long tradition of Adirondack hermits, lived in a hole in his woodpile for thirty-three years. All summer long he'd build teepees of firewood. He cut long poles of a good burning diameter and notched them almost all the way through at the appropriate lengths for his fire. He then leaned them together, leaving a passageway into the center of the stack. There he would live all winter, slowly using up the poles in his fire.

Rare photos of Rondeau show a man with a long but well-kept beard. He wore round spectacles and read whatever he could get his hands on, though astronomy was his favorite subject. He wrote his diary in a secret code, and "flapped his jacks in bear grease" before rolling them up like cigars and biting off bites to be washed down with a swig of syrup. Clarence Petty, a man now in his eighties who used to visit "old Noey" as a child, remembers that Rondeau kept skillets hidden in various hollow trees all over his neck of the woods so that if he got hungry while out on a hunting trip he wouldn't have to return to camp to cook.

When he was in his sixties, Rondeau built himself a semipermanent hovel at an abandoned logging camp near the Cold River Flow. Here he had a guest house of sorts that was slightly larger than his own place and was appropriately decorated in the rustic style of a Great Camp.

"This jointed shelter does have a window," wrote a reporter who visited him in 1947, "and more extensive decoration—the chalky shoulder blades of a dozen beavers, the antlers of bygone bucks and the skulls of two degreased bears. These rattle nicely in the breeze and add to the general cheer."

25   *The Long Good Fight*

"Look, I'm sitting over here listening to you," said Paul Schaefer at last, "and all I can think of is that you're all willing to accept peanuts when what we want is a full dressed meal."

It was late August of 1992, at an informal meeting of a dozen and a half leading Adirondack conservationists who were gathered at Schaefer's rustic hunting cabin just outside the Siamese Ponds Wilderness in the southern part of the park. Dan Plumley was there representing the Adirondack Council. Joe Mahay, the president of the Resident's Committee to Protect the Adirondacks, was there. The environmental writer Bill McKibben, whose home is in the park, was there as were several members of the Adirondack Northwoodsmen.

The meeting had been organized by David Gibson, the executive director of the venerable Association for the Protection of the Adirondacks, in the hope of jumpstarting a movement that appeared to be floundering in the wake of a string of setbacks. "They had all gotten discouraged," Schaefer recalled in his year-round home in Schenectady a few months after the event.

"It began with the defeat of the bond act," he went on. By the slimmest of margins, in 1990 New York voters for the first time ever rejected a bond issue that would have allowed the state to purchase significant pieces of private real estate for inclusion in the Forest Preserve. "But then on top of that, there was this business of Senator Stafford having control over all legislation in the park . . ." Schaefer's voice trailed off.

It is commonly believed in Empire State environmental circles that as part of a deal for support in his bid to become State Senate majority leader, Republican Ralph Marino of Long Island promised his colleague Ronald Stafford of Plattsburgh virtual veto power over all legislation affecting the Adirondack Park. Stafford, to put it mildly, is not considered by conservationists to be a friend of the park.

"The scale of this outrage has never been properly highlighted as it should have been," Schaefer fumed. "I can tell you a lot of things Tammany Hall did, most of them involved money. But it was never anything like this. It didn't involve priceless heritage, country . . ." His voice trailed off again.

Occasionally, at the ends of sentences, Schaefer's age is audible. He was born in 1908. But when he is exhorting the faithful, the powerful, or the unconvinced to fight the good fight for the sake of the Adirondack wilderness, there are no long pauses. There is no wavering. "There were a lot of small pieces of the Adirondacks that different people at that meeting wanted the state to get. And they were saying if we get some of these small ones we should be satisfied. And I said to them, NEVER. NEVER."

He pounded his fist on the coffee table. "I told them to go for something big enough to be a banner to rally under. Say you want something great, not that you want peanuts. Don't talk about some thousand-acre wetland down in the southern Adirondacks. Talk about the finest piece of private land in the whole park."

What he wanted his colleagues to do was unite behind an effort to get Albany to buy the fifteen thousand acres known as Follensby Park. Follensby Pond, where Ralph Waldo Emerson and his friends held the Philosophers' Camp in 1858, was more recently chosen by the Federal Fish and Wildlife Service as the best possible location in the Adirondacks to reintroduce bald eagles. An agreement between the state of New York and the present owner of Follensby, John S. McCormick, to buy the land was all set to go, but fell through when the bond act failure left the state without the reported five- to six-million-dollar price.

"I told them that Follensby is by far the most significant thing we've got to get. We've got to do everything we possibly can right now to get it. We've got to put pressure on the Senate, pressure on the governor. *Now,* I told them, not three years from now, not two years, but *now.* It's the finest piece of private land in the park."

When pressed as to whether his ranking of Follensby was a bit of hyperbole for the sake of the cause, Schaefer scoffed. "Oh, it's a gem," he said. "Twenty-two square miles. A three-mile-long lake. Bounded by the Raquette River. Heavily covered with big forest. Big pines, where eagles are nesting. They were introduced in 1984. *Eagles nesting there!* Feeding on the fish in the lake! The lake is filled with original strains of brook trout. It is simply the best.

"Sure, Whitney Park is fifty-one thousand acres and this is only fourteen thousand six hundred, something like that," he went on. Whitney Park is the largest remaining private family reserve in the park. "But the point is, Follensby has more ecological significance. With its location midway on the west side of the High Peaks wilderness, bordered by the Raquette River, on relatively low land with the High Peaks right there. No, it's unique. Nothing compares. In fifty years there has not been one better piece of land offered. This is the kind of land that a war could be fought over."

Paul Schaefer knows of what he speaks. The Adirondack Park is occasionally described as an accidental wilderness, in reference to the fact that its original promoters were far more interested in water supplies for their canals and their downstate cities than they were in the preservation of wild places. There is some truth to the assessment. Even Verplanck Colvin, whose eloquent writings on the mysteries of the region's wilds were "almost memorized" by a young Paul Schaefer, abhorred the notion of a preservation for preservation's sake. "The idea of such an unproductive and useless park we utterly and entirely repudiate," Colvin told the Legislature in the 1870s.

But Schaefer's lifework attests to the deeper truth that virtually nothing that has happened since the creation of the park and the Forest Preserve a century ago has been accidental. There have been many battles, some of them epic, over the future of the Adirondacks and the meaning of "forever wild." And ever since 1929, Paul Schaefer has been at or near the front lines. The Adirondacks are as remarkably wild and open as they are today only because he, and many others like him, lost fewer fights than they won.

Almost as soon as the State Constitution of 1894 was ratified, its forever-wild clause came under assault. During the very first session of the Legislature under the new charter both houses passed an amendment to permit the state to sell, trade, and lease pieces of the Forest Preserve. The measure passed both houses the following year, as required for constitutional amendments, but the voters rightly perceived it as a giveaway to the timber interests and rejected it overwhelmingly in 1896.

Other early attempts to weaken the constitution were beaten back by the Association for the Protection of the Adirondacks. But in 1913, the state's water interests succeeded where the loggers had failed. That year the voters approved a change allowing 3 percent of the Forest Preserve to be flooded for reservoirs. The Burd Amendment was the first significant crack in the forever-wild clause of the constitution and it would, in later years, come to haunt Paul Schaefer.

Before the dam builders arrived in the woods in earnest, however, the state bureaucracy itself attempted to redefine the Forest Preserve along lines more to its liking. In 1927, as a memorial to the veterans of World War I, the voters allowed a road to be constructed through Forest Preserve land to the summit of Whiteface Mountain. Two years later, the Conservation Commission (a predecessor of today's DEC) tried unsuccessfully to argue in the state courts that a bobsled run for the upcoming 1932 Lake Placid Olympic Games was a use of Forest Preserve that was compatible with "forever wild."

And in 1930, apparently at the direction of the master power broker of the period, State Council of Parks Chairman Robert Moses, several upstate legislators introduced what became known as the "Closed Cabin Amendment." This amendment would have allowed the state to build lodges, hotels, and various other recreational facilities on state land. It would have permitted soup kitchens all over the Forest Preserve.

About this time young Paul Schaefer met his mentor. "I was chairman of the Conservation Committee of the Mohawk Valley Hiking Club and I had seven members—seven guys with me," Schaefer recalled sixty-five years later. "And I was trying to find the key conservationist of the Schenectady area to help us to know what to do." After several false leads, Schaefer wound up at the door of John Apperson.

"When I found Apperson at last, he was an official at General Electric, and I set up a meeting with him and my gang. So we were together this one night and Appy started out sitting on a settee like this one I'm on, and we were all sitting on the floor around him. And first thing you know, he was sitting up on the back with his feet on the seat waving his arms and giving us all kinds of ideas. Telling us that there was a great big job to do, and that that job was to photograph the Adirondacks, and stop the nonsense of talking about stuff you haven't seen." Apperson made a point of always knowing the details of a contested place better than the opposition did, and having the photos and movies to prove it.

" 'You guys go to it,' he said to us. 'You're the first people that I can ever relate to that will carry on my work. Are you guys willing to do it?' " Schaefer paused, remembering. He smiled, and after a moment said, "Well, we were Appy's wheels after that."

Apperson and his new troops were instrumental in brokering a deal between Governor Franklin Delano Roosevelt and the Legislature that expanded the park by around a million and a half acres to include Lake George and the western shores of Champlain. After countless community meetings around the state, massive mailings of pamphlets, editorial submissions to newspapers large and small, they and the Association for the Protection of the Adirondacks handed Robert Moses one of the rare defeats in his long career. In 1932 the voters of New York State resoundingly defeated the Closed Cabin Amendment.

"Appy was unique," Schaefer reminisced. "He climbed Mount Marcy on skis in 1912; I have his picture here climbing that mountain, which you should see if I can catch my breath and try to remember where it is." He stood up and ran his hand through his thick white hair.

Paul Schaefer often ends sentences by rising and saying, "I want you to take a look at something." His house, which he built himself, is full to overflowing with photos, transcripts, letters, maps, pamphlets, and other documentary evidence of the long crusade. There are bits of Adirondack history from long before Schaefer's time as well. In one drawer is a map book used by British troops during the American Revolution that shows the Adirondacks as a great blank area with the handwritten legend, "This country by reason of mountains, swamps and drowned lands is impassable and uninhabitable." Near the stairs is a sketch by Verplanck Colvin.

On one wall of the largest room in the house, the vaulted and rustic "Adirondack room," is a twelve-foot-tall relief map of the park. It was handmade by painstakingly tracing onto cardboard and then cutting out each and every contour line on a complete set of topographic maps of the region. For nine years, Schaefer and fifty of his friends cut, glued, plastered, and painted the map. It dominates the room even more than the enormous fieldstone fireplace, where most winters Schaefer and his friends gather at least once to roast venison steaks and reminisce about the previous year's hunting trips to the park.

But despite the vastness of his collection of Adirondack memorabilia, it rarely takes Schaefer long to find whatever it is that he is seeking among the countless black three-ring binders. He soon returned with a binder full of photographs, including the desired one of John Apperson.

"Appy was a pioneer. He knew nothing about the constitution or the Adirondacks until he made that climb up Marcy on skis. Then he saw all this fantastic country that was protected by the constitution and decided to spend the rest of his life fighting for it. Not getting married or anything. And that's what he did. That's all he did: fight for article seven, section seven. That was Appy. He devoted his whole life to it.

"I was a contractor, trying to make a living for me and my family, restoring old places all over the state and Apperson wrote me once and said, 'You are of course right in saying that you must take care of your business. But if you could have as few regrets after a lifetime of fighting for the Adirondacks as I do, you will not regret having done it.'

"And I took his advice," Schaefer said matter-of-factly. "He and I became very close friends and he was with us right up to the beginning of the Moose River fight. And then we ran too fast for him. He couldn't keep up with us. One day he said, 'Paul, you're over my head, you don't need me anymore, take it away.' And so I did."

The Moose River fight was the first battle in what has been called the Black River War. It began with a proposal by a semipublic corporation called the Black River Regulating District to build a dam across the South Branch of the Moose River near Higley Mountain in the southwest quarter of the park.[1]

---

[1] A similar outfit called The Hudson River Regulating District succeeded in flooding the "great vale" that had supported the ducks hunted by Sir William Johnson and his butler, Pontioch, when it built the dam that created the Great Sacandaga Lake.

Had it been built, the dam would have inundated the Moose River Plains, the largest winter deer-yarding ground in the park. It would have eliminated a half dozen ponds, as well as significant stretches of the Red and Indian Rivers and several smaller streams. The fight to stop it was to be Schaefer's finest hour, or rather his finest decade. But when he and the other conservation leaders first became aware of the proposed dam, in 1945, the cause appeared to be virtually lost.

All the necessary papers for the project were already signed and in place. The Forest Preserve land to be flooded fell within the 3 percent allowable under the 1913 Burd Amendment. When Schaefer and a colleague named Ed Richard visited the state conservation commissioner they were told they were too late to do anything. The fight, Commissioner Perry Duryea told them, was over. And it hadn't even happened. Even the Association for the Protection of the Adirondacks was ready to concede after its lawyers advised that there was no legal recourse. As Schaefer wrote in his book *Defending the Wilderness,* "bulldozers were ready to move in past Fawn Lake and down the Red River valley."

With no legal avenues open, the only hope for the Moose River Plains lay in a public outcry loud enough to prod Governor Dewey and the State Legislature into action. Schaefer and company went to work, making movies, printing pamphlets, lining up allies. In addition to the various national environmental groups, they enlisted hunting clubs, fishing clubs, garden clubs, churches, labor unions, bird-watchers, and so on until eventually Schaefer's Moose River Committee claimed a membership of a thousand local and national organizations. Within two years, Governor Thomas Dewey changed his mind and packed the board of the Black River Regulating District with opponents of the Higley Mountain Dam.

It was an enormous victory. But two short weeks later, Dewey announced his support for an even bigger dam only twelve miles downstream at a place called Panther Mountain. He had clearly cut a deal with the dam builders. In fact, it soon became apparent that Panther was only the beginning. The State Water Power and Control Commission had approved the construction of more than thirty reservoirs throughout the Adirondacks.

The fight raged on with various twists and turns until 1953, when the voters effectively undid the Burd Amendment and made it once again unconstitutional to flood Forest Preserve land. Incredibly, the supporters of the dam managed to get the next two sessions of the fickle Legislature to pass another amendment allowing construction of the Panther Mountain Dam. But it was overwhelmingly quashed by the voters in 1956.

Panther was the last close call as far as dams in the Forest Preserve were concerned. A decade later, when the Army Corps of Engineers and the City of New York proposed a massive dam on the upper Hudson, the assembly unanimously rejected it. Not surprisingly, once again Schaefer was involved behind the scenes.

"Laurance Rockefeller—this is Laurance Senior—was chairman of the State Council of Parks and we used to meet down in Rockefeller Plaza . . . and during the course of this fight I got hold of him and got him to go up to the Rainbow Room with me. I gave him a brochure we had just taken off the press," Schaefer recalled.

"He said, 'Give me time to read it.' So we walked around the Rainbow Room while he read it. There was no one there but us. . . . And he came back and he said, 'Now what do you want me to do?' And I said, 'Get me every single Republican vote in the Senate.' He said, 'Okay, I'll try.' And he did."

The conservationists' victories on the Moose River and in the earlier Closed Cabin fight are significant not only because they preserved the wild qualities of the land involved. As important was the nature of the arguments successfully used by Schaefer and others in their defense of the Forest Preserve. Noticeably gone was the talk of watershed protection, with its implication that wilderness needs a better excuse for existence than the fact that it does exist. Nor did advocates of protection any longer feel the need to explain that the land was no good for farming anyway.

"Leave this valley of the South Branch of the Moose River alone," Schaefer demanded in a 1948 issue of his magazine *Forest Preserve*, "that it may serve its highest use which is preservation in its natural state."

This belief in the intrinsic value of wilderness was in synch with the thinking of contemporary leaders of the national wilderness preservation movement like Robert Marshall, who grew up in the Adirondacks, and Howard Zahniser, who owned a cabin there. And of course, it echoed the writings of John Muir and Aldo Leopold. But, armed with the state constitution, Schaefer went even further than they did.

"Evening on Lake Raquette, Adirondacks," 1874, by James David Smillie. COURTESY OF THE ADIRONDACK MUSEUM, BLUE MOUNTAIN LAKE.

"A citizen may not have title to his home, but he does have an undivided deed to this Adirondack land of solitude and peace and tranquillity," he wrote in *Forest Preserve*. "The issue concerns his basic rights as a citizen of New York State." Wilderness had become, to its strongest advocates in the Adirondacks, a civil right.

There have been numerous skirmishes over the integrity of the Forest Preserve in the decades since the Black River War. After the "Great Blowdown of 1950" knocked over trees in several hundred thousand acres of Forest Preserve, lumber companies were allowed to go in and "salvage" the timber in the name of fire prevention. Three hundred acres of Forest Preserve were lost in 1959 to the construction of Interstate 87, "the Northway." In 1967, yet another constitutional convention scared many conservationists but produced a charter that was rejected by the voters. And in 1973, a float-plane operator unsuccessfully challenged in court the newly created Adirondack Park Agency's decision to prohibit motorized vehicles in 45 percent of the Forest Preserve.

For the most part, though, the largest battles of the final third of the twentieth century have focused on attempts to regulate the pace of development on private land in the park. The issue first came to the forefront in 1967, when the chairman of the State Council of Parks, Laurance Rockefeller, proposed the creation of a large national park in the Adirondacks. His plan included the purchase by the National Park Service of 600,000 acres of private land in the heart of the mountains.

The idea of such a federal takeover was immediately and resoundingly rejected by conservationists and home-rule types alike. But the proposal served to publicize the threat to the wilderness character of the park posed by unrestrained development of the 57 percent of the park that is not in the Forest Preserve.

In 1967 the Adirondack Park boundaries, which were originally drawn primarily to guide future additions to the Forest Preserve, were still virtually meaningless in any practical sense. The only parkwide regulation in place was a ban on off-site billboards. The town of Lake George, some thought, was already unrecognizable because of the honky-tonk arcade, theme park, souvenir shop, night club, and motel developments that characterize it today. There was nothing to prevent the rest of the park from following suit.

So when the dust from the national park furor settled in 1968, Governor Nelson Rockefeller, Laurance's brother, appointed the Temporary Study Commission on the Future of the Adirondacks. Harold Hochschild, the mining executive who owned Eagle's Nest and founded the Adirondack Museum, became the chairman. Harold Jerry, the current chairman of the Public Service Commission, was the executive secretary. Lowell Thomas, the radio commentator, was on the commission as well, but he made it to only one meeting.

In December of 1970 they submitted their recommendations to the governor. Those regarding the Forest Preserve were relatively straightforward: the state constitution should be left alone; the federal government should be left out; the rivers should be left wild.

But the recommendations of the commission that dealt with private land represented a major departure from the laissez-faire past. The main element was the creation of an Adirondack Park Agency, the APA, which would have extensive power to regulate development on private lands in the park. Local governments, the commissioners argued, usually didn't have the money or personnel to undertake comprehensive land plans. Nor were the town boards, which are often dominated by local business leaders in a position to profit from real estate development, naturally inclined to defend the interest the rest of the state's population had in preserving the large open spaces of the Adirondacks.

"If the Adirondacks are to be saved," Harold Hochschild warned Governor Rockefeller when the commission presented its report, "time is of the essence."

The legislation that Rockefeller introduced in May of 1971 essentially followed all of his commission's recommendations. In fact, it was largely written by the commission. The usual conservation forces came out in strength to lobby for the cause, which helped convince Rockefeller to strong-arm his Republican majority in both houses to overcome any philosophical qualms they may have had over regional planning. This was, after all, an era when on the national front bipartisan majorities in Congress were supporting the Clean Water Act, the Clean Air Act, the Endangered Species Act, and the National Environmental Protection Act.

Downstate Democrats, meanwhile, who might have chosen to oppose the bill on partisan grounds, were swayed in part by the arguments of a Manhattan assemblyman named Peter A. A. Berle. Berle pointed out that for the better part of a century, voters from the cities and towns outside the park had sent their hard-earned tax dollars up to local Adirondack governments in the form of the property taxes paid by the state on the Forest Preserve land. The APA, he said, would finally end an unacceptable situation of taxation without representation. It would give voice to the interests of all New Yorkers in the affairs of their great park.

At heart, the argument was over whether or not it is possible to legislate a middle ground between the constitutionally protected wilderness of the Forest Preserve and the unbridled civilization that threatened to surround it. It was about blurring the old philosophical schism between the human and wild worlds, and getting closer to a more ancient relationship with the land. Could the law foster something resembling a thoroughly modern version of a Great Longhouse in the six million acres of the park, a place where citizens can live and work and earn good livings without destroying the wilderness character of the place?

It was a debate over what today is called sustainable development; it was radical for the time. But on June 7, 1971, the Republican-dominated Assembly passed the legislation creating the Adirondack Park Agency by a vote of 123 to 24. The Republican-dominated State Senate followed suit the next day by a margin of 22 to 14. The Republican governor promptly signed it.

A year later the new agency unveiled its State Land Master Plan, designating what types of activities were permissible in different parts of the Forest Preserve. After a series of public hearings Rockefeller approved it. "Wilderness" now became an official bureaucratic term with a legal meaning. Put simply, wilderness in the Adirondacks was defined to exist in inverse proportion to the evidence of human impact. In fifteen areas of the Forest Preserve, comprising around a million acres, all roads and power lines were to be removed and all things motorized were banned.

Roughly the same amount of the Forest Preserve was defined as "Wild Forest," where snowmobiles and the like were allowed on designated trails and floatplanes were allowed on the lakes. The remainder was divided among five other categories depending on intensity of use. The ski lifts up the side of the forever-wild Forest Preserve on Whiteface Mountain, for instance, are part of an "Intensive Use Area." Day-to-day administration of the Forest Preserve would continue to be done by the Department of Environmental Conservation.

The APA plan for private land, which was unveiled in 1973, also divided the park into categories depending on intended use. In the existing towns and villages, or "hamlets," there were virtually no regulations other than that the towns were expected to come up with long-term plans of their own. The agency did retain the right to veto these if it had reason to believe a town's plan would have adverse regional impact by polluting a river, say, or allowing high-rise hotels that would spoil the view from the surrounding mountains.

The rest of the 3.8 million acres of private land in the park was divided into six categories ranging from the least restrictive "Industrial Use Areas" to the most restrictive "Resource Management Areas." The latter category includes most of the large timber company lands and large private reserves.

Not surprisingly, zoning the park's private land was a good deal more controversial than the Forest Preserve plan. Accordingly, the legislation that created the Park Agency required more than just the governor's approval for the Private Land Use and Development Plan to become law. The Legislature again had to act.

The battle was fierce, but this time around it largely took the form of smoky-room horse-trading. A local government review board was created. More money for town planners was coughed up. Rockefeller promised to fight any future effort to discontinue the special status of state land within the park that allowed local governments to collect taxes from the state.

The most substantive changes had to do with the future of the undeveloped lakes in the park. "It was necessary on four separate occasions during the campaign to pass the act to compromise with the opponents," Harold Jerry remembers, "and in every instance it was to relax the standards on shorefront development. Of course, shorefronts are exactly where the most pressure to build is; everybody wants a water view. So we ended up with the ludicrous situation of lakes being less protected than backwoods forested land, when wild shorelines needed the most protection of all."

Rockefeller was strong enough to veto a delay bill and then force passage of the plan by a wide margin. He was helped by the fact that in 1972, as if on cue, a developer from Arizona bought 24,000 acres on the Grass River in the northwest quarter of the park. "Horizon" was only the largest of several big subdivisions in the works, but the timing of the Horizon project turned out to be a public relations boon for the fledgling agency; ten thousand new houses, multiple golf courses, ski slopes, and artificial lakes were exactly what most citizens of New York didn't want in the Adirondack Park.

"If there had been no Horizon," an agency staffer told the historian Frank Graham Jr., "we would have had to invent one."

"The Adirondacks are preserved forever," Rockefeller said when he signed the plan into law in 1973. But up north, the locals didn't think so. Over the next few years tempers raged among those who felt the state was trampling on the ability of local towns to control their own destiny, which to a degree it certainly was. Beyond the issue of home rule, though, many locals were convinced that regional planning would deprive the Adirondacks of a golden economic future. It didn't seem to matter that the region had failed as an agricultural center, failed as a mining center, and failed as a manufacturing center all by itself long before the advent of the APA.

For its part, the agency didn't have a particularly well developed sense of public relations. The first two cases of criminal zoning violations it pursued involved not greedy out-of-state developers but a DEC forest ranger and a local Boy Scout troop leader.

Those were rebellious years. Local patriots hurled eggs and left midnight truckloads of fresh manure at state office buildings. One man actually tried to burn the new agency headquarters down. He was caught by a late-working bureaucrat who, according to the lore, sat on him until the police arrived. And, of course, attorneys for various large landowners filed some fifty million dollars of lawsuits against the state.

As the seventies waned, though, tempers on both sides began to cool. The courts upheld New York's right to impose regional zoning, and the agency became somewhat more sophisticated about choosing its battles. A certain degree of normalcy began to reappear; maybe things hadn't changed so radically after all.

Which, as the 1980s began, is precisely what began to worry those who were looking closely at the progress of "progress" in the Adirondacks. It turned out that there were still many other sounds in the woods besides the voices of righteous townfolk hollering libertarian epithets in high school gymnasiums. There were chainsaws and bulldozers and nail guns; the noise of the "thousand houses a year" that became the rallying cry of conservationists as the park's centennial approached.

The houses weren't coming in massive developments of ten thousand at a time. But in ones, twos, fives, and even tens, here and there all over the park houses were sprouting up. They were houses, the conservationists realized to their dismay, that were completely in compliance with the Land Use and Development Plan.

In 1989, then-Governor Mario Cuomo spoke with typical eloquence of the need to protect the park for future generations. Like Rockefeller had two decades before, he appointed a temporary study commission. This one was chaired by Peter A. A. Berle, who had since left the Legislature and become president of the National Audubon Society. After a year of study this commission arrived at some dire predictions about the future of the park's open spaces and its timber industry if more was not done to contain development within the existing hamlets.

This time the antiregulation forces in the park didn't wait until after new laws were passed to raise the hue and cry. Protesters shut down traffic on the interstate highway through the park. In one incident, bullets replaced eggs and struck a passing state vehicle. The executive director of the commission, George Davis, received several anonymous telephone calls warning him that his house was going to be burned down. Anne LaBastille's barns *were* burned down; the author of *Woodswoman* and *Beyond Black Bear Lake,* she was a commissioner of the APA.

Cuomo chose to distance himself from his controversial committee's recommendations, which included everything from tighter control of resource management land to more money for guidance counselors in the local schools. In the absence of stronger leadership from Albany, the centennial of the forever-wild clause of the constitution came and went without any significant changes in the direction of development in the park.

After the collapse of the effort to further tighten controls on private land in the park, conservationists again focused on their more traditional strategy of attempting to enlarge the Forest Preserve. For a time, it seemed that major progress could be made. If, that is, the Environmental Quality Bond Act of 1990 could be passed. There were even some who dared to hope that the massive Whitney Park might become available.

But by a margin of less than half a percent, in November of 1990 the bond act failed to pass. Many were shocked; always in the past the voters had approved similar bond issues for purchases of Forest Preserve land. Upstate, antipark agitators noted with glee that the difference between yeas and nays was almost exactly the year-round population of park. Others pointed to the fact that there were no hotly contested races either statewide or in New York City to bring out the urban voters who traditionally supported the park.

Paul Schaefer had his own theory about the failure of the bond act. "The sportsmen were fragmented," he said in 1994. Hunting and fishing groups have always been key parts of every successful Adirondack coalition. "If they had been for the bond issue it would have passed. They didn't go against it. They just didn't go for it. It killed it. It was sad.

"But there's a war now," Schaefer continued cheerfully, referring to his effort to get the various demoralized battalions to unite behind an effort to find state funding for the purchase of Follensby Park. His exhortations in the cabin at the edge of the Siamese Ponds Wilderness had succeeded in uniting many of the conservationists.

"Before that meeting was over that day they all said, 'Yeah, we'll go for Follensby.' And Dan Plumley [of the Adirondack Council] said, 'As

soon as I get back to Elizabethtown I'll start writing a brochure,' "
Schaefer recalled.

"Did I show you our brochure?" he asked, standing once more and
crossing the room. "It's right over here somewhere." The brochure
had aerial photos of the lake under big bold type that read, "Save Follensby Park!" Schaefer personally sent out thirteen thousand of them.

"The pressure's been on Albany for two years now; so far [Sena-
tors] Marino and Stafford have been the enemy," said Schaefer when
he'd returned to his seat. "We've been attacking Stafford for having
veto power over ten thousand square miles the like of which no political person in the state of New York ever had before, and we've been
after Marino for giving it to him. But Stafford has now, at last, publicly
stated that he will vote for the Follensby Pond bill when it comes up
and . . . so has Marino.

"And McCormick, the man who owns Follensby, I have a letter from
him. I got in contact with him when we decided to fight for the state
to get it. He's a man eighty years old in a wheelchair. He says in his
letter here, 'I will not permit development on that land.' He's all for
selling it to the Forest Preserve.

"So the state's got to buy it. We can't even think about the state not
buying it. There'd be a revolution first, I'm telling you, this is a must.
If we get—no, I don't mean to say 'if,' I mean *when* we get Follensby—
the logjam of the Adirondacks acquisition will break and we can stop
worrying about the Adirondacks.

"After Follensby, the people of the state will want to see the other
remaining parcels we need in the Forest Preserve. After that, Finch
Pruyn [the lumber company] will stop being stupid and will go to the
state and beg them to buy an easement. But we have to have Follensby
first."

As Schaefer predicted, Marino and Stafford finally did come
around in the summer of 1994 and voted to appropriate money for
Cuomo's scaled-down environmental trust fund. Money was at last
available for the state to purchase Follensby. But then, for reasons
that remain unclear, at the last minute John McCormick backed out
of the deal.

At the end of 1996, Follensby was off the market until further
notice. Over at Whitney Park, meanwhile, owner Marylou Whitney
proclaimed to *Vanity Fair* magazine, "I don't call it subdividing if you're

going to sell somebody fifty acres." Her son Hobbs, meanwhile, grumbled about how difficult the "eco-socialists" were making life on the fifty-thousand-acre estate. And in early 1997, the Whitneys proposed a massive hotel and housing development project on their land.

The logjam was anything but broken for those who believe the park's future as the greatest wild remnant east of the Mississippi is not yet secure. If anything, the current seemed to have shifted in the opposite direction. There was a new governor in Albany. Judging from his handlers and advisors, George Pataki was apparently not cast from the same mold of Republicanism as the Rockefellers. With help from factions even more conservative than himself, Pataki rode into office promising to unharness the state's economy from what he felt was unnecessary regulation. One of his first Adirondack actions was to propose an expansion of "salvage" clear-cutting on private lands affected by the "Blowdown of 1995."

"I'm a regulatory ax murderer," one of his assistants explained to the commissioner of the APA in 1995. So much for strengthening the park's protection of private land. Pataki eventually brokered a solution to the salvage logging question that satisfied all but the most ardent protectionists, and he managed to get a more modest, though still important, bond act passed. Still, few expect Pataki's tenure to be marked by much progress in the cause of public conservation in the Adirondacks. Unless, that is, he manages to acquire the Whitney property for the Forest Preserve.

But Paul Schaefer, of course, didn't give up until the day he passed away in July of 1996. The Adirondack wilderness was his lifework, after all. As he said shortly after the 1990 bond act failed, "Here I've spent seventy years fighting for the Adirondacks and I'll spend more. So we won't give up; we'll do everything we can. That is what has been done by people who care about the place for a hundred years. And if it hadn't been done, you wouldn't have the park with its wild forest character and miles and miles and miles of marvelous country.

"At my cabin, for instance, which is on the east side of the Siamese Ponds Wilderness, I'm up two thousand feet. The boundary of the wilderness is thirteen miles away, and in that area are fifty-one mountains and sixty-seven lakes. My friends and I have gone hunting in there every single year for fifty-nine years. If you walk all the way through that wilderness you cross a thirty-foot highway and enter another wilderness area and you go thirty-five more miles through that. They have hundreds of lakes in there.

"And that's only two of the park's wilderness areas," he said, warming up. "South of Siamese Ponds Wilderness is the Silver Lake Wilderness and here's another two-hundred-square-mile wilderness area with another fifty-seven lakes in that.

"That's what the Adirondacks are like," Paul Schaefer said, looking up at the giant contour map on his wall as if gazing at a great devotional tapestry. "That's the Adirondacks."

26   *Wild Bureaucrats*

Bob Glennon sat grimly in his office at the Adirondack Park Agency. "The park is being nibbled to death. As I've said a lot of times before, the Adirondack Park is dying the death of a thousand cuts," he said. This was in July of 1995, and Glennon was in a decidedly grumpy mood about the future of both the APA and the twenty-five-year-old experiment in sustainable development in the Adirondacks.

Glennon was, at the time, the executive director of the agency and had just gotten the word from the new Republican governor in Albany that he needed to lay off fourteen people by the end of the year.

"We're only one deep in many positions," he fumed. "There's only one economic guy, one state land guy, and no legal counsel, and no public relations person. There are only three enforcement people. It's already a joke around here.

"So I put it in writing to my chairman that if they're going to do this they might as well put the APA out of its misery entirely." The decision-making power at the agency rests not with Glennon and his staff, but with the commissioners appointed by the governor. "And I was politely informed by the secretary of state that the people of New York elected George Pataki to downsize government. I was told that 'You know, a lot of times when these things happen there's some denial.'

"I have always said we are the second most controversial agency in the state, the first being the Low-Level Radioactive Waste Commission. No public relations person? I mean it's just stupid! If the state believed in the Adirondacks the state would do more than throw in here a rinky dink little agency with an immense mandate. We just can't cut that many people out of an agency this small. I happen to know I'm right and he's wrong." Glennon laughed bitterly.

Though he began at the agency as a young lawyer in the heady days of 1974 and worked his way up, which means he probably knows the intricacies of the agency better than anyone else, the position of executive director is essentially a political appointment. Glennon served at the pleasure of Mario Cuomo and his commissioners. Pataki's new chairman had already let him know he had only thirty more days on the job.

But Bob Glennon's no-holds-barred talk about the current regime in Albany, and about the state of affairs in the park, was not simply sour grapes from a man whose boss got defeated in the hustings and whose own days were numbered. Glennon was a vociferous and pessimistic executive director even back in 1992, when people were seriously talking about Cuomo being drafted to run for president of the United States. He griped then about "the death by a thousand cuts" to the reporters who had dutifully trudged north to write articles commemorating the centennial of the creation of the park.

"The law as it currently stands contemplates and plans for the destruction of the Adirondack Park as we know it," he told *Audubon* magazine. "The current regulations allow for as many as four hundred thousand more buildings in the Adirondacks," he said. He was speaking, of course, of the thousand houses a year. "This will be a very different park."

Neither the law, nor Glennon's assessment of the future, has changed in the intervening years. "I'm even more pessimistic now," he said when reminded of his long history of jeremiads. Along the far wall of his office, a pile of boxes was accumulating in anticipation of his impending departure.

"I'm only saying that [they should close the APA] as a squawking bureaucrat who sees a state government that really doesn't mean it when they say they want to preserve the Adirondacks for future generations of New Yorkers," he said. "It's just lip service. I've always said the state government should be twice its presence here if it wants the park to be a park.

"Don't forget that Rockefeller did something really neat when he got the agency law through in 1970. I don't know if he said it, but somebody said it was the biggest conservation battle in the state since 'forever wild.' The agency is still unique today, as near as I can tell. The failure was in the execution, not necessarily the idea.

"Surely, as the courts have upheld, there's a state interest in the Adirondacks on both public and private lands. And surely the regional zoning scheme is legally justified. But the staffing of the agency and the appointments to it have been uneven.

"And there have always been conflicting forces within it. We have those who believe that local government is king, and that as soon as the local plans are in place we should just wither away. And we have people like myself who believe that there is plenty of law in the state Environmental Quality Review Act to allow us to address cumulative impacts and say that in some places in this park, you are not going to get a subdivision permit."

Glennon raised his voice. "We should just say, 'Sorry, it's not a question of where does the house go, and is it behind some trees, or off the road? You're just not getting a permit. That's the habitat of the hoodia, or something.' " He shrugged.

"You just can't go on with an agency that accepts a basic premise of fragmentation of the park. At some point, someone has to say no. But I don't think there has ever been on this agency a board that could talk in those brave terms. The board has always been, 'Well, now, we want to be liked.'

"We were doing all right on the big developments for a while, but it's the thousand houses a year. There's just no evidence that the plan, if you want to call it a plan, is working at shaping, controlling, and guiding development to where the plan says it should go." Glennon pointed to the land-use map that hung opposite his desk, a patchwork of colors representing the different zoning categories.

"What's missing is a real land ethic. Even the damn agency doesn't have it. When they recently approved [a development called Oven Mountain Estates] they were fawning all over the developer."

Glennon, a blond man in his fifties with yacht-club good looks, sat sullenly on his couch for a moment, remembering the meeting of the commissioners on the Oven Mountain subdivision. He was wearing the chinos that seem to be the uniform of the agency, and a white shirt and tie. "Oh fuck 'em," he exploded after a few seconds. "Clowns."

It wasn't clear whether he was referring to the developers, the commissioners, the citizens of New York, or all of the above. But the long laugh that followed the expletives suggested that there was a part of Bob Glennon that was relieved to be leaving government service, even if the job of protecting the Adirondacks is unfinished.

When pushed on the issue, Glennon will say that the attempt to slow and direct development on private land in the park has not been a total failure. "I think the agency has accomplished something. The way I hear it expressed all the time is, 'Oh Bob, it would be much worse if we weren't here.' " The bitter laugh again.

"And I do believe that. But the real question should be how much better is it because we *were* here. Again the issue to me is not the weakness of the statute, the issue is philosophical. And it's quintessential America. Is development always good? Is land a commodity? You know. The old Aldo Leopold stuff. 'The land ethic.' "

In terms of impact on how environmentally conscious Americans think about their environment, Aldo Leopold is generally regarded in a league with Thoreau and Muir before him and Rachel Carson after him. While working for the U.S. Forest Service in the first decades of the twentieth century he was an early and persuasive voice for keeping part of the National Forests wild and roadless. "Of what avail are forty freedoms without a blank spot on the map?" he said.

But Leopold is most often remembered for writings he did after leaving the Forest Service to teach at the University of Wisconsin. In *A Sand County Almanac* and other works he proposed a new moral structure that he called "the land ethic." Society must expand its conception of right and wrong beyond the bounds of relations between humans, he said, to include "soils, waters, plants, and animals, or collectively, the land." Laws are not enough to save us from ourselves, Leopold implied, when the problem is as basic as how we conceive of the nonhuman world.

"We've always had an agency that espouses a land ethic to some degree," Bob Glennon went on, "but it has never had the guts to say, 'No, I'm not sure development is going to be good.' We tried to gather the literature on the economic impacts of development, and most of it actually shows that the effect on the tax burden of all the new roads and schools and all that jazz is actually negative after a very short time. I'm not sure if that holds in regard to second homes, but again, do they stay second homes?

"If you had personnel here, as you did in the early days, who truly believed in a land ethic, and if they were charismatic enough to go out and take it on the stump, perhaps you'd make some progress at generating a stronger ethic in the wider population. And if you had some backers who stood up for it.

"But I haven't ever really felt much environmental pressure. You come to an agency meeting and see who's yammering there. The Adirondack Local Government Review Board, and local officials. The Adirondack Council sends one guy. He's a very nice guy. But he doesn't stand up and say, 'God you're screwing up on this, fools! Don't you know this is the Adirondack Park, and what's the matter with you? Why are you sitting at your desk? Did you take an oath of office?' There's not been that kind of pressure.

"From where I sit, it would have helped to have had a lot more vociferous, angry pressure, instead of Hail fellow, well met. But the conservationists probably felt that they had to deploy their resources elsewhere."

Later, he said, "I got in trouble a couple of years ago for proposing that we do a regular taking of the ecological temperature of the park. We should be putting out a report every year that says, This many acres got subdivided, this many houses got built, this many acres of wetland got filled, this many power lines got strung across formerly open land. We should do that.

"But again that would put the park agency in a position where more people are going to shoot at it. 'What's the matter, don't you like development? You're not here to stop it. You're here to mitigate it. You're here to make sure it doesn't pollute offsite. Remember, it's a land use *and* development plan.' "

He gazed again at the multicolored land use map. "The statute simply came too late to save a lot of the park," he said. "Paul Smith was subdividing shorelines in 1896. So when you see our map with the red shorelines [red means high density]—Christ, a lot of those were gone in the fifties. . . .

"I've said we can't go on like this. Go down to the back road of Lake Placid and find Averyville Road and drive out Averyville Road. I used to

"AuSable Lake, Adirondack Mts.," 1868, by George Henry Smillie. Courtesy of the Adirondack Museum, Blue Mountain Lake.

drive out there just because it was so gorgeous. Drive out there now, and practically every house out there is a new house. A new house with a park agency permit! It's a failure of will. It's tough to say to a private landowner, God this is beautiful, we're not going to let you develop it."

His voice grew loud. "But we should have had the will to drive out there and say, This is gorgeous, it's wonderful, it's an asset. North Elba ought to tell people it's one of the most beautiful parts of the park; 'Go down and see it and then come back to our town and spend all your money and then go home.' "

He paused. Then in a very quiet and sorrowful voice he said, "But instead we just let it go." He paused again. "And it's not as pretty as it used to be."

Millions of Americans whose home turf has been split up and changed might have said the same thing about the back road to wherever. But there was difference in Glennon's tone. He lives in a place that he believes passionately is supposed to be a park; a park that he spent twenty-one years of his professional life fighting for.

"I'm the guy who was working late and caught the arsonist trying to burn down the agency," he said at one point. "And I didn't sit on him, I kneeled on him while dialing the police."

So when Bob Glennon talks of the spoiled roads he knows, and he knows spoiled roads all over the park, it is not with the same confused passivity of the average citizen who wonders when it was the old hometown lost control of its destiny.

"There's still a lovely farm out there on Averyville Road," Glennon added. "There's still obviously open space, but it ain't what it used to be." It ain't, you can almost hear him thinking, what it might still have been.

27 *The Global Park*

A month later, Bob Glennon packed up the rest of his office and went to work for George Davis. Davis was the staff person on Nelson Rockefeller's 1968 commission who, perhaps more than anyone else, was responsible for conceiving and drawing the multicolored maps of the Adirondack land use plans.

Davis worked for the APA in the early years, but in the late seventies, according to Glennon, Governor Hugh Carey told his appointed commission chairman Robert Flacke to "tame that agency or I'll kill it." By the end of Carey's term George Davis no longer worked for the state. A decade later, however, when Mario Cuomo created his ill-fated Commission on the Adirondacks in the Twenty-First Century, Davis was given Harold Jerry's old title of executive director. It was not exactly fun. More than once during those years, members of the Davis family picked up the telephone and heard anonymous voices threatening violence and arson.

Davis still lives at the eastern edge of the park, and the offices of his company, Ecologically Sustainable Development, are located next to those of the conservationist Adirondack Council in Elizabethtown. Though he says he hasn't read a local newspaper in five years—"There was so much pain at the end of the Cuomo commission"—on one wall of his office hangs a framed copy of the Adirondack land use map.

On an adjacent wall, over the couch, is another map. Like the Adirondack map, this one has various areas blocked out in different colors, representing different appropriate uses for different types of land. This map's legend, however, is in the Cyrillic alphabet: it is a map of the Lake Baikal region, "the Yellowstone of the Russian Federation." Baikal is a big place. The lake itself contains 20 percent of the world's supply of fresh water; more than fifteen Adirondack Parks would fit into the area represented on the map.

Still another map hangs near Davis's long, curving, built-in desk. This one is just a traditional political map of the world, but there are a half dozen pins stuck in it. Each represents a place where Davis has been involved in devising long-term regional development plans in the years since his direct involvement with the Adirondack Park. Pins for Baikal and the Adirondacks are joined by those for groups of indigenous Americans in British Columbia and in Nicaragua. There's a pin in Mongolia, and one in the Altai Republic of Russia's Far East.

Finally, on the wall behind Davis's desk hangs a collection of diplomas and awards. The only one that is legible from the couch and chair across the room is for the MacArthur fellowship—the "genius grant"— that Davis received in 1989.

"As I've gone around the world I've learned a lot of lessons, but one of them was not how we should have done things differently in the Adirondacks from a cultural or political standpoint," Davis said a few weeks before Bob Glennon was scheduled to arrive to work at Ecologically Sustainable Development. Davis laughed a big hearty laugh, which is something he does quite regularly.

"On the other hand, I go around the world and I always come back feeling better about the world as a whole. Which maybe is a dichotomy in a way, because where I go I see areas that have been devastated environmentally. Or areas of extreme poverty, where you say to yourself, How can these people care about their land when they have to be so concerned about where the next meal is coming from?"

He stopped talking and looked at the map with the pins for a moment. "Yes, I think everywhere we've gone, with the possible exception of the area we're working in China, the people have a much more sincere and deep respect for the land and water resources than we have here in the Adirondacks and elsewhere in this country.

"And I've thought a lot on why this is. And the only thing I can come up with is the cultural difference that we are a young nation and we really haven't developed our culture that much, except kind of the culture of the frontier ethic. And that is kind of dying out, and we're in the throes of evolving a culture. We've only been around for two hundred years so it's hard to look ahead five hundred years.

"Part of the problem is also the lack of a sense of home here. You can pack up the car and move on, or the covered wagon. We've always had somewhere to move on to. I, as an individual, can always move on to Oklahoma and my hundred and sixty acres or whatever it is. We've had this never-ending resource. . . .

"So first of all our culture isn't very deep. Secondly, there's always been plenty. Thirdly, the private land ethic is tied in there; you really can 'own' land here as opposed to seeing yourself as a steward on it temporarily. All of these things come together; the lack of anything in the past and 'Why worry about the future if there's always more.' There just isn't a concept of the future.

"Whereas if you look at the Mongols, or you look at the Russians, or you look at the indigenous people by Lake Baikal, or you look at either the Slavic or the indigenous people in the Russian Far East or in the Altai Republic, they all have this cultural background that ties them to the earth. Even the people who were moved to Lake Baikal by the central government under the Communists seem to feel it. Because it's still 'Mother Russia.'

"So it's not that we can just go back and glorify the Native Americans and say, well if they had stayed in the majority things would have been different. It's not just to say that as soon as you take the [nonindigenous] people away you're done. At least in Russia, it's not the case.

"There are exceptions to all of this, of course. I could point to a lot of places within any of these countries that really have been treated badly. But usually, the real environmental disasters have occurred because orders came down from Moscow, or Beijing, or whatever, to do this or that."

Davis took a pack of Marlboro Lights from the pocket of his open-collared short-sleeve shirt, shook one out, and lit it. With a laugh he explained that he quit smoking for fourteen years before going to work in China and Russia. "Trying to get things done in China can drive you to smoke," he said. "Their problem sometimes seems to be the reverse of ours, that they have too much of the long view. They think, China's been here two thousand years, it will be here a thousand years from now. And we won't, so what's the hurry."

In other ways, Davis believes the Chinese may have a similar cultural weakness in the area of land preservation. "Interestingly, the Chinese we work with are also used to being moved around," he said. "And they have strong ties to their culture, which in their case is very old, but which, like ours, isn't tied specifically to the land. They are used to doing things for the betterment of China, and if, as in the area we're working, that means filling in the wetlands to make farms, well, so be it. The people have a concern for the cranes that nest there, but I think it's because the birds are in their paintings and therefore qualify as a part of the culture. It's not the land directly.

A little later he said, "I'm afraid that unfortunately a government cannot create a land ethic where there is not one." It sounded, though he didn't say it, as if this might be one of the hard lessons he learned in the Adirondacks. "It's just like any other ethic, I suppose. As much as they might try, regulation is simply not going to do it, and sometimes it actually works against the development of such an ethic because people become resentful that they're being told what to do.

"I don't know if that has really happened in the Adirondacks. But I'm equally unsure whether the landowners here today have any stronger land ethic personally than they had when the park agency act passed, or than they would have had now if there hadn't been a park agency. And indeed with some of them there's probably less of such an ethic. You hear this all the time, that some of them did actually feel a land ethic and believe in it before the regulations came on them. That, you know, 'After all, we've protected the Adirondacks all these years, why do we need the agency?'

"Most of that is bullshit, to be sure, but there was a certain grain of truth too," he said.

"The thing that may have happened is that partly because of the park agency, the land ownership pattern may have changed or may be changing in the Adirondacks. There may be more people buying land here now because they say to themselves, 'Hey, this is a protected area.' Those are the type of people who presumably have some kind of land ethic to start with, coupled with the selfish motive that, 'Well this is a protected area so once I have mine, I don't want anyone to have theirs next to me.' These people are going to end up, in the long run, being the ones who save the park.

"But in the meantime, in our present culture there's nothing to indicate that anyone but outsiders can save a natural area. Whether you're talking about the greater Yellowstone ecosystem, or Alaska, or the Adirondacks, the people actually living in it still have this frontier ethic. The majority on the inside still are not, unfortunately, the people who want to save it."

The philosophical implications of outsiders looking in at wilderness and wishing to save it hung there over the conversation for a moment, but attempts to reach an overarching answer having to do with some fatal Cartesian divorce of mind from body, of human from wild, of sense from reason, proved fruitless. It has always been outsiders who protected the Adirondacks; as if the park were an alter ego that had to grow progressively wilder as the more urban parts of the state became increasingly uncivilized in other ways.

"A lot of the problem is, both in this country and elsewhere, we've always tended to fight over the lines rather than thinking about how we treat the rest of the land," Davis said later. "We think, 'Well, we won that, that's a park.' Or on the other side: 'Yup, we won that, we can go harvest trees there.' But we're never going to protect biodiversity or the whole concept of life, which is then reflected in the quality of human life, if we just say, 'Let's have a protected area here,' and then we go after the rest of the land with abandon.

"Because really, of course, the future depends on what happens to the rest of the land. Not just from an ecological standpoint, either. That's also where our jobs are going to come from. That's where we need to be sure the resources regenerate. That's where people are going to live. That's what they will see of the world in many cases.

"Therefore, the nonprotected areas are what need to be focused on much more. And those of us interested in preservation have to focus on that. Because to be selfish and just say 'Gee, let's just get these protected areas,' even if we get the wildlife corridors between them, is not going to work in the future. Unless we live humanely in the areas that are not in the Forest Preserve, or the National Park, or wherever, it's not going to work."

Davis shrugged, smiled, frowned, and took out another cigarette.

"I fall somewhere between Paul Schaefer and Bob Glennon in terms of my level of optimism about the Adirondacks. Paul has [had] the gift of turning everything around, even the greatest defeat in the world, so that somehow the next morning he's got a smile on his face and he's figured out how it's going to help us in the long run.

"Maybe that's what's kept him going all these years. The ability to do that, and the ability to rally people with the positive force. It's hard to rally people if you're muttering behind your breath that the place is lost already or that it's going to be lost.

"And I think Bob is overly pessimistic, though in the long run he may be right. The park is certainly going to be much different thirty years from now or fifty years from now. And it will be different in a way that he and probably myself would not be happy with. But I don't think it's going down the tubes totally either. I think we really are leaving a legacy behind us, it's just not quite as nice a legacy as Bob might have hoped. Or I might have hoped. Or Harold Jerry might have, or any of the people involved. . . .

"But I guess partly because I've been working in all these other places I don't get as panicky as Bob does. I think, 'Hey, eventually, what's happening in the rest of the world is going to come full circle and come back around to the Adirondacks.' The park agency is no longer even in the forefront of protecting private land. It's no longer the only agency you can point to. When we bring people over from wherever else we're working we take them to the Pacific Northwest, to Tahoe, to the New Jersey Pine Barrens, and to the Adirondacks.

"So certainly the Adirondacks are not 'it' anymore as far as sustainable development goes. They were once but now they're just one of a number of experiments. There are stricter regional zoning plans right here in America. Probably even the New Jersey Pine Barrens are in some ways better protected than the Adirondacks."

An associate of Davis's appeared at the door to his office to remind him that he was scheduled to make an international phone call in two minutes. He looked up, looked at his watch, nodded, and immediately commenced speaking again.

"Still, there are two things that come immediately to mind as major breakthroughs in the Adirondacks," he said. "The first is the whole concept of total preservation on the Forest Preserve. The idea that we're going to set this land aside and let nature run its course there. That goes back a hundred years.

"And the second was the acceptance of the basic concept thirty years ago of zoning different types of land uses and different intensities of land use on private land based on what the land can bear and what is compatible with the park as a special place. Those were both *major* steps forward. Conceptually, for their times, they were breakthroughs. As it stands now, though, we haven't quite achieved the second step.

"That's just a failure in culture, I guess. I don't know how else to have done it. You could say political will, but it took a lot of political will at various times to achieve some of the things that we did. At the time that it happened forty-two-acre zoning—that's not how I would describe it, but it's referred to that way—was really far ahead of its time. That took a lot of political will.

"So there's been political will along the way. But to really save the park sheerly by political will would mean going in and trying to do the whole thing by regulation. And that's not the American way.

"So it was really culture. People just aren't ready to think in long terms about the land. They see it all as a threat."

Davis was silent for a moment, thinking. "And maybe it really is a threat to our way of life," he said. "Maybe our lifestyle has to back up. Maybe we can't go on forever with five percent of the world's population using up whatever it is—thirty percent of the world's resources. You don't have to think about that for more than a little while and you say, Hmm, maybe we can't really do that forever."

Something about this struck him as very funny and he laughed his big hearty laugh. "So maybe we're terrified," George Davis said between guffaws.

28 *Wild Trout*

"Hey, did you guys get as far as this pile of otter shit?" Leo Demong called out, and the answer came back, "Yeah, Leo, we're all right on this side all the way to that big dead maple." Demong gave the lever near his left hand a couple of pumps to add pressure to the plastic tank that was strapped to his back, and moved off toward the middle of the swamp. In his right hand, he held a hose with a squeeze valve and a long metal wand.

"Look," he said a moment later, "bear tracks," and then gave a nearby puddle a good squirt from the hose. The water turned milky white. "Let me know if there's any water over there I need to get," he said, and trudged on farther through the muck.

The place was actually pretty dried out. Late in the week before, Demong and his crew spent a day breaching the dozen or so beaver dams and sub-dams that created the swamp. The largest of these was an impressive structure around five feet tall and seventy-five feet long, through which they had chopped a channel two feet wide. They also jumped up and down on the lodge a few times, to encourage the animals to stay inside for a few days.

And just to make sure the beaver hadn't rebuilt things, over the weekend, on Sunday, Demong hiked the several

miles back up here to look around. A few half-hearted repairs had been
made to the main dam, but nothing that he wasn't able to pull back out.

"I don't think there were too many beaver left at this colony anyway," he now explained as he passed the large lodge and squirted liberally into the pool around it. "They had pretty much eaten everything
around here for them to eat. Most of them had already moved on to
somewhere else."

Demong, a small and strongly built man in his forties, doesn't hike
into the Forest Preserve on his day off and pull down dams just to
harass beaver. Controlling overly ambitious rodents is better left to
trappers like Bob Inslerman, whose office at the DEC in Ray Brook is
just down the hall from Demong's. In fact, the rotenone Demong and
his crew of five were spraying from their backpacks into the remaining puddles of water has no known effect on beaver or other air-
breathing animals. It rarely even causes problems for pollywogs, of
which there were countless numbers in the swamp.

But this collection of beaver ponds happened to lie at the upstream
edge of Moose Mountain Pond at the southern end of the park, and it
was Leo Demong's intention that week to kill every single fish in that
body of water. If even a handful of minnows were left behind in some
obscure backwater, he and his crew would be wasting their time and
the state's money.

So here they were, in their hip boots and tank packs, occasionally
up to their thighs in mud, spraying forever-wild puddles. At the very
top of the swamp, where the original stream was just a trickle coming
out of the rocks, they set up a device to slowly drip rotenone into the
flow for the next few days.

Rotenone is extremely good at killing fish. Once in the water, it
breaks down quickly and essentially disappears from the ecosystem;
there are indigenous peoples in South America and Africa whose traditional method of fishing is to grind up the roots of rotenone-
producing plants and throw them into rivers. But while it lasts, even
in small concentrations, rotenone prevents the cells of fish from
absorbing oxygen. They suffocate.

Earlier that morning Demong had sent a person over to nail some
signs onto trees near the lean-to where most visitors to this area camp.
A bright orange one said, "Fish have been eradicated from Moose
Mountain Pond. This water was reclaimed on 6/26/95 by the Department of Environmental Conservation. A fish toxicant was applied to

eliminate undesirable fish. When the water is no longer toxic it will be restocked with trout. DO NOT USE THE WATER FOR DRINKING, COOKING, OR SWIMMING."

Perhaps because this sign had the potential to alarm unsuspecting Forest Preserve lovers, a second was also nailed nearby. This one, intended to be permanent, is primarily a plea for anglers to follow the regulations and refrain from using bait fish, and it goes into much greater detail about the program. It explains that the majority of the "undesirable" fish are not native to the Adirondacks, and that these exotic fishes often outcompete the natives. "Most of the ponds that historically contained only brook trout have been lost to the invasion of other species," it says. In other words, the sign tries to reassure its readers that the state is merely attempting to put the wilderness back the way it probably once was at Moose Mountain Pond.

"If you read the textbooks, they will talk about this being a boreal habitat," said Demong's boss, Larry Strait, a month before the rotenone mission to Moose Mountain Pond. Strait is a wiry man with an academic manner to him. The bookshelves in his office in Ray Brook overflow with piscatorial texts, old and new. The walls are hung with images of various fish diseases, and of lamprey eels.

"These ponds are a relic from when the last glaciers were here," he went on. "Because of high elevations, the ice left here late when compared to low-lying surrounding areas. Also, the habitat is rigorous, cold. It left very few fish species; it left many waters with only one or two species, or even none. The brook trout was one of the fishes that was in these simple environments. Also round whitefish, which is on the state's endangered species list.

"It's interesting to contrast that with the sort of pop ecology of the moment that says we want to increase or maintain the diversity, which on the surface is usually interpreted to mean a lot of species. However that is not the natural situation here. Naturally, there were very few species here.

"And they were ill equipped, it turns out, to compete with lots of other species. They were very well equipped to live here on their own, absolutely, but when you throw in other species on top of them, intense competition results. The new fish can eat the same food organisms as the trout, there can be direct predation on the native species, there can be impacts on eggs.

"So by these various mechanisms things like suckers, golden shiners, and yellow perch rapidly outcompete the native brook trout, round whitefish, and some of the other less common fishes.

"It's an insidious process," he went on, genuinely warming up to his subject, even though it was clear he had explained these things hundreds of times before. "The water looks clean and bright, just the way it did, but what's in that water may have changed dramatically. The smaller ponds, the smaller waters, and the smaller lakes would have had the fewest species to start with and were the ones that would have had things like brook trout and round whitefish in them. They are the ones that are truly devastated by this situation."

Larry Strait considers nonnative species a more widespread threat to the fishes of the Adirondacks than the much more publicized effects of acid rain. According to some estimates, dozens of ponds and lakes in the park reach acidity levels that are toxic to aquatic animals each year. Acidification disproportionately threatens small bodies of water at high altitudes, which is to say the same trout ponds most affected by nonnative fishes.

But acid rain's havoc is concentrated primarily in the western reaches of the park, rather than the central and eastern sections. This is because when the eastward-moving weather systems, which are laden with sulfur dioxide from the smokestack industries of the Midwest, hit the western foothills of the Adirondacks the resulting precipitation cleanses the air of the lion's share of its poison. In the long run acid rain may prove the greater evil, with its potential to kill the surrounding forest, but for now the Bureau of Fisheries is trying to make the best of a bad situation. Most of the reclamations that take place in the western Adirondacks, Strait said, don't even require rotenone. The DEC waits instead for the rain to kill the pond, and then restores the water's pH balance with lime before restocking with brookies.

Strait believes the declines in trout fishing reported by writers as early as the nineteenth century were quite possibly being caused not only by the long strings of twenty-pounders the romantic anglers consistently boasted of landing but also by introduced fish. "The waters are just as productive as they ever were historically in the park," he explained, "they just don't yield as much in the way of fish that people want to catch. Every time you add a species, the total amount of fish flesh may increase, but not what people want to catch. So the fishing can get worse while the pond is as productive biologically as it ever was.

"By the time of the first comprehensive fisheries survey of the park in the 1930s, introduced fishes were already widely established. Initially they were introduced with good intentions. The brown bullhead was probably always common in the park, but not nearly as common as it is today because folks like to eat brown bullhead and they were widely distributed. Also things like yellow perch, which can eliminate our native brook trout and other native fishes very rapidly, are good to eat and were probably introduced on purpose." Loggers often introduced bullheads and perch into the ponds near their camps because they breed fast, taste good, and are easier to catch than trout.

"Even today, the smelt is considered by many people to be the optimum forage for, say, the lake trout. And in addition, folks like to eat smelt directly. So maybe they place burlap on the bottom of the stream where some fish they want to move spawn, then they roll the burlap up, keep it wet, and away they go. It's on purpose, but ill-advised. Unauthorized introductions that are on purpose still happen all the time. There are very few large lakes in the park now that don't have smelt in them.

"Bass is another good example of fish that were introduced on purpose. And northern pike, which tend to stunt here in the Adirondacks. The pike become very abundant, they reproduce so successfully. But the ratio of available prey to reproduction is such that very few of them ever end up getting very big. There just isn't enough food, so you end up with a system dominated by predators versus a balanced system where there would be more prey per fish.

"More recently, most introductions have been unintentional, very often through release of bait fish. Minnows principally, but also yellow perch, bullheads, and suckers get introduced because they come along in the bait pail for the ride. And at the end of the day, the fishermen don't want to kill the poor little minnows so they go into the lake. This can be devastating in some circumstances."

At one point Strait said, "I must make it clear, though, that in the appropriate circumstance all these introduced species are fine. In many of the large lakes the introduced fish are very important parts of the community, and that's fortunate because we can't do anything about them anyway. We're talking about largemouth bass, northern pike, smallmouth bass, yellow perch. There are some very desirable critters out there that were introduced.

"Frequently the introduced fish provides something for folks directly. They get big enough to eat or they are themselves a game species. But it's important to understand that they weren't here historically. And that they're actively managed to provide the greatest benefits to human beings.

"So generally we would not be looking, say, to eliminate largemouth bass from a variety of places in the park because they provide a very valuable fishery and a tremendous amount of food and recreation for folks. And in the right circumstances they do not cause massive ecological changes. In a circumstance where we have a pond that is incapable anyway of supporting a cold-water fish like the brook trout there may be very few impacts. In the appropriate circumstance, in small, warm-water ponds that can never be reclaimed we might even introduce smallmouth bass.

That he and his department are not opposed to the introduction of nonnative fish under any circumstances was a point Larry Strait made repeatedly, in various ways. "This is management of a fishing resource," he said more than once, with the emphasis on "management." Another time he said, "Our job, principally, is to provide fishing-related benefits to society: angling, recreation, economics. And those benefits interface quite nicely with the wilderness qualities here in the park."

Ever since a day in fourth grade when his teacher put up pictures of all the birds in the state, Larry Strait intended to become a wildlife manager. But when he came to work in the Adirondacks after getting degrees from Cornell and Michigan State, he discovered that the stern protection of trees provided by the forever-wild provision of the constitution severely limited what wildlife managers could do in terms of habitat manipulation in the Forest Preserve.

"I found the wildlifers had no potential to manage," he said, "they have no real ability to have a positive impact." Bob Inslerman, Strait's wildlife counterpart, puts it somewhat differently, but without changing the underlying sentiment. "Wildlife management," Inslerman said several times that day trapping on Upper Saint Regis Lake, "is really all about managing people."

So Larry Strait went into fisheries management, where there are lots of things that can be done to alter the available populations of animals without violating the constitutional ban on interfering with the trees. This doesn't, of course, mean there are not those who believe he is interfering with the spirit of the Forest Preserve, if not the letter of the state's charter.

"We've been successfully stocking domestic fish for a hundred years in the Adirondacks," he said when asked about periodic concerns by some anglers and wilderness advocates that stocked fish are not the same thing as wild fish, and that they can even drive out the natives they are meant to augment. "That concern is held by well-intentioned, but misinformed, environmentalists. There may be some reproduction by the domestic fish we stock, but they have never caused a collapse of the [native] breeding stock.

"The streams and rivers in particular are a much more rigorous habitat than the lakes or ponds, and there the native trout really do have the competitive advantage over any introduced fish. The issue in the rivers is not food supply but habitat loss, from sand from highway maintenance mainly. Sand-sized particles imbed the spawning gravels and don't wash away easily. You literally would have to get in there and dig up the bed. It's a result of human development; sedimentation, sand on the roads, overall development, excessive runoff. Picture the streets of Lake Placid at the end of March when all of that sediment and sand is running off the roads into the West Branch of the Ausable River.

"So it boils down to the question, Is there room for those stocked fish in that particular environment? I mentioned the West Branch. There is simply not enough reproduction there to reach the carrying capacity of the stream." So the DEC adds fish, he said, mostly hatchery-raised brown and rainbow trout.

"The rearing of pure wild trout is extremely difficult," Strait said, "so there never will be a goal to only stock wild. There are examples, however, where we would use only native fish. In a wild steelhead stream, for instance, you may not want to introduce [hatchery fish]. Not because a domestic rainbow is ever going to cut the mustard as long as a wild steelhead is around. The steelhead is a much tougher fish. We're getting into some fine nuances of management here, but you may not want to do that because you want to maximize the steelhead."

The nuances, it turns out, are endless. Depending on a range of circumstances, most often geological features affecting breeding habitat, trout reproduction in two equally wild Adirondack ponds can range from extremely successful to relatively dismal. But which circumstance is better depends entirely on your perspective. "In Nellie and Bessie," Strait said, referring to two small ponds in the heart of the Saint Regis Canoe Area, "trout will probably never get much bigger than fourteen inches because the reproduction is so successful that they compete with one another for the available food and space.

"At another pond we work with, the only fish in it are brook trout and a little fish called the creek chub. Reproduction there is minimal and it commonly produces brook trout over twenty inches long. It's called—" Strait stopped talking and asked that the name of this particular pond be kept confidential. He is himself a fisherman, it turned out.

"Other ponds range through all the circumstances in between," he continued. "In some, the trout barely hold on year to year. Some we don't need to restock no matter how hard they get fished. Some we have very restrictive regulations. In a perfect world we would have separate regulations for each pond. As it is we have regs that cover a variety of circumstances ranging from no-kill to ten a day." Even in fisheries the bulk of successful management turns out to be controlling the actions of humans beings loose in the wilds.

People occasionally ask Larry Strait whether or not these non-native species would have eventually gotten into the ponds on their own; whether reclamation is really just an arbitrary selection of some historical situation, some imagined pre-white-man wilderness that was going to give way sooner or later.

"The way I always answer that," he says with a patient smile, "is that these simple Adirondack systems persisted for ten thousand years. The answer can't be no, these species would never get here on their own, because the environment is dynamic. Yes, mountains get worn down, waterfalls become no longer barriers to fish migration. The bird hypothesis is common, but again, there were ten thousand years for the birds to distribute fish eggs here and they didn't do it. So"—he paused to find a scientifically acceptable way to say impossible—"let's just say it's a slow process." He laughed, uncrossed his legs, and then promptly recrossed them the other way.

"But this idea of a wilderness without people is most definitely a twentieth-century idea," he said a few minutes later. "Quite frankly, we can't recreate that wilderness in the Adirondacks. It's preposterous. Every pond, every water, every little bit of habitat has evidence of human intervention. Sixty-five percent of the ponds surveyed by the Adirondacks Lake Survey had nonnative fish in them. The hand of man is pervasive here. Trails are everywhere. It's a semblance of wilderness. It isn't the real thing . . . if wilderness is defined as the absence of the hand of man.

"This homogenization of nature accompanies humans wherever they go. What we're trying to do here in the Adirondacks is keep it knocked back, either for human use or in order to maintain examples of these natural systems. But we'll never finish. It's management, remember. It's like pulling weeds in your garden."

Even when the weed fish are gone, Moose Mountain Pond won't actually be exactly the way it once was. Originally it most likely had its very own, recognizable strain of brook trout, a strain that is long since extinct. Larry Strait believes there were once as many as four hundred distinct varieties of Adirondacks brook trout.

But Moose Mountain Pond will be as close to its prehumanized state as science, technology, and historical accident can get it. When reclaiming remote ponds the DEC usually restocks with one of the handful of surviving "heritage" strains of brook trout it has discovered in ponds and lakes in the Adirondacks that were spared from degra-

"Leaping Trout," by Winslow Homer, 1889. Courtesy of the Museum of Fine Arts, Boston.

dation by their sheer remoteness or other circumstances. One of these, the Horn Lake brookie, is remarkably red in the fall, almost vermilion, and the tips of its dorsal fins are white. Another, from Stink Lake, is unusually yellow.

There have been other attempts over the years to put missing pieces of the original Adirondack wilderness back into place. Though it got off to a little bit of a rocky start, the most successful effort was the reestablishment of beaver. In 1905, seven Canadian beaver that had done duty at the Louisiana Purchase Centennial Exposition in Saint Louis were put under the care of a man named Ned Ball. He built a spacious forty-foot lodge in a trout pool at the Old Forge hatchery for the animals to live in over the winter until they could be released in the spring.

But the seven, it turned out, wouldn't live together; five of them ganged up on the other two. So Ball built another house for the outcasts. These two wouldn't live together either, though, so he built a third lodge. This worked until one spring morning workers at the hatchery awoke to the sound of irate beavers. One of the two in solitary confinement had escaped and broken in to visit the other five. But these apparently hadn't missed him as much as he had missed them, and in the fracas that broke out, the intruder was killed.

Shortly thereafter, the survivors were separated, taken to the Moose River, and released. A year later, twenty more beaver from Yellowstone were released. A decade later there were estimated to be twenty thousand *Castor canadensis* chewing away in the park. Today, Bob Inslerman regularly fields calls from camp owners whose wilderness getaways are suddenly without phones, or whose driveways are underwater, or whose favorite stand of birches is crashing to the ground in the first hours of dawn.

In the 1970s the federal government successfully returned bald eagles to the park, establishing a pair at Follensby Pond. And peregrine falcons were reestablished around the same time. But an effort to restore the lynx fizzled when most of the animals released were hit by cars. There have been numerous misbegotten attempts to reintroduce moose to the region, going back to the turn of the century. By the time the animals got from Maine or Canada to the Adirondacks, most often in boxcars, they had usually become too accustomed to being fed to leave the settlements for big woods.

There was some talk a few years ago of a renewed state effort to bring the moose back, but it got no further than a couple of public meetings. Part of the reason was the DEC didn't know if it could get the money for such an undertaking when moose were already occasionally crossing the ice from Vermont on their own. Most of all though, according to some in the department, the idea was dropped out of a fear of lawsuits when someone inevitably ran into a moose with their car.

For similar reasons there are no official plans to bring wolves back to the park, though wolf lovers throughout the northeast periodically agitate for their reintroduction. And it would be a brave wildlife manager indeed who would publicly suggest spending millions of tax dollars to reintroduce panthers to the Adirondacks. Unverifiable but not entirely unsubstantiated reports of sightings of wolves and big cats are on the rise in the park, however.

For the time being, then, the handful of ponds that get reclaimed each year are the only places where human beings are actively trying to return missing native species to the Adirondack Park. And even though only a small subset of former trout waters qualify for the program—lakes can't be too large, or have too much wetland around them, or be part of an extensive watershed—the job is never really finished.

A small subset of three thousand Adirondack lakes is, after all, still a lot of lakes. And sadly, there are backsliders among them. Inevitably, somebody uses bait, or thinks they know better what might be good for their favorite fishing spot, and throws smelt or something else in. Less likely, though still possible, is that despite Leo Demong's best efforts a prolific pair of minnows might occasionally slip by unnoticed in some overlooked puddle.

"This is management of a wilderness resource," Demong said at one point while collecting insect larvae from the muck at the edge of the pond for the "before and after" part of his final report. Like Larry Strait, he emphasized the word "management." Rotenone reclamation has been undertaken off and on in various places in the park for almost fifty years, he said. Though some remote ponds were reclaimed thirty years ago and are still free of undesirable fish, a pond near a road might require reclamation every seven to ten years. "It's not something we'll ever be able to say Okay, that's the last one, we're done."

The Adirondacks will never be a wilderness that stays as wild as its handlers would like.

Moose Mountain and the other fish restoration projects are also the only places in the park where, in order to recover the desired pre-humanized environment, such drastic measures must be taken. Established populations of seemingly equally wild, if biologically mis-placed, animals must first be eliminated. If the wilderness that Amer-icans originally found in the Adirondacks, then debauched, and now desire to see again, is to be reborn then this other wilderness that they have since created must first pass away.

Not surprisingly, this is an equation that has not always sat well with everyone. For years, Leo Demong never scheduled reclamations on Mondays. He knew that at the end of the day on the Friday before, a certain vigilant fish-rights activist was likely to file a last-minute injunction against the operation. Demong reserved Mondays for get-ting such motions thrown out of court.

There was also trouble for a while convincing the watchdogs at the APA to let the DEC use its helicopters and motorboats for reclama-tions in the legally designated wilderness areas, where motorized vehi-cles are not permitted. People who didn't particularly care one way or the other about the lives of immigrant bait fish occasionally ques-tioned whether the effort was really being made for the sake of this thing called wilderness. After all, no one, least of all the managers at the DEC, suggests that state money would be spent to reclaim the pond for little white minnows if the species were reversed and magnif-icent vermilion-spotted trout were the impostors.

Reclamation got caught up in the seemingly endless debate in the park over how much a "wilderness" can be "managed" for human use and still be "forever wild." That debate continues on other fronts, most recently over the question of "salvage" logging of trees felled on the Forest Preserve by the freak summer storm of 1995, and over how best to regulate human traffic in the most popular sections of the High Peaks. It's an argument that will no doubt continue until there are fewer people in the world in need, as Aldo Leopold was, of "wild country to be young in." Or until there are more places like the Adirondacks to hold them.

For now, though, it is the unified policy of both the APA and the DEC that, as much as is practical, Adirondack brook trout should be returned to the park. So at Moose Mountain Park Leo Demong and his crew sprayed the soggy areas around the edge, and then moved into their boats and started their rotenone pumps.

When the fish first began to die, it looked from the shore as if a great feeding frenzy were taking place. It was as if all over the surface of the pond some magnificent hatch of tasty insects were occurring, and every scaly resident of the place were rising greedily to the feast.

But up close, near the shore, it was obvious there was something quite different going on. Some fish were flopping erratically around on the surface. Fish were careening off at weird angles. Fish were swimming up on shore. Fish were swimming upside down. Fish were already dead.

"They're in distress now," said Leo Demong. He squinted a little as he looked out at the bright water from beneath the shade of the trees. He noted the time and wrote something in his log book. On the lake, one of the three boats that had been flown in the day before on an army surplus helicopter neared the shore and made a U-turn. It then headed back up the pond on a course that was parallel and just to one side of the path it had taken coming down, as if mowing a lawn. From that distance, the sound of the outboard and the sound of the rotenone pump melded together into a single motorized drone.

"That was relatively quick," Demong added, "but there should be even more fish coming up when we treat the surface layer."

Later in the afternoon, the thousands and thousands of floating fish no longer struggled much. The wind blew them together into great curving shapes and slowly moved them down the surface of the water. From the top of the cliffs down at the far end of the pond, they looked remarkably like silvery birch leaves prematurely fallen from some mysterious grove of trees.

By the time the big yellow helicopter came in low over the ridge and settled its large gray pontoons onto the surface of Moose Mountain Pond, most of the fish were gone. They sank, or blew down below the overhanging canopy of the trees at the far shore. The morning sun had given way, too, and it looked like rain.

Demong and his crew rushed to get the aircraft loaded. One boat could go at a time, sticking out of the sliding doors on either side of the helicopter. A couple of pumps were strapped in here and there, along with as many of the empty, bright yellow five-gallon rotenone cans as would fit. It took four trips in all to get everything back to the Schroon Lake airstrip.

When the helicopter lifted off, the surface of the pond was whipped up into an ever-widening circle of disruption that then slowly disappeared as the big machine withdrew into the sky, playing out in miniature the previous three centuries of human endeavor in the Adirondacks. From the tailgunner's seat at the back, pressed up against the throbbing hot engine, it was possible to see through the open doors the outlet of Moose Mountain Pond winding its way down to another ribbon of water called the Berrymill Flow. There were beaver dams in places. There were houses, too, here and there. To the west, under a sky that couldn't make up its mind what to do, range after range after purple range of the Adirondacks faded back into the evening sun.

Below and to the rear, rapidly disappearing now behind Owl Pate Mountain, lay Moose Mountain Pond, a little wilderness utterly devoid of fish until the day that Leo Demong and his team of fellow managers would return with a helicopter load of wild, wild Adirondack brook trout.

NOTES

One of the best things about the Adirondacks from a storyteller's point of view, and one of the most intimidating things from a writer's point of view, is the astounding amount that has already been written about the place. Americans began writing in earnest about the region a century and a half ago and never stopped. The *Adirondack Bibliography* (published by the Adirondack Museum, Blue Mountain Lake, NY), which is the best resource a researcher could hope for, now runs to three chunky volumes.

For the most part, then, this book is a retelling and reorganizing of tales others have told before. And while all the sources I consulted were helpful in some way, the following books were so important to my effort that they deserve special acknowledgment: *A History of the Adirondacks,* 2 vols. (1921; reprinted 1992 by Purple Mountain Press, Fleischmanns, NY), by Alfred L. Donaldson; *The Great Forest of the Adirondacks* (1994, North Country Books, Utica, NY), by Barbara McMartin; *Durant: The Fortunes and Woodland Camps of a Family in the Adirondacks* (1981, Adirondack Museum, Blue Mountain Lake, NY), by Craig Gilborn; *Forever Wild: A Cultural History of Wilderness in the Adirondacks* (1985; paperback ed. 1994 by Syracuse University Press, Syracuse, NY) and

Wildlife and Wilderness: A History of Adirondack Mammals (1993, Purple Mountain Press, Fleischmanns, NY), both by Philip G. Terrie; *The Adirondack Reader* (1982, Adirondack Mountain Club, Glens Falls, NY), edited by Paul Jamieson; and *The Adirondack Park: A Political History* (1978; paperback ed. 1984, Syracuse University Press, Syracuse, NY), by Frank Graham Jr.

In the specific notes below, I've put the original date of publication immediately following the title. If I used a reprint or later edition, I've put that in parentheses following the first reference to a source. Also, though I did often read the sources that other writers referred to in their works, out of courtesy to earlier researchers I have credited quotes to the source where I originally found them.

Chapter 1

The majority of this chapter is derived from numerous conversations and travels with Bob Inslerman that took place between the fall of 1994 and the summer of 1996.

"It does, however work . . ."—The anecdote in this paragraph was told to me by Greenleaf Chase in the fall of 1993.

"One quarter of a beaver is tail . . ."—Much of the information regarding biology of beaver is from an enjoyable article on the return of the animal by Jessica Maxwell that appeared in *Audubon* magazine in March 1994.

"In addition to beaver . . ."—Lists of species come from a variety of sources, but most importantly from the appendix of *Adirondack Wildguide: A Natural History of the Adirondack Park*, 1984 (Elizabethtown, NY), by Michael G. DiNunzio.

"In most places . . ."—By far the best book on the status and makeup of the Adirondack forest is Barbara McMartin's statistical masterpiece *The Great Forest of the Adirondacks*, and the estimates of remaining old-growth and virgin forest are hers. The final chapter is especially useful to those in search of old trees.

"New York has her wilderness within her own borders." From *The Maine Woods*, 1848, as quoted in Jamieson, p. 1.

Chapter 2

Most of the information about Iroquois custom and politics, and experience of various explorers and captives, comes from the following books: *League of the Iroquois,* 1851 (1993, Secaucus, NJ), by Lewis Henry Morgan; James Thomas Flexner's biography of William Johnson, *Lord of the Mohawks,* 1959 (1979, Boston); Harmen Meyndertsz Van Den Bogaert, *A Journey into Mohawk and Oneida Country, 1634–35,* 1988 (Syracuse, NY), Charles Gehring and William Starna, translators; *Apology to the Iroquois,* by Edmund Wilson (1959, New York); *A New World,* 1994 (Boston), by Arthur Quinn; *The Works of Francis Parkman,* 1898 (Boston); *Wildlife and Wilderness,* by Philip G. Terrie; and *The Jesuit Relations,* 1896–1901 (Cleveland), R. G. Thwaites, translator. Also, *The Fur Trade in Colonial New York,* 1974 (Madison, WI), by Thomas Elliot Norton, for details of the trade.

"Grapes and Pompions . . ."—Norton, p. 3.

Etymology of "Mohawk"—Gehring and Starna (from the "Linguistic Notes"), p. 23.

"The line between the Mohawks . . ."—from *Historical Sketches of Northern New York and the Adirondack Wilderness,* by Nathaniel Sylvester, 1877 (1973, Mamaroneck, NY). Sylvester's information is presumably derived from Morgan's *League,* and should be taken only as a rough guess.

"They had three great palisaded river towns . . ."—There seem to be as many different spellings of the Mohawk towns as there are books that refer to them. These two are from Flexner's biography of William Johnson.

"Leave these filthy swine . . ."—speech recorded in the *Jesuit Relations* of 1645.

"When I saw them making a move to fire . . ."—Champlain's quote, as appeared in Francis Parkman's *The Jesuits in North America* (slightly different translations of the famous story appear in other texts).

"My pen has no ink . . ."—*Relations des Hurons, 1650,* as quoted in Sylvester, p. 18.

"Hideous and desolate . . ."—Both Bradford's and Mather's quotes and a discussion of their context appear in *Wilderness and the American Mind,* 3d ed., 1982 (New Haven, CT), by Roderick Nash, pp. 24–36.

"In Jogues's descriptions . . ."—Jogues's epic story is probably best told by Francis Parkman in *The Jesuits in North America,* though *The Jesuit Relations* (vols. 28, 31, 39) makes for good reading as well and is the source of the Jogues quotes. The same is true of the story of Marie's escape from her Onondaga captors that follows.

Chapter 3

The best source for biographical information about Sir William Johnson is *Lord of the Mohawks*, by James Thomas Flexner, though there is
also some entertaining, if somewhat less authoritative, material in
Jeptha Simms's *Trappers of New York*, 1871 (1980, Harrison, NY). For
the course of the French and Indian War battles on Lakes George and
Champlain, the most enjoyable and breathtakingly complete sources
by far are the works of Francis Parkman, especially *A Half Century of
Conflict*, and *Montcalm and Wolfe*, though *A New World*, by Arthur Quinn,
was also very useful. *Documents Relative to the Colonial History of the State
of New York* (Albany, NY) and *Papers of Sir William Johnson* (Albany, NY)
were also helpful, though, I confess, mainly to verify quotes found previously by Flexner or Parkman. *Robert Rogers of the Rangers*, 1988 (Ticonderoga, NY), by John R. Cuneo, is the source for much of the material
related to Rogers's Rangers. Norton's *The Fur Trade in Colonial New York*
was also very helpful.

"Should any French priests . . ."—Parkman, *Half Century*, p. 211.

"The deference paid to them . . ."—The 1710 conference, as well
as the general outline of the fur trade during the period are described
in Norton, pp. 34 ff.

"The style abounds with noble images . . ."—as quoted in Flexner,
p. 39.

"Joined in their games . . ."—Parkman, *Half Century*, p. 211.

"Whole areas of his mind . . ."—Flexner, p. 38.

"Poor as ratts . . ."—as quoted in Parkman, *Half Century*, p. 213.

"Dined with Sir Wm. . . ."—as quoted in Parkman, *Conspiracy of Pontiac*, footnote on page 158.

"George Clock . . ."—as quoted in Parkman, *Half Century*, p. 213.

"Man Who Undertakes Great Things . . ."—Flexner, p. 40.

"I nevertheless . . ."—as quoted in Flexner, p. 223.

"Warts, pimples, blisters . . ."—Nash, p. 45. Nash is also the primary source for the discussion of Romanticism in the next paragraph.

"Sir William told us how to lay . . ."—Simms, p. 45.

"That damned Irishman . . ."—Flexner, p. 25.

"Every house was set on fire . . ."—as quoted in Parkman, *Half Century*, p. 253.

"The collected farmers . . ."—The notion that the regular volunteers were alarmed to see Johnson cavorting with his Mohawk

friends is implied by Parkman, and the quote of Seth Pomeroy in the next paragraph appears on page 306 of Parkman, *Montcalm and Wolfe,* vol. 1.

"Not only in honor . . ."—as quoted in Parkman, *Montcalm and Wolfe,* vol. 1, p. 306.

"The more there are . . ."—as quoted in Parkman, *Montcalm and Wolfe,* vol. 1, p. 311. The additional quotes by Hendrick, Johnson, and Dieskau describing the battle are from the same source.

"[There are] about twenty-five hundred men . . ."—as quoted in Parkman, *Montcalm and Wolfe,* vol. 1, pp. 414–15. Quote from Captain Duchat in paragraph that follows is from the same source on page 393.

"Excepting some few casks of brandy . . ."—from Rogers's journal as quoted in Cuneo, p. 38.

"Imagine a great assembly . . ."—as quoted in Parkman, *Montcalm and Wolfe,* vol. 1, p. 494.

"I sang the war song . . ."—from Bougainville's journal as quoted by Parkman in *Montcalm and Wolfe,* vol. 1, p. 490.

"I believe you will think it proper . . ."—as quoted by Parkman in *Montcalm and Wolfe,* vol. 1, p. 511. Montcalm's quote a few paragraphs down is from the same source (p. 513), as is Robaud's description of the carnage a few paragraphs below that (p. 520), and Bougainville's journal entry (p. 521).

"I was about six yards from him . . ."—as quoted in Cuneo, p. 85.

"In Lord Howe . . ."—as quoted in Parkman, *Montcalm and Wolfe,* vol. 2, p. 102. The Parkman quote that follows is from the same source.

"The scene was frightful . . ."—Parkman, *Montcalm and Wolfe,* vol. 2, pp. 110–11.

Chapter 4

Most of this chapter is based on conversations and visits with Toby Edwards that took place in the spring and summer of 1994. Additional information about the nature of the fur business in the Adirondacks today also comes from conversations with Bob Inslerman and Gordon Bachelor, both of the New York State Department of Environmental Conservation.

"A survey of trappers in the state . . ."—"Characteristics, Motivations and Involvement of Trappers in New York," 1991, DEC document.

340

"The most vicious and abandoned wretches . . ."—as quoted in *Adirondack Wilderness: A Story of Man and Nature,* 1980 (Syracuse, NY), by Jane Ebelen Keller, p. 22.

"How to Be an Advocate . . ."—from "Advanced Trapper Training Seminar" handout entitled "Trapping Responsibility in the 1990s" (1993, Albany, NY).

"There are a dozen small-type pages . . ."—The annual trapping regulations for New York State are typically printed on the back of large maps, so the "pages" mentioned are, in reality, sections of the folded map.

Chapter 5

Much of the information on Nick Stoner and Nat Foster comes from Jeptha Simms's somewhat anecdotal book, *Trappers of New York.* I also consulted the rather hagiographic *The Life and Adventures of Nat Foster,* 1897 (1976, Harrison, NY), by A. L. B. Curtiss. Alfred L. Donaldson's two-volume *A History of the Adirondacks* was also useful for details.

"It was because the varmints . . ."—The story of Elisha Beldon, including the quote, is from *Home Sketches of Essex County,* 1858 (Keeseville, NY), by Flavius J. Cook.

"I watched 'em as they came toward the bridge . . ."—This quote and those that follow are from Curtiss, pp. 211 ff.

"Unlike virtually every other marketable species . . ."—The best analysis of Adirondack deer populations in the park, and on the ethics of various hunting methods mentioned a few paragraphs later, appears in *Wildlife and Wilderness,* by Philip G. Terrie.

"I did a pretty good afternoon's work . . ."—as quoted in Curtiss, p. 190.

"C. Hart Merriam concluded . . ."—as quoted in Keller, p. 19.

Chapter 6

The primary source for material about the Brown family of Providence, Rhode Island, is *John Brown's Tract: Lost Adirondack Empire,* 1988 (Canaan, NH), by Henry A. Brown (a descendant who uncovered a trove of family correspondence) and Richard A. Walton. The book also contains much that is of interest about the nature of land speculation in the years immediately following the American Revolution. Donaldson's *History of the Adirondacks,* vol. 1, was also valuable on both the history of Brown's Tract and on Adirondack speculation in general. Also see *Adirondack Country,* 1954 (1985, Syracuse, NY), by William Chapman White, and Nathaniel Sylvester's *Historical Sketches* for information on William Gilliland. *The Great Republic,* 1977 (Lexington, MA), by Bernard Bailyn et al., was also helpful for general background information.

"One thousand and fifty whole chests . . ."—as quoted in Brown and Walton, p. 88.

"When Brown was informed . . ."—from Donaldson, vol. 1, p. 97.

"John Quincy Adams . . ."—as quoted in Donaldson, vol. 1, p. 92.

"Pray remember that my securing . . ."—as quoted in Brown and Walton, p. 112.

"You'll be sure to note . . ."—as quoted in Brown and Walton, p. 125. Quote that follows is from the same source.

"I therefore contemplate . . ."—as quoted in Brown and Walton, p. 137.

"No other purpose but to accommodate . . ."—as quoted in Keller, p. 26.

"Hasterpudding . . ."—as quoted in Brown and Walton, p. 128. Quote that follows is from the same source, p. 139.

Chapter 7

The primary sources for this chapter are the same as those noted for chapter 6: Brown and Walton, Donaldson, White, etc. As mentioned in the text itself, Flavius Cook's *Home Sketches* was also very useful for descriptions of early farm life in the Champlain Valley.

"We had heard that Ti . . ."—as quoted in Cook, p. 34.

"Men scraped their own axe-helves . . ."—Cook, p. 32.

"After I married . . ."—as quoted in Cook, p. 34.

"On the north side of Black Mountain . . ."—*Adventures of an Angler in Canada, Nova Scotia and the United States,* 1848 (New York), by Charles Lanman, p. 66.

"Set fire to an old dead tree . . ."—as quoted in Brown and Walton, p. 234. Quote in following paragraph is from the same source, p. 236.

"Crow shed tears . . ."—Simms, p. 191.

"A judge who threatened . . ."—as quoted in Brown and Walton, p. 282.

"Will be found an excellent country . . ."—from *Third Annual Report of the Survey of the Second Geological District,* 1839 (Documents of the Assembly of the State of New York), p. 224.

"The day shall arrive in which . . ."—as quoted in Jamieson, p. 67. The quotes by Joel T. Headley that follow also appear in Jamieson on pages 72–73.

Chapter 8

Both Alfred L. Donaldson and William Chapman White provide a little information about Castorland, but the most complete source by far is *Castorland: French Refugees in the Western Adirondacks, 1793–1814,* 1985 (Harrison, NY), by Edith Pilcher. Donaldson was also useful for material on the abolitionist John Brown, as was Steven Oates's *To Purge This Land with Blood: A Biography of John Brown,* 1970 (1984, Amherst, MA).

"I am something of a pioneer . . ."—Oates, p. 65.

"We were all ranged at a long table . . ."—Dana's account of meeting John Brown appeared in the *Atlantic Monthly* in July 1871.

"Every thing you see . . ."—Oates, p. 66.

"How mysterious . . ."—*Atlantic Monthly,* July 1871.

"Dead clearings"—Charles Fenno Hoffman, *Wild Scenes in the Forest and Prairie,* 1843 (New York), p. 20.

Chapter 9

This chapter comes entirely from conversations the author had with Janice Allen and Janet Tucker at the Willsboro Public Library in Willsboro, New York, in the summer of 1994, and over the phone in the summer of 1996.

Chapter 10

As with earlier sections on John Brown of Rhode Island, the best source on his son-in-law Herreshoff is Brown and Walton's *John Brown's Tract.* For more general information about the early mining industry in the region, see *The Great Forest of the Adirondacks,* by Barbara McMartin; *Adirondack Forests, Fields, and Mines,* 1974 (Lakemont, NY), by Floy S. Hyde; and Donaldson's *History* (of course).

"I will settle the tract . . ."—as quoted in Brown and Walton, p. 202. All the quotes from Herreshoff's correspondence that follow are from the same source, pp. 202–57.

"Sent a boat with Skene's . . ."—as quoted in White, p. 92.

"Just then came the freshet which destroyed . . ."—as quoted in White, p. 93.

"Put an end to his life by discharging . . ."—Brown and Walton, p. 256.

"The right side of his temple . . ."—Simms, p. 186.

Chapter 11

Geology of New York: A Simplified Account, 1991 (Albany, NY), Y. W. Isacksen, et al., gives the best overview of the last few billion years of history in the state. On Ebenezer Emmons and his geological survey, see *The First One Hundred Years of American Geology,* 1924 (New Haven, CT), and *Contributions to a History of American State Geological and Natural History Surveys,* 1926 (Washington, DC), by George P. Merrill; Terrie's *Forever Wild* and *Wildlife and Wilderness;* Donaldson's *History,* White's *Adirondack Country,* and the January 1891 issue of *American Geologist.*

"The principal object of the survey . . ."—as quoted in Merrill, *Contributions,* pp. 327–29.

"This district, still almost entirely unexplored . . ."—as quoted in Terrie, *Forever Wild,* p. 34.

"Sunday commenced Saturday . . ."—*American Geologist,* January 1891.

"A region of country . . ."—White, p. 99.

"Some convulsion of nature . . ."—Merrill, *First One Hundred Years,* p. 227.

"It makes a man feel . . ."—as quoted in White, p. 14.

Chapter 12

In addition to the general sources mentioned at the beginning of chapter 11, add *The MacIntyre Mine: From Failure to Fortune,* 1962 (Blue Mountain Lake, NY), by Harold Hochschild. Also see McMartin's *Great Forest of the Adirondacks;* and finally, the November 1943 issue of *Mining and Metallurgy,* which was entirely devoted to mining in the Adirondacks. Additional information came from several conversations with George Cannon in 1993 and 1994. Cannon, the town manager of Newcomb, is a former employee of the National Lead operation at Tahawus.

"Never was a vein . . ."—as quoted in Terrie, *Forever Wild,* p. 34.

"A strapping young Indian . . ."—as quoted in Jamieson, pp. 58–59.

"If land in that wilderness is to have any value . . ."—letter from Henderson to McIntyre on March 14, 1845, as quoted in Hochschild, p. 25.

"John, you must have left . . ."—as quoted in Hochschild, pp. 8–9.

"Here on this log I sat . . ."—Joel T. Headley, *The Adirondack: or, Life in the Woods*, 1849 (New York), chap. 6.

"Work was dropped just as it was . . ."—Hochschild, p. 11.

"Steady and relentless . . ."—*Mining and Metallurgy*, p. 480.

"It should not be concluded . . ."—*Mining and Metallurgy*, p. 475.

Chapter 13

This chapter is drawn entirely from conversations and visits with Don Mellor and Ed Palen during the winter of 1995.

Chapter 14

The primary sources for this chapter are the early travel books mentioned in the text: *Wild Scenes in the Forest and Prairie,* by Charles Fenno Hoffman; *The Indian Pass,* 1869 (1993, Fleischmanns, NY), by Alfred Billings Street; *In the Wilderness,* 1878 (1990, Syracuse, NY), by Charles Dudley Warner; *Adventures in the Wilderness,* 1869 (1970, Syracuse, NY), by William H. H. Murray; *The Adirondack; or, Life in the Woods,* by Joel T. Headley; *Adventures of an Angler,* by Charles Lanman. My interpretation of the above writers, though somewhat different in detail and angle, was influenced by Roderick Nash's classic work *Wilderness and the American Mind: The Idea of Wilderness,* 1991 (New Haven, CT), by Max Oelschlaeger, and Terrie's *Forever Wild.* Also, *Up the Lake Road,* 1987 (Keene Valley, NY), by Edith Pilcher, was helpful for details on the early years in Keene Valley. And, of course, Donaldson was the starting place.

"Strange to find so wild . . ."—Hoffman, p. 29.

"If it didn't involve an anachronism . . ."—Hoffman, p. 30.

"Just returned from an excursion . . ."—as quoted in *The Life and Works of Thomas Cole,* 1964, (Cambridge), by Louis Legrand Noble, p. 178.

"For lodging, food and drink . . ."—as quoted in Hochschild, *MacIntyre Mine,* p. 18.

"It was not a very long leap . . ."—Terrie, *Forever Wild,* p. 19. The discussion of the importance of Edmund Burke's thinking, described in the previous paragraph, to the development of the romantic notion of wilderness is also discussed by Terrie.

"The territory is getting so much notice . . ."—letter from Henderson to McIntyre, March 27, 1837, as quoted in Keller, *Adirondack Wilderness* (Syracuse), p. 110.

"In conclusion, I remark . . ."—as quoted in Donaldson, vol. 1, p. 164.

"At last we reached the point . . ."—Street, pp. 23–24.

"I had expected, from paintings . . ."—Headley, chap. 7.

"One of the most savage and stupendous . . ."—Hoffman, p. 40.

"The impression of the whole . . ."—Headley, chap. 6.

"What I have never been wearied . . ."—Hoffman, p. 22.

"I was a 'distinguished stranger' . . ."—Lanman, p. 60.

"I have gazed on many mountain prospects . . ."—Headley, chap. 16.

" 'Every Natural Process,' Emerson wrote . . ."—from the essay "Nature," 1836 (1964, *Selected Writings of Ralph Waldo Emerson,* New York), p. 209.

"The wilderness has unfolded to them . . ."—Murray, p. 38.

"For when the good dominie . . ."—Murray, pp. 24–26.

"Moist from its long dalliance . . ."—This and the quotes in the next few paragraphs are all collected from Headley's introduction and chapters 1–3.

"Adorned with every ornament . . ."—as quoted in Parkman, *Montcalm and Wolfe,* vol. 1, p. 494.

"Up with the dawn . . ."—from "The Adirondacks," as quoted in Jamieson, pp. 74–76.

"Sufficiently educated to understand . . ."—Headley, p. 272.

"Meager utilitarianism . . ."—Cole, as quoted in Nash, *Wilderness and the American Mind,* p. 97.

"Things are in the saddle . . ."—Emerson, "Ode, Inscribed to W. H. Channing," as quoted in Nash, p. 87.

"An attack on the brain"—Headley, introduction.

"Why, Doc, you ain't no heavier . . ." Donaldson, vol. 1, p. 247.

"A bleak blackguard beggarly climate . . ."—from *The Letters of Robert Louis Stevenson* (1910, New York), as quoted in Jamieson, p. 208.

"Uncontaminated with the vicious habits . . ."—Murray, pp. 36–37.

"The better qualities of both conditions . . ."—Cooper, as quoted in Nash, p. 94.

"I had heard of some of his feats . . ."—Hoffman, p. 30.

"Huge, powerful and hairy Nimrod . . ."—Lanman, p. 90.

"Shook his honest hand . . ."—Headley, p. 250.

"If ever a man . . ."—This, and the quotes in the following five paragraphs, are from Warner, pp. 48–73.

"The summit of Dix . . ."—Phelps's manuscript was cleaned up and published under the title *The High Peaks of Essex: The Adirondack*

Mountains of Orson Schofield Phelps, 1992 (Fleischmanns, NY), by Bill Healy. The quoted material appears on page 23.

"When the primitive man . . ."—Warner, p. 73.

"The life of a guide . . ."—from *American Angler,* September 22, 1883, p. 186.

Chapter 15

The general sources for this chapter are essentially the same as those for chapter 14, with addition of *Wildlife and Wilderness,* by Philip G. Terrie, and *Guides of the Adirondacks: A History,* 1994 (Utica, NY), by Charles A. Brumley. Also, for information on the early development of grand hotels in the region see: *An Adirondack Resort in the Nineteenth Century: Blue Mountain Lake, 1870–1900,* 1962 (Blue Mountain Lake, NY), by Harold Hochschild; *Durant: The Fortunes and Woodland Camps of a Family in the Adirondacks,* 1981 (Blue Mountain Lake, NY), by Craig Gilborn; and *Great Camps of the Adirondacks,* 1986 (Boston), by Harvey H. Kaiser.

"I finally fixed a trap under the water . . ."—This quote, and the story of Cheney's trapping of the last beaver, appear in chapter 7 of Lanman.

"Being a little curious . . ."—This quote, along with many other stories of Cheney's prowess, is from chapter 8 of Headley, pp. 76 ff.

"The demolition of the pine forests . . ."—Hoffman, p. 28.

"The only manly way . . ."—as quoted in Terrie, *Wildlife and Wilderness,* p. 52. Terrie's general discussion of hunting methods in the pages around this quote is also well worth reading.

"I sat and shivered . . ."—Headley, chap. 15.

"I can't help it, my speckled beauty . . ."—Headley, chap. 2.

"It's wrong, it's wrong . . ."—Hoffman, p. 59.

"I wish I could get my living . . ."—Lanman, chap. 7.

"Only the mountain . . ."—from "Thinking Like a Mountain," in *A Sand County Almanac: and Sketches Here and There,* 1949 (1989, New York), by Aldo Leopold, p. 129.

"What caused the moose to all leave . . ."—as quoted in Brumley, p. 112.

"Awoke from a piscatorial dream . . ."—from Lanman, preface. The quotes in the paragraph that follows are from pages 50–60.

"By the time I had taken ten or fifteen . . ."—Headley, p. 250.

"One of the most harmless and least vexatious . . ."—Murray, p. 56.

"There is nothing in the trip . . ."—Murray, p. 19.

"Between the fish-hog . . ."—*Forest and Stream,* July 12, 1888, p. 489. This quote and Charles Dudley Warner's comments in the paragraphs that follow appear in Philip Terrie's discussion of class snobbery in the Adirondacks on page 72 of *Forever Wild.*

"Embryo sportsmen . . ."—as quoted in White, p. 131.

"It appears evident . . ."—*Forest and Stream,* December 22, 1888, p. 529.

"About certain changes which have taken place . . ."—This and the Piseco quotes in the paragraphs that follow are from an article that appeared in the May 3, 1883, issue of *Forest and Stream,* pp. 262–64.

"Your guide if he knows his business . . ."—from *Forest and Stream,* May 6, 1880, p. 264.

"A royal dinner . . ."—from an article in *Frank Leslie's Illustrated Weekly Newspaper,* November 1858, as quoted in Terrie, *Forever Wild,* p. 50.

"Tree after tree came down . . ."—Headley, chap. 6.

"Tormented lightning . . ."—Hoffman, pp. 44 ff.

"The storm did not set in . . ."—Lanman, p. 95.

"Got your pork . . ."—Brumley, p. 105.

"Ten scholars . . ."—from "The Adirondacks," as quoted in Jamieson, p. 74.

Chapter 16

This chapter is taken entirely from conversations and travels with Brian McDonnell that took place in the winter and spring of 1995.

Chapter 17

This chapter is based entirely on a visit with John Courtney III that took place in February of 1995.

Chapter 18

McMartin's *Great Forest of the Adirondacks,* and *Lumberjacks and Rivermen in the Central Adirondacks, 1850–1950,* 1962 (Blue Mountain Lake, NY), by Harold Hochschild, were both indispensable sources for my chapters dealing with the timber industry. Graham's *Adirondack Park* was also of great help, especially regarding the rise and organization of preservationist sentiments in the wake of logging in the region, as were the previously mentioned works of Terrie and Nash.

"An ocean of mountain summits . . ."—Phelps's descriptions in the paragraphs to follow are from Healy, pp. 20–22.

"Covered with great and high forests . . ."—Champlain, as quoted in Keller, p. 79.

"Roll on a hardwood log . . ."—as quoted in McMartin, p. 24.

"Driving trees . . ."—Headley, p. 29.

"The jam stretch . . ."—from "The Big Boom," by Peter Fosburgh, reprinted from *New York State Conservationist,* in *North Country Life,* summer 1947, pp. 52–55.

"Whereas, the undersigned . . ."—Full text of the agreement appears as an appendix in Hochschild's *Lumberjacks.*

"As late as 1885 no more than . . ."—McMartin, p. 68.

"Great northern forest contained . . ."—McMartin, p. 65.

Chapter 19

The primary sources for this chapter are the same as those for chapter 18, with an added emphasis on the work of Nash, Terrie, and Graham.

"If the Adirondacks are cleared . . ."—January 23, 1890, issue of *Forest and Stream,* as quoted in Terrie, *Forever Wild,* p. 96.

"The operation of causes set in action . . ."—as quoted in Terrie, *Forever Wild,* p. 94.

"I desire to call your attention . . ."—as quoted in Graham, p. 70.

"In any event . . ."—Graham, p. 96.

"I shall hereafter show . . ."—*Report on the Topographical Survey of the Adirondack Wilderness of New York for the Year 1873,* 1874 (Albany, NY), by Verplanck Colvin, p. 6.

"An unproductive and dangerous desert . . ."—The official report of the Sargent commission was actually published in early 1885, as quoted in Graham, p. 104.

"Taking the forester . . ."—Graham, p. 150.

"Despoiling the Forests . . ."—as quoted in Terrie, *Forever Wild,* p. 101.

"The wood pulp men cut all the trees . . ."—as quoted in Hochschild, *Lumberjacks,* p. 9.

Chapter 20

The first half of this chapter is derived from conversations and travels with John Courtney Jr. that took place in the early winter of 1995. The second half is largely the result of a conversation with Harold Jerry during the spring of 1995.

Chapter 21

As the opening paragraph suggests, *Camp Chronicles*, 1952 (1964, Blue Mountain Lake, NY), by Mildred Phelps Stokes Hooker, was an important starting place for the chapter. The most important sources, however, were Gilborn's *Durant*, and *Great Camps of the Adirondacks*, by Harvey H. Kaiser, for material on the development of the camp aesthetic. Four books by Harold Hochschild—*Adirondack Steamboats on Raquette and Blue Mountain Lakes*, 1962; *Life and Leisure in the Adirondack Back Woods*, 1962; *Dr. Durant and His Iron Horse*, 1962; and *An Adirondack Resort in the Nineteenth Century: Blue Mountain Lake, 1870–1900*, 1962 (all Blue Mountain Lake, NY)—were very useful, as was Howard Kirschenbaum's *The Story of Sagamore*, 1990 (Raquette Lake, NY). And, as always (of course), Donaldson was essential.

"Was so charmed by the beauty . . ."—Hooker, p. 1.

"Chicken Coop Island . . ."—Hooker, p. 10.

"If ever an exact little word . . ."—Donaldson, vol. 1, p. 6.

"These camps are never really completed . . ."—Stoddard, as quoted in Kaiser, p. 80.

"I never saw anything like it . . ."—as quoted in Jamieson, p. 293.

"No one will be received . . ."—as quoted in White, p. 137.

"Suburb of New York . . ." *New York Times*, as quoted in Kaiser, p. 39.

"Unquestionably the most picturesque . . ."—as quoted in Gilborn, p. 19.

"It became the show place . . ."—Donaldson, vol. 2, p. 92.

"If you have to ask . . ."—as quoted in Gilborn, p. 92. (Gilborn is the source for the whole tale of Durant's legal troubles with his sister that follows.)

"The finest trio . . ."—as quoted in Kaiser, p. 176.

"Before [Pine Knot] . . ."—Donaldson, vol. 2, p. 92.

"I firmly believe . . ."—as quoted in Gilborn, p. 5.

"No confidence in her brother . . ."—Gilborn, p. 87.

"Cost me a great deal more . . ."—as quoted in Kirschenbaum, p. 20.

"This property came into . . ."—as quoted in Gilborn, p. 136.

Chapter 22

The primary sources for this chapter are essentially the same as those for chapter 21, with the addition of Edith Pilcher's *Up the Lake Road*.

"Some of us took a firm stand against evening clothes . . ."—This quote, and those of Hooker's in following paragraphs, are from her *Camp Chronicles*, pp. 25–35.

"I want it finished the day I get back . . ."—as quoted in White, p. 147.

"We should turn wild . . ."—as quoted in Oelschlaeger, p. 9.

"And here we venture a suggestion . . ."—*New York Times*, August 9, 1864.

"Of all the things that I have experienced . . ."—as quoted in Graham, p. 43.

"Let's have dinner . . ."—Pilcher, *Up the Lake Road*, p. 152.

"Strictly as a factory of wood . . ."—Graham, p. 137.

"All felt as lazy as possible . . ."—Excerpts from the diary kept at Camp Stott appear as Appendix B in Gilborn. This quote appears on page 152.

Chapter 23

This chapter is primarily derived from a conversation with Howard Kirschenbaum at White Pine Camp that took place during the summer of 1995. Additional information came from the general sources already mentioned above.

"The Manor House had become . . ."—Gilborn, p. 103.

Chapter 24

Most of this chapter is based on a conversation with Clarence Petty that took place in the winter of 1991. The rest of it, including the quote at the end, came from an article, "The Hermit of Cold River Flow," by Clayton B. Seagears that appeared in the *New York State Conservationist*, October–November 1946, p. 8.

Chapter 25

Most of the material in this chapter is derived from conversations and visits with Paul Schaefer that took place between 1991 and 1995. Schaefer's book *Defending the Wilderness*, 1989 (Syracuse, NY), was also an important source, as were additional conversations with David Gibson, George Davis, Harold Jerry, and Robert Glennon. Finally, Graham's *Adirondack Park* was indispensable.

"The idea of such an unproductive . . ."—as quoted in Graham, p. 77.

"Bulldozers were ready to move . . ."—Schaefer, p. 65.

"Leave this valley . . ."—from July 1948 issue of *Forest Preserve*. Both this and the quote two paragraphs below are included in Schaefer, p. 66.

"If the Adirondacks are to be saved . . ."—Graham, p. 247.

"If there had been no Horizon . . ."—Graham, p. 249.

"I don't call it subdividing . . ."—from "Mary, Queen of Spots," by Michael Schnayerson, in *Vanity Fair*, August 1995.

Chapter 26

This chapter is derived primarily from conversations with Robert Glennon at the Adirondack Park Agency in Ray Brook, New York, that took place between 1991 and 1995.

" 'The land ethic.' . . ."—Leopold, pp. 201–25.

Chapter 27

This chapter is primarily derived from conversations with George Davis that took place in the spring of 1995. Other details came from earlier conversations with Davis and/or from published sources already mentioned above.

Chapter 28

This chapter is primarily derived from conversations, visits, and travels with Leo Demong and/or Larry Strait during the spring and summer of 1995.

"Under the care of a man named Ned Ball . . ."—The story of Ball's difficulty with the Canadian beavers is told in more detail in *Up Old Forge Way*, 1948 (Rochester, NY), by David H. Beetle.

ACKNOWLEDGMENTS

I am indebted above all to my wife, Nina Bramhall, without whose encouragement, insight, and above all, patience, this book would not have been written. Others whose reading of early versions improved the book significantly include Pat Schneider, Peter Schneider, Mark Marvel, Kib and Tess Bramhall, Philip Terrie. There are many writers and thinkers, like Philip Terrie, without whose published works this book could not have been written, and they are credited in the reference notes.

I am also grateful to the many kind people of the Adirondacks I met during the course of researching this book, especially those who appear in its pages. Most especially, this refers to the late Paul Schaefer, the tireless warrior to whom all residents of the northeast who cherish wild places are indebted. Without the generous help of Barbara Parnass and others at the Saranac Lake Free Library, and Jim and Tracy Meehan at the Adirondack Museum, I would never have found the wonderful illustrations included in the book. Thanks as well to the staff of the New York Public Library, the Empire State's other great underappreciated and inadequately funded treasure. And to Roger Cohn of *Audubon* magazine, who first sent me to the Adirondacks with an assignment to write.

Finally, I'd like to thank my agent, Kim Witherspoon, for introducing me to Jack Macrae, whose guidance from conceptualization to completion was indispensable.

Index